Successfully Implementing Problem-Based Learning in Classrooms

Successfully Implementing Problem-Based Learning in Classrooms

Research in K–12 and Teacher Education

Edited by Thomas Brush & John W. Saye

Purdue University Press, West Lafayette, Indiana

Printed in the United States of America

Cataloging-in-Publication data is on file with the Library of Congress.

Cloth ISBN: 9781557537805
ePDF ISBN: 9781612494944
ePUB ISBN: 9781612494951

Cover image *Hand Drawing* by Kalawin/iStock/Thinkstock

Contents

Part II: Problem-Based Learning in K–12 Contexts

Conclusion

Problem-Based Learning in K–12 and Teacher Education: Introduction and Current Trends

Thomas Brush and John Saye

Welcome to this edited volume focusing on research exploring the use of problem-based learning (PBL) in preservice and inservice teacher education. Currently, there is a major debate regarding the most effective methods for providing the best educational experiences for K–12 students that will afford them with the experiences they need to succeed in the 21st century. Recent definitions of the requirements for high-quality teaching emphasize not only content and pedagogical knowledge but also the use of innovative instructional strategies to support students' acquisition of a more flexible knowledge base as they engage in complex problem solving (Bell, 2010; Lombardi, 2007; Saye et al., 2013; U.S. Department of Education, 2010). PBL represents a widely recommended best practice that facilitates both student engagement with challenging content and students' ability to utilize that content in a more flexible manner to support problem solving. In PBL, curriculum is anchored within authentic, ill-structured problems. Teachers guide and support students as they apply content knowledge toward problem solutions (Barrows & Kelson, 1993; Hmelo-Silver, 2004; Savery, 2015).

Current Trends of PBL in K–12 Education

Extensive research conducted over the past decade demonstrates that PBL can be an effective strategy for enhancing both student engagement with challenging content and students' academic achievement with that content in K–12 settings (Brush et al., 2013). A number of meta-analyses focusing on the implementation of PBL in K–12 environments conclude that PBL instruction is more effective than traditional, teacher-centered instruction with regard to student achievement (Ravitz, 2009; Strobel & Barneveld, 2009; Walker & Leary, 2009). Wirkala and Kuhn (2011) explored the effectiveness of PBL with middle school social studies students and determined that students engaged in PBL instruction versus lecture-based instruction performed better on a number of outcome variables including content knowledge and argumentation. Linn and colleagues' extensive research focusing on both the web-based science environment and "knowledge integration" framework continues to demonstrate the effectiveness of problem-based instruction when compared to typical instructional activities (Chiu & Linn, 2014; Linn & Eylon, 2011). Liu and colleagues (2014) and Pedersen and Liu's (2002) research with *Alien Rescue* suggests that PBL can be an effective method for both student academic achievement in science and (perhaps more importantly) for students to transfer knowledge to both similar problems and different situations. Saye and colleagues (2013) analyzed the teaching practices of numerous middle- and high school teachers and found a strong positive correlation between teachers who engage in problem- and inquiry-based teaching practices and their students' performance on achievement tests.

PBL has also been found to have a positive impact on a wide range of student abilities. For example, Glazewski and colleagues (2016) collaborated with a high school biology teacher on a problem-based unit focused on genetics. Results of the implementation of this unit with ninth grade students not only indicated that students had significant content knowledge gains in science (specifically genetics) but that students who were struggling with science content had significantly greater gains from pretest to posttest than their peers. Similar research demonstrating the positive impact of PBL with struggling students has been found in the areas of economics (Mergendoller, Maxwell, & Bellisimo, 2006) and scientific thinking in social science (Jewett & Kuhn, 2016).

PBL Versus Project-Based Learning

While extensive PBL research has been conducted in the areas of secondary science, social studies/history, and mathematics (e.g., Trinter, Moon, & Brighton, 2015), the research in the area of English language arts (ELA) is more limited. In addition, research focusing on PBL implementation at the elementary level is also limited. This may be due to the distinction between *problem*-based learning and *project*-based learning. Much of the literature examining inquiry-based curricular models implemented in the ELA curriculum and/or with elementary-age students tends to focus on project-based learning. This is even the case with new educational trends such as the maker movement, which tends to have students be more product/maker focused as opposed to problem focused (Halverson & Sheridan, 2014; Peppler & Bender, 2013; Smith, 2013). For example, Smith (2013) discussed an inquiry project with seventh and eighth grade ELA students in which they digitally fabricated pop-up books. The researcher specifically discussed how these types of "maker" initiatives should be considered project-based as opposed to problem-based.

From our perspective, PBL curricular models are distinct from many models proposed for project-based learning (Saunders & Rennie, 2013; Savery, 2015; Saye & Brush, 2004). In PBL, an authentic problem or central question is the overall focus of a unit; with project-based learning, the *project* or activity is the central focus of the unit of instruction (Savery, 2015). This sometimes can lead down a path in which the project takes over the curricular focus with little regard for the need for students to demonstrate any understanding of substantive, authentic problems. Barron and colleagues (1998) dismissed project-based learning that focuses on "doing for the sake of doing" (p. 273), or "action without appropriate reflection." They define worthy projects as ones that integrate "doing with understanding" (p. 274). However, for Barron and colleagues, PBL is most meaningfully used when embedded in complex projects.

The Buck Institute for Education, a leading organization for development and promotion of project-based learning, has published what they refer to as "essential design elements" for any project-based curricular initiatives. They specifically state that "[t]he heart of a project ... is a problem to investigate and solve, or a question to explore and answer" (Buck Institute for Education, 2015, p. 2). Similarly, Parker and colleagues (2011) used project-based learning to characterize a substantial problem-based curriculum project. Noting that project-based learning often refers to "a broad and often unspecified umbrella term for a wide range of pedagogies" (p. 538), they make clear that their use of the term *project-based* emphasizes activities in which students engage in deep, disciplined inquiry structured around authentic *problems*.

Thus, the distinction between PBL and project-based learning may become less of an issue as inquiry-based instructional models become more accepted in K–12 settings. However, the conceptualization of "problem-based learning," "problem-based projects," and "project-based learning" may warrant further discussion and clarification as we continue to explore the most effective methods for promoting inquiry in K–12 settings. In particular, the lack of PBL models in ELA and elementary settings may benefit from continued exploration of the commonalities between PBL and project-based learning.

The Need to Prepare Teachers to Implement PBL

The increasing evidence that PBL has a positive effect on a wide variety of student outcomes with a broad range of students is leading more K–12 schools to adopt PBL as an overarching model for their curriculum. School models such as Da Vinci Schools (2013), New Tech High (New Tech Network, 2015), and High Tech High (2014) have adopted technology-enhanced PBL approaches to their curriculum. With support from the U.S. Department of Education, Sammamish High School in Bellevue, Washington, has adopted an integrated PBL curriculum throughout their school, and the school district has plans to expand the curriculum to all schools in the district (Edutopia, 2013).

Given these trends, it seems appropriate and important for teacher educators to attempt to integrate effective PBL teaching practices into both preservice teacher education programs and professional development opportunities for practicing teachers. Unfortunately, many preservice and inservice teacher education programs still approach teaching methods with conventional practices (Feiman-Nemser, 2008; Kiggins & Cambourne, 2007), and few current and future teachers have clear conceptualization regarding effective design, development, and implementation of PBL instruction (Saye, Kohlmeier, Brush, Mitchell, & Farmer, 2009; So & Kim, 2009).

Some teacher education programs have attempted to address the need for teachers prepared to meet the instructional needs of these new school models by incorporating more PBL into their courses. A study of one program that introduced technology-enhanced PBL instruction to preservice teachers found that participating novice teachers indicated that they planned to utilize PBL in their future classrooms (Park & Ertmer, 2008). In another study, preservice teachers who had opportunities to develop collaborative PBL lessons in their methods classes demonstrated enhanced knowledge of PBL theory and practice (So & Kim, 2009). However, while more teacher education programs are recognizing the need to integrate PBL into their programs (Edwards & Hammer, 2006; Murray-Harvey & Slee, 2000), the research focused on methods to prepare both current and future teachers to successfully integrate PBL strategies in their classrooms remains limited.

The content of this volume begins to address this issue. This volume is an extension of a special issue of the *Interdisciplinary Journal of Problem-based Learning* (volume 8, issue 1) that focused on the topic of PBL in teacher education settings. Several of the chapters are versions of papers published in the special issue. However, this volume extends the focus of the special issue to include new chapters that focus on the integration of PBL strategies within both teacher education programs and teacher professional development in K–12 settings across a wide range of grade levels and content areas. This includes strategies to assist both K–12 teachers and teacher education faculty with implementing PBL within their teaching methods experiences as well as instructional approaches to assist preservice teachers with exploring the integration of PBL strategies into their future classrooms.

Overview of Volume

Based on the need to provide strategies for assisting both preservice and practicing teachers with implementing PBL in their classrooms, this volume is divided into two parts: "PBL Research in Teacher Education" and "PBL Research with Practicing Teachers." Readers will find a wide range of strategies and models presented in these sections—all of which have been implemented in teacher education programs and/or K–12 classroom settings. A wide variety of grade levels are represented, including both elementary and secondary educational settings. In addition, the chapters represent a range of content areas including mathematics, science, and social studies/history. Throughout the volume, we ask "What strategies and models help prepare current and future teachers to *effectively* design and implement PBL teaching and learning activities?" The chapters included in this text attempt to provide insight into this question while identifying challenges and unresolved issues that invite further research on this important topic.

Part I discusses a variety of different PBL strategies that have been implemented in various preservice teacher education programs. In Chapter 1, Strutchens and Martin provide an overview of their teacher education curriculum in secondary mathematics (including methods experiences, field experiences, and student teaching), in which they assist preservice teachers in developing research-based teaching strategies and practices to create classroom environments that foster mathematical problem solving and sense making. In Chapter 2, Glazewski, Shuster, Brush, and Ellis present a specific model of PBL known as socioscientific inquiry and discuss how they integrated the model into a graduate-level teaching methods class in science to help prepare prospective teachers utilize this model to teach a variety of science content. In Chapter 3, Brush and Saye describe problem-based historical inquiry, a PBL model specific to the areas of history and social studies. They discuss how they adapted this model to integrate persistent issues in history into a teacher education program and how preservice teachers applied this model as they developed PBL history units.

We have noted that there has been little empirical research investigating problem-based learning in elementary education—particularly with respect to preparing future elementary teachers to implement PBL in their classrooms. In Chapter 4, Lottero-Perdue discusses how she inducts her preservice teachers into PBL practices for the elementary science/engineering curriculum. She integrates a model of PBL known as design problem solving (Jonassen, 2000) to provide a venue for preservice teachers to introduce advanced science and engineering concepts to elementary students.

Part II provides models and strategies for collaborating with practicing teachers on the implementation of PBL in their classrooms. In Chapter 5, Hjalmarson and Diefes-Dux discuss a model of PBL known as model-eliciting activities and examine how middle school mathematics teachers use this model to develop tools to support student problem solving and presentation of problem solutions. In Chapter 6, Ertmer, Schlosser, Clase, and Adedokun discuss an intensive professional development program for secondary science teachers in which the teachers applied PBL principles toward the development of a STEM unit focused on sustainable energy as well as the impact the experience had on their self-efficacy toward teaching science and their knowledge of science concepts. In Chapter 7, Saye and Brush describe their line of research, exploring methods to support secondary social studies teachers as they integrate problem-based historical inquiry into their curriculum, and how various types of scaffolding (specifically referred to as hard scaffolding and soft scaffolding) can be used by teachers to support student inquiry. Finally, in Chapter 8, Goodnough and Hung describe how elementary teachers used a nine-step PBL design model to develop and implement units focused on science concepts and the impact that the use of the model had on teachers' pedagogical content knowledge and their willingness to integrate PBL practice into their future instructional activities.

Grant and Glazewski provide a summary chapter in which they discuss both common themes among the chapters as well as gaps in the current research in PBL and the need for additional exploration in specific areas (e.g., elementary education and ELA). They particularly highlight the need for more PBL research that examines sustainability of PBL curriculum efforts in both preservice and inservice teacher education, and call for longitudinal research that explores promising practices such as the ones described in this volume over a longer time period.

Technology to Support PBL Practice

While the use of digital technologies is by no means a prerequisite for the implementation of PBL in K–12 classrooms, technology is a theme throughout the various projects described in this volume. How technology is integrated within PBL can range from very specific applications to a broader suite of resources that support PBL development and implementation in multiple ways. Strutchens and Martin describe a variety of web-based tools and "apps" they have integrated into their mathematics education overall program. Glazewski and colleagues discuss how their students integrate online tools to develop their socioscientific PBL units. Saye and Brush describe a set of digital tools (*Decision Point*) specifically designed to support problem-based historical inquiry with both students and teachers. Ertmer and colleagues discuss the integration of technology as a crucial component of their professional development program with teachers as they design and develop PBL units. Thus, *technology* can be defined in many ways, and the various methods in which technology can be used to support PBL is diverse. However, it is important to note that in virtually all of the projects described in this volume, PBL can be effectively implemented without technology. When preparing current and future teachers to effectively implement PBL in their classrooms, the focus should always be on the pedagogical principles that make PBL an effective instructional model. Technology can definitely support the implementation of PBL, but technology is not a *requirement* for PBL.

Conclusion

While policymakers and K–12 school leaders continue to advocate for the adoption of more inquiry-oriented instructional models, many teacher educators have yet to fully integrate these practices into their preservice or inservice instruction. The lack of models for effectively preparing teachers to adopt a problem-based teaching practice exacerbates this problem. This volume provides multiple models for implementing problem-based learning in K–12 settings and for preparing teachers to apply these models to develop PBL instructional activities. We would like to thank the contributing authors for their scholarship and dedication in conducting exciting, innovative research that will expand our knowledge of PBL in K–12 and teacher education settings. We hope that this work will also stimulate further exploration of the continued challenges and issues that serve as barriers for successful implementation of PBL in schools.

References

Barron, B., Schwartz, D., Vye, N., Moore, A., Petrosino, A., Zech, L., Bransford, J., & The Cognition and Technology Group at Vanderbilt. (1998). Doing with understanding: Lessons from research on problem- and project-based learning. *The Journal of the Learning Sciences, 7*(3/4), 271–311.

Barrows, H. S., & Kelson, A. M. (1993). *Problem-based learning: A total approach to education.* Springfield: Southern Illinois University School of Medicine.

Bell, S. (2010). Project-based learning for the 21st century: Skills for the future. *The Cleaning House: A Journal of Educational Strategies, Issues, and Ideas, 83*(2), 39–42.

Brush, T., Glazewski, K., Ottenbreit-Leftwich, A., Saye, J., Zhang, Z., & Shin, S. (2013). The PBL-TECH project: Web-based tools and resources to support problem-based learning in pre-service teacher education. In L. Liu, D. Gibson, & C. Maddux (Eds.), *Research highlights in technology and teacher education 2013.* Chesapeake, VA: AACE.

Buck Institute for Education. (2015). *Gold standard PBL: Essential project design elements.* Retrieved from http://bie.org/object/document/gold_standard_pbl_essential_project_design_elements

Chiu, J., & Linn, M. (2014). Supporting knowledge integration in chemistry with a visualization-enhanced inquiry unit. *Journal of Science Education and Technology, 23*(1), 37–58.

Da Vinci Schools. (2013). *Da Vinci Schools.* Retrieved from http://davincischools.org/index.shtml

Edutopia. (2013). *Reinventing a public high school: A case study of integrating problem-based learning.* Retrieved from http://www.edutopia.org/sammamish-problem-based-learning-school-reform

Edwards, S., & Hammer, M. (2006). Laura's story: Using problem based learning in early childhood and primary teacher education. *Teaching and Teacher Educator, 22*(4), 465–477.

Feiman-Nemser, S. (2008). From preparation to practice: Designing a continuum to strengthen and sustain teaching. *Teachers College Record, 103*(6), 1013–1055.

Glazewski, K., Brush, T., Shin, S., & Shin, S. (2016, June). *Implementing socioscientific inquiry in high school biology: Teacher and student perspectives.* Paper presented at the 2016 PBL Congress, Zurich, Switzerland.

Halverson, E., & Sheridan, K. (2014). The maker movement in education. *Harvard Educational Review, 84*(4), 495–504.

High Tech High. (2014). *High Tech High.* Retrieved from http://www.hightechhigh.org/

Hmelo-Silver, C. E. (2004). Problem-based learning: What and how do students learn? *Educational Psychology Review, 16*(3), 235–266.

Jewett, E., & Kuhn, D. (2016, March). Social science as a tool in developing scientific thinking skills in underserved, low-achieving urban students. *Journal of Experimental Child Psychology, 143*, 154–161.

Jonassen, D. H. (2000). Toward a design theory of problem solving. *Educational Technology Research and Development, 48*(4), 63–85.

Kiggins, J., & Cambourne, B. (2007). The knowledge building community program: A partnership for progress in teacher education. In T. Townsend & R. Bates (Eds.), *Handbook of teacher education* (pp. 365–380). New York, NY: Springer.

Linn, M. C., & Eylon, B. S. (2011). *Science learning and instruction: Taking advantage of technology to promote knowledge integration.* New York, NY: Routledge.

Liu, M., Rosenblum, J., Horton, L., & Kang, J. (2014). Designing science learning with game-based approaches. *Computers in the School, 31*(1/2), 84–102.

Lombardi, M. (2007). *Authentic learning for the 21st century: An overview.* Report of the EDUCAUSE Learning Initiative. Retrieved from http://net.educause.edu/ir/library/pdf/eli3009.pdf

Mergendoller, J. R., Maxwell, N. L., & Bellisimo, Y. (2006). The effectiveness of problem-based instruction: A comparative study of instructional methods and student characteristics. *Interdisciplinary Journal of Problem-based Learning, 1*(2). http://dx.doi.org/10.7771/1541-5015.1026

Murray-Harvey, R., & Slee, P. (2000, December). *Problem based learning in teacher education: Just the beginning.* Paper presented at the Australian Association for Research in Education, Sydney, Australia.

New Tech Network. (2015). *New Tech Network student outcomes report: Re-imagining teaching and learning.* Retrieved from http://32dkl02ezpk0qcqvqmlx19lk

-wpengine.netdna-ssl.com/wp-content/uploads/2016/08/newtechnetwork2015studentoutcomesreport.pdf

Park, S. H., & Ertmer, P. A. (2008). Impact of problem-based learning (PBL) on teachers' beliefs regarding technology use. *Journal of Research on Technology in Education, 40*(2), 247–267.

Parker, W., Mosborg, S., Bransford, J., Vye, N., Wilkerson, J., & Abbot, R. (2011). Rethinking advanced high school coursework: Tackling the depth/breadth tension in the AP US Government and Politics course. *Journal of Curriculum Studies, 43*(4), 533–559.

Pedersen, S., & Liu, M. (2002). The transfer of problem-solving skills from a problem-based learning environment: The effect of modeling an expert's cognitive processes. *Journal of Research on Technology in Education, 35*(2), 303–320.

Peppler, K., & Bender, S. (2013). Maker movement spreads innovation one project at a time. *Phi Delta Kappan, 95*(3), 22–27.

Ravitz, J. (2009). Summarizing findings and looking ahead to a new generation of PBL research. *Interdisciplinary Journal of Problem-based Learning, 3*(1), 4–11.

Saunders, K., & Rennie, L. (2013). A pedagogical model for ethical inquiry into socio-scientific issues in science. *Research in Science Education, 43*(1), 253–274.

Savery, J. (2015). Overview of problem-based learning: Definitions and distinctions. In A. Walker, H. Leary, C. Hmelo-Silver, & P. Ertmer (Eds.), *Essential readings in problem-based learning: Exploring and extending the legacy of Howard S. Barrows.* West Lafayette, IN: Purdue University Press.

Saye, J. W., & Brush, T. (2004). Promoting civic competence through problem-based history learning experiments. In G. E. Hamot, J. J. Patrick, & R. S. Leming (Eds.), *Civic learning in teacher education* (Vol. 3, pp. 123–145). Bloomington, IN: The Social Studies Development Center.

Saye, J., Kohlmeier, J., Brush, T., Mitchell, L., & Farmer, C. (2009). Using mentoring to develop professional teaching knowledge for problem-based historical inquiry. *Theory and Research in Social Education, 37*(1), 6–41.

Saye, J., & the Social Studies Inquiry Research Collaborative (SSIRC). (2013). Authentic pedagogy: Its presence in social studies classrooms and relationship to student performance on state-mandated tests. *Theory and Research in Social Education, 41*(1), 89–132.

Smith, S. (2013). Through the teacher's eyes. *Journal of Research on Technology in Education, 46*(2), 207–227.

So, H., & Kim, B. (2009). Learning about problem based learning: Student teachers integrating technology, pedagogy and content knowledge. *Australasian Journal of Educational Technology, 25*(1), 101–116.

Strobel, J., & Barneveld, A. V. (2009). When is PBL more effective? A meta-synthesis of meta-analyses comparing PBL to conventional classrooms. *Interdisciplinary Journal of Problem-based Learning, 3*(1), 44–58.

Trinter, C., Moon, T., & Brighton, C. (2015). Characteristics of students' mathematical promise when engaging with problem-based learning units in primary classrooms. *Journal of Advanced Academics, 26*(1), 24–58.

U.S. Department of Education. (2010). *Transforming American education: Learning powered by technology.* Retrieved from http://www.ed.gov/sites/default/files/netp2010-execsumm.pdf

Walker, A., & Leary, H. (2009). A problem based learning meta analysis: Differences across problem types, implementation types, disciplines, and assessment levels. *Interdisciplinary Journal of Problem-based Learning, 3*(1), 12–43.

Wirkala, C., & Kuhn, D. (2011). Problem-based learning in K–12 education: Is it effective and how does it achieve its effects? *American Educational Research Journal, 48*(5), 1157–1186.

PART I

PROBLEM-BASED LEARNING IN TEACHER EDUCATION

1

Transforming Preservice Secondary Mathematics Teachers' Practices: Promoting Problem Solving and Sense Making

Marilyn E. Strutchens and W. Gary Martin

Introduction

Since the 1970s, there have been calls for changes in mathematics instruction emphasizing problem solving, culminating with the recommendation by the National Council of Teachers of Mathematics (NCTM) in 1980 that "problem solving be the focus of school mathematics" (p. 1). Throughout the 1980s, there was considerable research on how to promote students' problem solving in mathematics (cf. Charles & Lester, 1984; Goldin & McClintock, 1984; Schoenfeld, 1985). Near the end of the decade, a distinction was drawn between a focus on problem solving as an end of instruction (i.e., "teaching about problem solving") and a focus on problem solving as a means of instruction (i.e., "teaching via problem solving") (Schroeder & Lester, 1989, p. 32). This process view of problem solving promotes students' development of a relational understanding of mathematics (Skemp, 1976/2006) in which students understand both mathematical procedures and the reasoning behind those procedures.

In the NCTM's first set of national standards, both perspectives were valued; the first standard for each of its three grade bands was "Mathematics as Problem Solving," which called for students to "use problem-solving approaches to investigate and understand mathematics content" as well as "to develop and apply strategies to solve a wide variety of problems" (1989, p. 23). The subsequent *Professional Standards for Teaching Mathematics* (NCTM, 1991) described ways of supporting students' development of problem solving through the use of worthwhile tasks, classroom discourse, and an effective learning environment. This primary focus on problem solving in mathematics education was maintained through multiple "NCTM standards" documents produced over the following two decades (NCTM, 1995, 2000, 2006, 2009). As stated in *Focus in High School Mathematics*: "In the three decades since the 1980 publication of *An Agenda for Action*, NCTM has consistently advocated a coherent prekindergarten through grade 12 mathematics curriculum focused on mathematical problem solving" (NCTM, 2009, p. xi). *Focus in High School Mathematics* further framed problem solving in terms of "reasoning and sense making"—that is, reasoning is "the process of drawing conclusions on the basis of evidence or stated assumptions," while sense making requires "developing understanding of a situation, context, or concept by connecting it with existing knowledge" (p. 4).

In 2010, the National Governor's Association (NGA) and the Council of Chief State School Officers (CCSSO) developed the *Common Core State Standards for Mathematics*, which more than 43 states and territories adopted as their state course of study. In addition to promoting a more "coherent and focused" mathematics curriculum (p. 3), the document includes a required emphasis on problem solving and mathematical sense making in the *Standards for Mathematical Practice*, process and proficiencies that students should develop across the grades. These practice standards require that students develop the ability to make sense of problems and persevere in solving them, reason abstractly and quantitatively, construct viable arguments and critique the reasoning of others, model with mathematics, use appropriate tools strategically, attend to precision, look for and make use of structure, and look for and express regularity in repeated reasoning (NGA & CCSSO, 2010).

While the *Common Core* set both content and practice standards for K–12 mathematics, the document did not provide guidance for how schools and teachers might support students in achieving those standards. In response, the NCTM released *Principles to Actions: Ensuring Mathematical Success for All* in 2014. This document describes "essential elements" of school mathematics programs that will support student attainment of the *Common Core*, along with research-informed "mathematical teaching practices" to support students' mathematical learning, which is explicitly described to include problem solving and sense making. This latest standards-genre document from the NCTM is quickly gaining support as a primary source in framing discussions around mathematical teaching and learning.

In this chapter, we discuss how we work to transform the mathematical teaching practices of preservice secondary mathematics teachers to develop an equitable, inquiry-based approach to teaching in a manner that will help them to create classroom environments that foster mathematical problem solving and sense making. We discuss a range of pedagogical strategies and describe how these strategies might be introduced in methods courses and reinforced during teacher candidates' clinical experiences, including early field experiences and student teaching.

Instructional Practices to Promote Problem Solving and Sense Making

In this section, we describe research-based instructional practices that promote problem solving and sense making. These are the targets for our preparation of secondary mathematics teachers. We begin by describing tenets related to teaching and learning mathematics, consider the importance of the classroom environment, and, finally, discuss specific mathematics teaching practices described by the NCTM in 2014 to promote students' mathematics learning of problem solving and sense making.

Foundational Tenets for Teaching and Learning Mathematics

As teacher candidates begin to conceptualize how to teach mathematics in a meaningful way, they need to understand some tenets that should undergird their development of lesson plans and how they enact those lessons with students.

Relational versus instrumental understanding. Skemp (1976/2006) defined relational understanding as "knowing what to do and why" and instrumental understanding "as rules without reasons" (p. 89). Preservice secondary mathematics teachers need to know the difference between the two kinds of understanding because most preservice secondary mathematics teachers have largely experienced learning mathematics in an instrumental way. Realizing the differences between the two types of understanding, experiencing learning mathematics in a relational manner, and seeing the results of students developing relational understanding of concepts are important experiences for secondary mathematics preservice teachers.

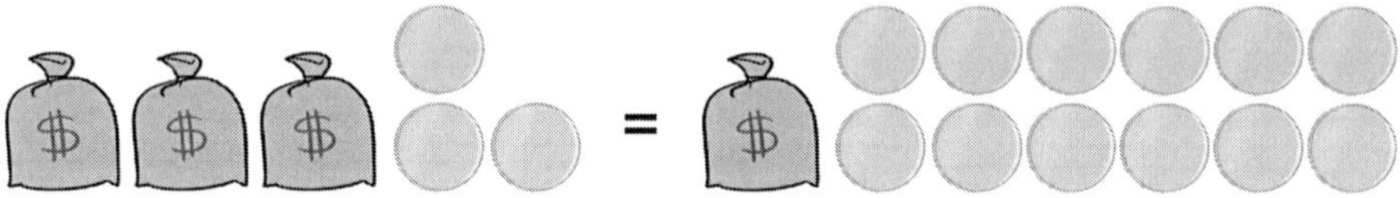

Each pouch contains the same number of one-dollar gold coins.
The number of gold coins on both sides of the equality sign is the same, but some coins are hidden in the pouches. Try to find the number of gold coins in each pouch.

Figure 1.1 Task promoting meaningful use of equations. (From *Moving Straight Ahead: Linear Relationships* by G. Lappan, J. T. Fey, W. M. Fitzgerald, & S. N. Friel, 2014, Upper Saddle River, NJ: Prentice Hall. Reprinted with permission.)

Placing preservice secondary mathematics teachers in situations in which they develop a relational understanding of a concept helps them to see the difference between relational understanding and instrumental understanding. For example, allowing preservice secondary mathematics teachers to work with mystery pouches and coins can help them understand how to solve equations in a meaningful way. Preservice teachers are given a picture such as the one in Figure 1.1.

The pouches in the figure are related to the variables in an equation, and the coins represent the constants. The equation represented by the picture is $3x + 3 = 2x + 12$. In thinking about the picture, the students know that each of the pouches contains the same number of coins. In balancing the equation, they know that the two pouches on each side are equal and three of the coins on the right side are the same number as three of the coins on the left side. They then know that each pouch has to contain nine coins in order for the equation to be true because they are left with one unmatched pouch on the left side of the equation. These problem types enable preservice teachers to understand that variables represent unknown quantities, which will make the equation true.

In addition to asking preservice teachers to solve these types of problems, they are asked to reflect on their thinking and to think about how helping students to develop a relational understanding of concepts and skills such as this will enable them to reason and make sense of mathematics. In addition, showing preservice teachers videos of students solving problems and presenting their solutions in a relational manner helps to confirm why it is important to teach mathematics in a relational manner.

Furthermore, Pesek and Kirshner (2000) posited that in order "to balance their professional obligation to teach for understanding against administrators' push for higher standardized test scores, mathematics teachers sometimes adopt a two-track strategy: teach part of the time for meaning (relational learning) and part of the time for recall and procedural-skill development (instrumental learning)" (p. 524). Moreover, they specifically addressed the problems that might occur when rote-skill development (instrumental understanding) occurs prior to teaching for relational understanding. In addition, they found that students who were taught area and perimeter via instrumental instruction before they received relational instruction "achieved no more, and most probably less, conceptual understanding than students exposed only to the relational unit" (pp. 537–538). Pesek and Kirshner also found that students who learned area and perimeter as a set of how-to rules referred to formulas, operations, and fixed procedures to solve problems, whereas students whose initial experiences were relational used conceptual and flexible methods to develop solutions. Finally, the authors shared that extensive time spent on routine exercises to consolidate rote or procedural knowledge does not lead to the kind of learning that takes place through the time given to students' intuitive and sense-making capabilities.

Equity. Another tenet of inquiry-based teaching is equity. Understanding that all students need the opportunity to reach their full mathematics potential is crucial for secondary mathematics preservice teachers. Preservice secondary mathematics teachers need to understand what it means to achieve equity in a mathematics classroom, examine barriers related to student engagement and achievement, develop equitable pedagogical strategies, and examine their beliefs about students from different race/ethnicity, socioeconomic status, gender, ability, and sociolinguistics groups, and confront the negative beliefs (NCTM, 2014; Strutchens, 2000).

Preservice teachers need to think about the meaning of equity from different perspectives. They should understand that "equity does not mean that every student should receive identical instruction; instead, it demands that reasonable and appropriate accommodations be made as needed to promote access and attainment for all students" (NCTM, 2000, p. 12). Equity also means "being unable to predict students' mathematics achievement and participation based solely upon characteristics such as race, class, ethnicity, sex, beliefs, and proficiency in the dominant language" (Gutiérrez, 2007, p. 41). Teachers should also think of equity as a bidirectional exchange—which is different from equity as primarily benefitting growth of students and student groups that have historically been denied equal access, opportunity, and outcomes in mathematics to a reciprocal approach where teachers are learning from the students and what they bring from their cultural backgrounds (Civil, 2007). In addition, the concept of equity includes "the equitable distribution of material and human resources, intellectually challenging curricula, educational experiences that build on students' cultures, languages, home experiences, and identities; and pedagogies that prepare students to engage in critical thought and democratic participation in society" (Lipman, 2004, p. 3). In addition, according to a joint position statement of the National Council of Supervisors of Mathematics and TODOS: Mathematics for All (2016), "a social justice stance requires a systemic approach that includes fair and equitable teaching practices, high expectations for all students, access to rich, rigorous, and relevant mathematics, and strong family/community relationships to promote positive mathematics learning and achievement. Equally important, a social justice stance interrogates and challenges the roles power, privilege, and oppression play in the current unjust system of mathematics education—and in society as a whole" (p. 1).

These conceptions of equity are made concrete to preservice teachers when they actually experience equitable pedagogy as students in their methods classes, and then practice implementing equitable pedagogy in their field experiences. According to Banks and Banks (1995), equitable pedagogy focuses on the "identification and use of effective instructional techniques and methods as well as the context in which they are used," "challenges teachers to use teaching strategies that facilitate the learning process," and "provides a basis for addressing critical aspects of schooling and for transforming curricula and schools" (p. 153). Teachers may use mathematics autobiographies and other means to get to know their students and foster positive mathematics identities in students. Teachers may ask students to engage in social justice activities, such as studying statistics related to racial profiling and determining whether injustices have occurred, and then suggesting what steps should be taken next (Gutstein, 2003). Teachers may ask students to develop and explore mathematical problems related to situations that they have observed in their community, such as comparing convenience store prices to those in a major grocery store and discussing which store has the better deals and why (Tate, 1995). Teachers may ask students to write and share reports on the contributions of various cultures to the advancement of mathematics (NCTM, 1991). These strategies, along with the NCTM's (2014) mathematics teaching practices discussed in a later section, will enable teachers to foster reasoning and sense-making skills in students from a variety of backgrounds.

Mathematical habits of mind. Mathematical habits of mind are ways of thinking that are indigenous to mathematics (Cuoco, Goldenberg, & Mark, 2010). In the middle grades, students develop habits of mind beyond what they learn in elementary school, such as abstracting regularity from calculations and articulating a generalization using mathematical language, which are both related to algebraic thinking (Mark, Cuoco, Goldenberg, & Sword, 2010). At the high school level, students develop general habits of mind and habits of mind that are more subject specific (Cuoco, Goldenberg, & Mark, 2010). Some of the habits of mind discussed by Cuoco, Goldenberg, and Mark (2010) are: performing thought experiments; finding, articulating, and explaining patterns; creating and using representations; articulating generality in precise language; generalizing from examples; expecting mathematics to make sense; modeling geometric phenomena with continuous functions; seeking regularity in repeated calculations; and chunking—changing variables to hide complexity. In addition to the aforementioned habits of mind, the NCTM (2009) contended that students should develop reasoning habits such as analyzing a problem and implementing a strategy, which are described as "productive way[s] of thinking that become common in the processes of mathematical inquiry and sense making" (p. 9).

The mathematical habits of mind and the reasoning habits are in alignment with the Standards for Mathematical Practice of the CCSS (CCSSO & NGA, 2010). The Standards for Mathematical Practice were built on the NCTM's (2000) process standards of problem solving, reasoning and proof, communication, representation, and connections, as well as the strands of mathematical proficiency specified in the National Research Council's report *Adding It Up* (Kilpatrick, Swafford, & Findell, 2001).

Throughout their program of study, preservice secondary mathematics teachers should experience tasks and problems that help them to develop the mathematical habits of mind, reasoning habits, and the skills and proficiencies embedded in the Standards for Mathematical Practice. These reasoning and sense-making skills are paramount for teachers who will be facilitating an inquiry-based classroom.

Curriculum coherence. It is necessary for preservice secondary mathematics teacher candidates to understand the importance of using a set of curriculum materials that are well aligned with their course of study and that are problem based with the Standards for Mathematical Practice or other reasoning and sense-making skills embedded. It is also important that preservice secondary mathematics teacher candidates are able to examine curricular materials to determine which ones are more in alignment with the problem-based approach to teaching. They should also be provided an opportunity to look across grades to determine how the curriculum grows and how topics are connected. Examining learning trajectories (Confrey, Maloney, & Corley, 2014; Daro, Mosher, & Corcoran, 2011) is also helpful.

Assessment. Assessment in an inquiry-based classroom should be in alignment with the type of mathematics teaching that is occurring. Preservice teachers need the opportunity to examine and experience a variety of tasks that lead to more information about what students know and can do. Equitable assessments include open-ended, open-middle, and a small number of closed tasks. Preservice secondary mathematics teachers should learn about exit slips, writing prompts, projects, portfolios, and other measures of student mathematical understanding. They should also learn about and use rubrics in evaluating student work. Preservice secondary mathematics teachers should learn the difference between formative assessment and summative assessment, and the affordances of each. Formative assessment is particularly important in the inquiry-based classroom. Formative assessment is any assessment for which the first priority is promoting students' learning. Furthermore, formative assessment aids in the learning process when it provides feedback that teachers and students can use to modify the teaching and learning activities in which they are engaged (Black, Harrison, Lee, Marshall, & Wiliam, 2004).

Classroom Environment

The classroom environment for a problem-based inquiry classroom is one of the main determinants of successful implementation. Students need to know that teachers care about and value their opinions. How teachers interact with students around problem solving will impact students' mathematics identities. Creating a classroom environment in which students are empowered because they are able to see themselves as capable of participating in and being doers of mathematics is important (Solomon, 2007). Solomon asserted that when students identify themselves as participatory and doers of mathematics, they make positive connections and are motivated to achieve at high levels.

Cooperative learning groups. One important component of a problem-based inquiry classroom is the opportunity for students to work in cooperative learning groups. Cooperative learning groups have been shown to improve academic achievement, improve behavior and attendance, increase self-confidence and motivation, and increase liking of school and classmates. In a cooperative group, members discuss their approaches to solving a math problem, explain their reasoning, and defend their work. However, cooperative learning involves more than placing students into groups. Students need to be taught how to work effectively in groups.

Complex instruction (CI) is a form of cooperative learning where students are assigned open-ended, interdependent group tasks and serve as academic and linguistic resources for one another. Their teacher addresses status issues to ensure that all students have the opportunity to be heard and to participate well (Cohen, Lotan, Scarloss, & Arellano, 1999). In CI, teachers use cooperative group work to teach at a high academic level in diverse classrooms. One goal of this approach is to let students make mistakes, figure out why things did not work, and then try to think of new ways to solve the problems they have encountered. The teacher should be very involved in the following activities: (1) observe students, (2) listen to the discussions in the groups at a proper distance, (3) ask questions to groups who are stuck, (4) provide positive feedback to individuals and groups, (5) watch for who is participating and who is not, and the reasons for this, and (6) remind the groups about rules, roles, and norms (Kujansivu & Rosell, 2000).

Boaler (2006) found that when CI is implemented well, an added benefit for students and teachers occurs—relational equity. Relational equity is the respectful relationships that students develop through a collaborative problem-solving approach in which students work together and learn to appreciate the diverse insights, methods, and perspectives that different students offer in the collective solving of problems (Boaler, 2006, 2008; Boaler & Staples, 2008). Preservice teachers need to be engaged in cooperative group work as learners of mathematics and facilitators of student learners. Figure 1.2 provides a list of rules and roles that can be shared with preservice teachers to help them facilitate cooperative learning.

Differentiated instruction. Differentiation consists of the efforts of teachers to respond to variance among learners in the classroom. It is an approach designed to improve classroom learning for all students. At least four classroom elements can be differentiated based on student readiness, interest, or learning profile: (1) content: what the student needs to learn or how the student will get access to the information; (2) process: activities in which the student engages in order to make sense of or master the content; (3) products: culminating projects that

Rules for Cooperative Learning

1. Each member of the group has a responsibility to contribute to the group work.
2. Each member of the group should be willing to help any other member of the group who asks for help.
3. Each member of the group is accountable for the learning progress of the group.
4. Within your group, you will respect one another and listen to what each member has to say.
5. When a question is asked of the group, each member should be able to answer the question and state what the group's thoughts are.
6. Each member of the group has a role.
7. You can only ask for help when all members of the group have the same question.
8. Members of a group should speak in a voice that can only be heard by its members.
9. Members of the group will be evaluated individually and collectively.

Roles for Cooperative Group Members

Group Facilitator:	Keep the group on task
Materials Manager:	Obtain, maintain, and return materials needed for the group to function
Recorder:	Record all group activities and processes
Reporter:	Report group processes and accomplishments to the teacher and/or the entire class

Figure 1.2 Rules and roles for effective cooperative learning.

ask the student to rehearse, apply, and extend what he or she has learned in a unit; and (4) learning environment: the way in which the classroom works and feels (Tomlinson, 2000). Furthermore, Small (2009) listed three elements that are essential to effectively differentiating instruction:

1. The focus of instruction must be on the big ideas being taught to ensure that they are addressed across all levels.
2. Pre-assessment is essential to determine what needs different students have.
3. There must be some aspect of choice for students, whether in content, process, or product. (p. 4)

Differentiated instruction in the problem-based classroom can be implemented through using multiple entry-level tasks and tasks designed to meet students at their levels of mathematics understanding. Moreover, flexible grouping is also a hallmark of effective differentiated instruction. It is important for preservice secondary mathematics teachers to understand what it means to provide effective differentiated instruction.

Classroom discourse. As first defined by the NCTM in 1989, "[t]he discourse of a classroom—the ways of representing, thinking, talking, agreeing and disagreeing—is central to what students learn about mathematics" (p. 34). The teacher is envisioned as an orchestrator or facilitator of rich exchanges in which students share their ideas about mathematics, consider the ideas of others, and question the teacher and others. Such discourse effectively promotes students' engagement in mathematical problem solving and sense making. Moreover, it helps to surface the shift from everyday use of language to more mathematical and precise use of language that is essential for effective communication about mathematics (Moschkovich, 2007). Preservice secondary mathematics teachers need to understand the importance of classroom discourse in promoting student learning, as discussed further in the following section.

Mathematics Teaching Practices

In 2014, the NCTM proposed a set of eight mathematics teaching practices, which is quickly gaining currency as a useful "framework for strengthening the teaching and learning of mathematics" (p. 9), including work with preservice mathematics teachers. These practices are grounded in research that has been conducted over the past four decades on how to promote students' ability to build relational understanding of mathematics through engagement with challenging mathematics problems. Each of these practices is briefly described in the following sections.

Establish mathematics goals to focus learning. Hiebert and colleagues (2007, as cited in NCTM, 2014) stated: "[F]ormulating clear, explicit learning goals sets the stage for everything else." Those goals should not be established in isolation but should rather be situated within a progression of mathematics learning. The goals established will guide decisions about the tasks that are selected, the directions that classroom discourse should take, and assessments of student learning.

Implement tasks that promote reasoning and problem solving. This practice states that "effective teaching of mathematics engages students in solving and discussing tasks that promote mathematical reasoning and problem solving and allow multiple entry points and varied solution strategies" (NCTM, 2014, p. 10). The selection of tasks should be in alignment with the goals that are set for students. Moreover, tasks should be selected that allow many students to approach them but provide challenge for all. Consider, for example, the following task:

A slab of soap on one pan of a scale balances three-quarters of a slab of soap of equal weight and a three-quarters-pound weight on the other pan. How much does the slab of soap weigh? (Adapted from Kordemsky & Parry, 1992, as cited in NCTM, 2009.)

Students might solve the problem using a variety of methods, including:

- Writing an algebraic equation and solving it: $x = 3/4x + 3/4$.
- Reasoning arithmetically: Remove three-quarters of a slab from both sides of the scale. That means one-quarter of a slab measures three-quarters of a pound. Since there are four quarters in a pound, the weight must be 4 x 3/4, or three pounds.
- Guess and check: Let's guess that it's a pound. Then the weight on the left pan will be 3/4 + 3/4, or 1.5 pounds. That's more than one pound, so let's try a larger amount. If it weighs two pounds, then the left side will be 3/4(2) + 3/4, or 9/4. That's still too much, so let's try three pounds. 3/4(3) + 3/4 = 3. So it weighs three pounds.

Note that students can approach this problem at a variety of levels, which may increase student engagement in the problem and provide students with an opportunity to learn from and with one another.

Use and connect mathematical representations. Mathematical representations "embody critical features of mathematical constructs and actions" (NCTM, 2014, p. 24). Representations can be physical, visual, verbal, or symbolic. The use of representations, and connecting among representations, is essential to developing deep mathematical understanding and effective problem solving (NCTM, 2014). For example, students might explore what happens when one multiplies one more than a number by one less than that same number by making a drawing, making a chart, or using a symbolic representation, as shown in Figure 1.3. These representations become both a tool for problem solving and for students to communicate their reasoning with others.

Facilitate meaningful mathematical discourse. As stated in the previous section, mathematical discourse is essential for developing mathematical problem solving and sense making. In particular, Smith and Stein (2011) describe five practices for effectively orchestrating classroom discourse:

1. *Anticipating* student responses prior to the lesson
2. *Monitoring* students' work on and engagement with the tasks

Drawing

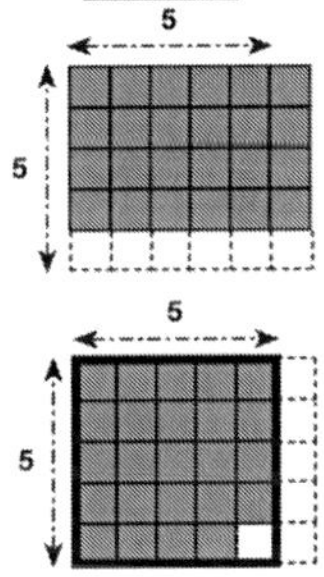

Table

N	N+1	N-1	(N+1)(N-1)	N^2
1	2	0	0	1
2	3	1	3	4
3	4	2	8	9
4	5	3	15	16
5	6	4	24	25
6	7	5	35	36
7	8	6	48	49

Symbolic

$$(N + 1)(N - 1)$$
$$N(N - 1) + 1(N - 1)$$
$$N^2 - N + N - 1$$
$$N^2 - 1$$

Figure 1.3 Representations of multiplying one more than a number by one less than that same number.

3. *Selecting* particular students to present their mathematical work
4. *Sequencing* students' responses in a specific order for discussion
5. *Connecting* different students' responses and connecting the responses to key mathematical ideas

These practices provide a mechanism through which teachers can move from initial discourse about a mathematical task that may be occurring in pairs or small groups to discourse of the full mathematics classroom that is aimed at allowing students to share problem-solving methods and the sense they are making of mathematical problems with the goal of developing common mathematical understandings.

Pose purposeful questions. A teacher's use of effective questioning is essential in promoting students' mathematical reasoning and sense making (NCTM, 2014), as such questions encourage students to share their thinking and reflect on the thinking of others. According to the NCTM (2014), two critical issues must be addressed. First, rather than relying on questions that primarily count on the recall of facts, teachers must ask effective questions that encourage students to discuss mathematics, make connections among ideas, and justify the validity of their work. Second, teachers must use effective patterns of questioning. A funneling pattern, in which a series of questions is used to guide students to a desired outcome, is all too frequently implemented with minimal attention to divergent perspectives, whether or not they may be productive (Herbel-Eisenmann & Breyfogle, 2005). Alternatively, a teacher may use a pattern of questioning that focuses on student thinking. In this pattern, the outcome of the discussion is guided by the students' thoughts, and alternative perspectives are encouraged. The teacher's goal is to encourage students to clearly communicate their thinking and to reflect on what other students say. This latter pattern is foundational to developing deep discourse that supports mathematical learning and problem solving.

Build procedural fluency from conceptual understanding. Procedural fluency requires more than recall of facts and procedures. As stated by Martin (2009): "Students must be able to do much more than carry out mathematical procedures. They must know which procedure is appropriate and most productive in a given situation, what a procedure accomplishes, and what kind of results to expect. Mechanical execution of procedures without understanding their mathematical basis often leads to bizarre results" (p. 165). Such procedural fluency is built on a solid base of relational understanding that is developed through engagement with meaningful problem situations. A "rush to fluency" is, however, not productive, as it may cause mathematics anxiety and decrease interest in the study of mathematics (NCTM, 2014, p. 42). On the other hand, development of procedural fluency is essential, as it forms a solid base for students' expanding problem solving and sense making, allowing them to focus on the more challenging aspects of a problem while off-loading its more trivial aspects.

Support productive struggle in learning mathematics. As students face a challenging mathematics problem, they may feel that they are unable to solve it if they do not readily see its solution. Teachers must resist the inclination to become overly helpful in the face of student frustration and encourage students to persist in attempting to solve the problem. This corresponds with the first standard for mathematical practice in the *Common Core*, which states that students must "[m]ake sense of problems and persevere in solving them" (CCSSO & NGA, 2010, p. 6). All too often, mathematics students have a fixed mind-set in which they consider mathematical ability to be an innate characteristic of a person that cannot be changed (Dweck, 2008). Building a growth mind-set in which students recognize that mathematical ability can be improved through hard work and persistence requires teachers to expect their students to persist. They praise effort over perceived intelligence and provide feedback on students' progress in becoming more proficient (NCTM, 2014).

Elicit and use evidence of student thinking. "Effective teaching of mathematics uses evidence of student thinking to assess progress toward mathematical understanding and to adjust instruction continually in ways that support and extend learning" (NCTM, 2014, p. 10). This mathematics teaching practice is essentially formative assessment. An example of an effective way to elicit students' thinking is a strategy called "My Favorite No" (Teaching Channel, n.d.). Students are given an entry task/warm-up, which serves as a review problem. Students are asked to write their solutions on index cards. Next, the teacher collects the cards, and then chooses the "best" wrong answer to share with the class, usually a misconception that the teacher wants to highlight so that students will learn from the solution. The teacher rewrites the solution so that students cannot tell who solved the problem in that manner. The teacher displays the solution to the problem so that the students can analyze the solution to determine its strengths and weaknesses. Next, the teacher asks the students to tell her what they think she likes about the thinking displayed in the solution. After discussing what is right about the solution, the class talks about where the error occurred. This discussion helps the teacher to assess the thinking of multiple students and provides the class with immediate feedback on the problem they just solved. This strategy leads to growth in students' ability to recognize their weaknesses and identify exactly where they need to improve.

Practices to Foster Preservice Teachers' Facility With Effective Instruction

In this section, we discuss experiences integrated into our secondary methods program that can help preservice secondary mathematics teachers gain familiarity and facility with instructional practices that promote and support mathematical problem solving and sense making. In our program, students are required to take three methods courses:

- CTSE 5040, Technology and Applications in Secondary Mathematics. This course focuses on the use of technology that supports mathematics teaching and learning.
- CTMD 4010, Teaching Mathematics in the Middle School. This course focuses on teaching middle school mathematics and the middle school mathematics curriculum.
- CTSE 4030, Curriculum and Teaching in Secondary Mathematics. This course focuses on teaching high school mathematics and the high school mathematics curriculum.

Throughout these methods classes, students are exposed to the importance of mathematical problem solving as the core of school mathematics by careful analysis of the Standards for Mathematical Practice, which are presented as required content that they will need to address as mathematics teachers. We also emphasize the importance of "teaching via problem solving" as a way to both meet the practice standards and make sense of mathematics. A variety of readings (NCTM, 2009, 2014; cf. Schroeder & Lester, 1989; Skemp, 1976/2006), vignettes, videos, and in-class "laboratory experiences" are used to illustrate these points, as well as an extensive microteaching experience in CTSE 4030. These approaches are described in more detail in the following sections.

"Laboratory Experiences" With Problem Solving

A major obstacle in preparing preservice secondary mathematics teachers to teach mathematical problem solving and sense making is that they themselves may not have developed proficiency in these areas. Moreover, they frequently lack the relational understanding of core mathematical topics in the secondary mathematics curriculum needed to promote their students' learning. Volumes such as *The Mathematical Preparation of Teachers II* (Conference Board of the Mathematical Sciences, 2012) recommend rethinking the mathematics courses preservice teachers take to integrate attention to mathematical practices and processes, including changing how mathematics courses are taught and adding mathematics courses specifically designed for mathematics teachers. While implementing these recommendations is a long-term goal for our program, in the short term we compensate by including "laboratory experiences" within the methods courses where students explore mathematics concepts using problem solving. Particular focus is placed on building their mathematical habits of mind, especially the Standards for Mathematical Practice.

These experiences generally incorporate the use of appropriate tools and technology that are useful in making sense of mathematics and problem solving. Physical manipulatives (or their virtual, online counterparts) can be useful in helping students visualize mathematical relationships. While emphasis is often placed on using manipulatives with younger children, they can also be very useful with secondary mathematics students (NCTM, 2014). Technology also provides a useful context for mathematical problem solving, particularly the use of "mathematical action technologies" (Dick & Hollebrands, 2011), which "perform mathematical tasks and/or respond to the user's actions in mathematically defined ways" (p. xii). As argued in NCTM (2014), given the pervasiveness of technology in students' lives, it should be an inherent part of doing mathematics in classrooms.

CTSE 5040, experiences with technology as a learner. A major focus of CTSE 5040 is developing the preservice teachers' own mathematical problem solving and sense making. Technology provides a context in which they can build their experiences with problem solving, taking them out of their comfort zone. They explore a wide range of mathematical action technologies that can be accessed via tablet devices (e.g., iPads) or laptops. Applications used include spreadsheets (e.g., Microsoft Excel or Google Sheets), dynamic geometry software (e.g., Geogebra or Geometer's Sketchpad), computer algebra systems (e.g., WolframAlpha or TI-Nspire), statistical analysis software (e.g., Fathom or Core Math Tools), and software designed to explore specific mathematical concepts (e.g., the NCTM's Illuminations website or the Shodor Interactivate website).

Students are generally given "labs" in which they use particular mathematical tools in order to solve mathematical problems. A sample activity from the first day of class follows. Students are directed to a web-based app, pictured in Figure 1.4, and are asked to complete the following directions:

1. What does changing the black slider do?
2. Consider the purple slider:
   a. How does changing its value change the line? The equation?
   b. What happens when the number is large? A negative number? Zero?
3. Consider the green slider:
   a. How does changing its value change the line? The equation?
   b. What happens when the number is large? A negative number? Zero?
4. In the equation $y = mx + b$, summarize what m tells you and what b tells you.

The preservice teachers typically work on lab activities in pairs so they can discuss their thinking in a safe environment. The course instructor then facilitates full-class discourse around their solutions, keeping their focus on their own mathematical solutions rather than discussing how secondary students might solve the problems. Thus, the instructor is essentially modeling instruction designed to promote mathematical problem solving without directly addressing instruction. Only after the discussion of their mathematical problem solving and sense making is complete does the discussion turn to a reflection on the activity from the perspective of a preservice teacher, including the methods the instructor used to facilitate instruction, the approaches secondary students might use to solve the problem, and how the activity or technological tool

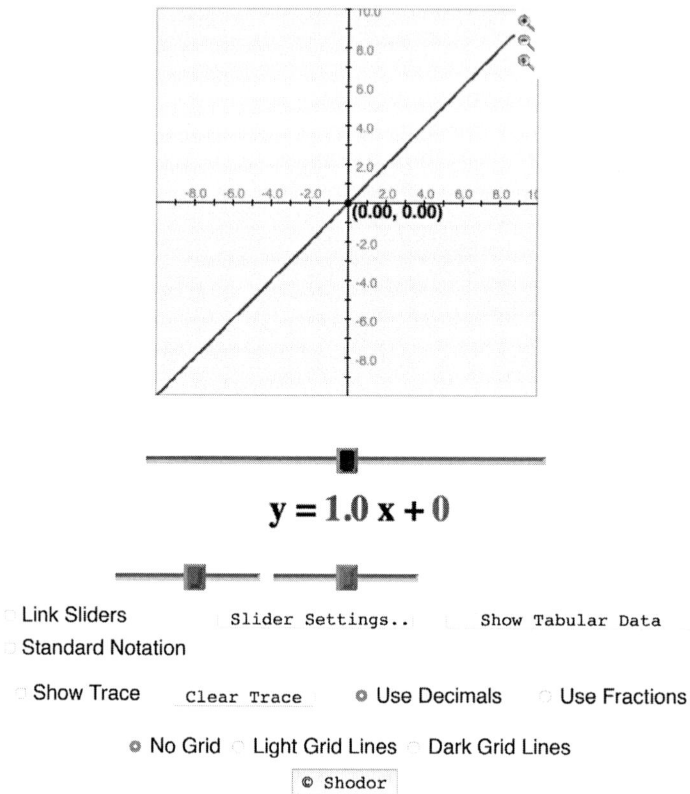

Figure 1.4 Web-based app exploring slope-intercept form at http://x.co/mwjU.

might be used to promote mathematical problem solving and sense making in the secondary classroom.

Throughout the course, the preservice teachers are given open-ended projects to complete, in which they solve extended mathematics problems that may take several days to complete. For example, following several labs focused on dynamic geometry, students were given their choice of several problems to pursue, such as the following (adapted from Dick & Hollebrands, 2011):

> Two brothers are part of an expedition that discovers a new island. From the sky, they notice that the island is shaped like an irregular convex quadrilateral. They are not sure of the actual dimensions of the island, but they want to determine a way that they can fairly divide the island between the two of them. The older brother suggests that they divide the land along one diagonal, and each would take one triangular part. He states that this is a fair method since it creates two triangles, and each will receive one triangle.

1. Is this method fair? Why or why not?
2. Devise another method that is more fair.
3. Can you come up with other approaches that will be more advantageous?

Note that this task is amenable to multiple solution paths and is likely to engage multiple mathematical habits of mind. Use of dynamic geometry software, such as Geogebra or Geometer's Sketchpad, is very helpful in supporting preservice teachers' exploration of the problem. Figure 1.5 shows a possible exploration of the problem in the NCTM's Core Math Tools. Students can investigate various subdivisions of the quadrilateral to see which meet the conditions of the problem.

In the project write-up, the preservice teachers are asked to discuss their own mathematical problem solving; in a second section, they are asked to discuss how that problem might be incorporated into a mathematics classroom.

CTMD 4010, experiences with manipulatives as a learner. In this course, preservice teachers use a variety of physical models or manipulatives to solve problems in order to develop a relational understanding of mathematical concepts and skills. They solve problems and reflect on their problem-solving processes and think about

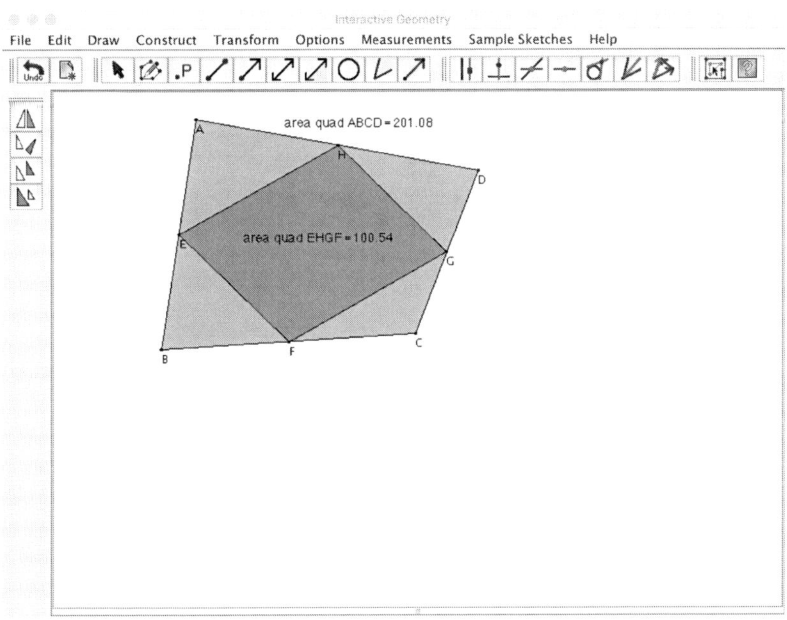

Figure 1.5 Exploration of the "island problem" using NCTM's Core Math Tools.

how students in the middle grades would solve the same type of problem and what the students would learn from solving the problem. A sample problem with a variety of solutions is shown in Figure 1.6.

The "sharing the money" problem allows students to see multiple ways to solve the problem and that a fraction is relative to the whole. They also may use Cuisenaire rods, fraction circles, or counters to solve the problem.

CTSE 4030, experiences as a learner of high school mathematics. Throughout CTSE 4030, preservice teachers are asked to solve challenging problems that focus on the development of mathematical habits of mind within key areas of the high school mathematics curriculum. Given that CTSE 5040 is a co-requisite for this course, the preservice teachers are expected to integrate the use of technological tools

Problem: A father gives half the money in his pocket to his wife, a fourth of what is left to his son, a third of what is left to his daughter; he then splits the remainder with his youngest son. If the youngest son got $2, how much did the father start with?	
Solution 1: Draw a picture or use Fraction Factory Pieces Rectangle 1 represents the original amount of money in the father's pocket. Rectangle 2 shows that the father gave half of the money to his wife. Rectangle 3 shows that he gave a fourth of what remained to his oldest son. Rectangle 4 shows that he gave a third of what was left to his daughter. Rectangle 5 shows that he split what was left with his youngest son. From the rectangles one can see that everyone got an eighth except the mother. Thus since the youngest son received $2.00, the daughter, the oldest son, and the father also received $2.00 each. Together the youngest son, the daughter, the oldest son, and the father received $8.00. So the mother received $8.00 and the total amount the father had was $16.00.	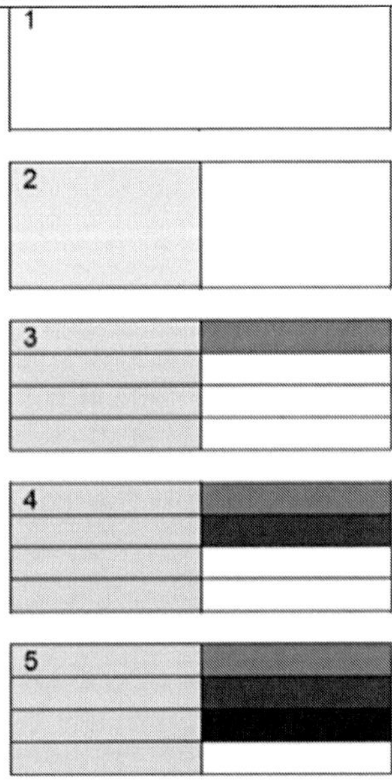
Solution 2: Use a variable	Let x = whole amount 1/2x = the amount given to the mother 1/4 * 1/2x = 1/8x = the amount given to the oldest son 1/3* 3/4 * 1/2x = 1/8x = the amount the daughter received 1/2* 2/4 * 1/2 x = 1/8x = the amount given to the youngest son So 1/8x = 2 8 *1/8x = 2 * 8 x = 16

Figure 1.6 "Lab" problem along with possible solutions.

into their problem-solving activities, as appropriate. For example, they use spreadsheets to model the concentration of a drug in a person's blood for given dosages and filtration rates by the kidneys (NCTM, 2000). This problem both builds their mathematical habits of mind and familiarizes them with an area of the high school curriculum that they may not have experienced, functions that are defined recursively.

A number of problems incorporate use of physical manipulatives; for example, algebra tiles are used to explore operations with polynomials. While the preservice teachers may be able to carry out the algebraic procedures, they often do not possess a relational understanding of why those procedures work. For example, they explore the algebraic technique of "completing the square"; using algebra tiles makes it evident that they are literally completing a square, as shown in Figure 1.7 (NCTM, 2009).

The preservice teachers are generally asked to work on the problems in small groups, with a subsequent full-group discussion led by the instructor, modeling instructional approaches that promote the development of mathematical problem solving and sense making. While the initial focus of the discussion is on developing their mathematical habits of mind and knowledge of the curriculum, subsequent discussion considers the problems from the perspective of a high school mathematics teacher, including common ways students may think about the problem and instructional approaches that may help students develop productive ways of thinking.

Case Studies

In order for preservice teachers to fully understand the instructional practices that promote mathematical problem solving and sense making, such as the mathematical teaching practices (NCTM, 2014), they need to see depictions

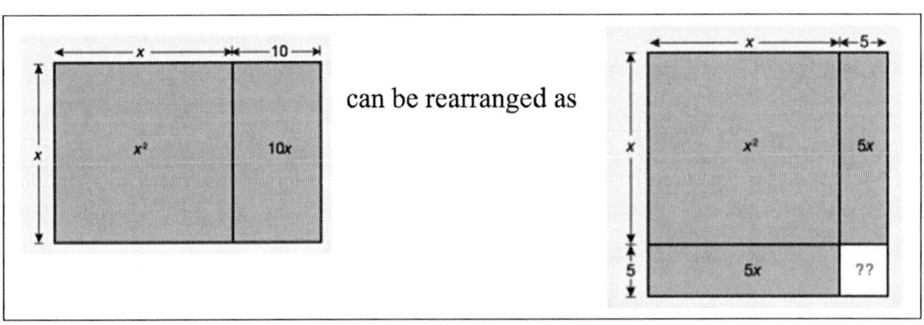

Figure 1.7 Visual representation of completing the square.

of such instruction within the context of high school classrooms. While they participate in school classrooms as a part of their field experiences, those experiences are not common across the preservice teachers within a given course. To provide a common base for discussion and reflection, we use classroom cases—either textual vignettes or videotapes. The prototypical approach used is to begin by having the preservice teachers participate as a class in the activity depicted in the case and to subsequently analyze its potential for promoting student learning. Consider, for example, the "Pay It Forward" task (Smith, 2014), presented to the CTSE 4030 class:

> In the movie "Pay It Forward," a student, Trevor, comes up with an idea that he thought could change the world. He decides to do a good deed for three people and then each of the three people would do a good deed for three more people and so on. He believed that before long there would be good things happening to billions of people. At stage 1 of the process, Trevor completes three good deeds. How does the number of good deeds grow from stage to stage? How many good deeds would be completed at stage 5? Describe a function that would model the Pay It Forward process at any stage. (p. 1)

The vignette or videotape is then shown to the class, including appropriate reflection questions. In the case of the "Pay It Forward" task, a case titled *Exploring Exponential Relationships: The Case of Ms. Culver* (Smith, 2014), which details a teacher's attempt to teach the task, was presented to the class along with the following reflection questions:

- How does this classroom compare to the typical high school classroom?
- Which of the Standards for Mathematical Practice did you observe?
- What did the teacher do to support students' use of the Standards for Mathematical Practice?

As is typical with our use of vignettes or videotapes, the preservice teachers first discussed the vignette in small groups, and then shared their responses with the class as a whole.

Lesson Plan Format

Preservice teachers write lesson plans for each course that are designed for problem-based classrooms. The lesson plans contain three major phases that are centered around worthwhile tasks that support what students should know and be able to do: launch, explore, and summarize. A sample lesson plan is provided in the Appendix.

Launch. In the first phase, the teacher launches the problem with the whole class. This involves helping students understand the problem setting, the mathematical context, and the challenge. The following questions can help the teacher prepare for the launch:

1. What are students expected to do?
2. What do the students need to know to understand the context of story and the challenge of the problem?
3. What difficulties can I foresee for students?
4. How can I keep from giving away too much of the problem?

The launch phase is also the time when the teacher introduces new ideas, clarifies definitions, reviews old concepts, and connects the problem to previous experiences of the students. It is critical that, while giving students a clear picture of what is expected, the teacher leaves the potential of the task intact. He or she must be careful not to tell too much and lower the challenge of the task to something routine or to cut off the rich array of strategies that may evolve from an open launch of the problem.

Explore. In the explore phase, students work individually, in pairs, in small groups, or occasionally as a whole class to solve the problem. As they work, they gather data, share ideas, look for patterns, make conjectures, and develop problem-solving strategies. The teacher's role during this phase is to move about the classroom, observing individual performance and encouraging on-task behavior. The teacher helps students persevere in their work by asking appropriate questions and providing confirmation and redirection where needed. For students who are interested in and capable of deeper investigation, the teacher may provide extra challenges related to the problem. The following questions can help the teacher prepare for the explore phase:

- How will I organize the students to explore this problem? (Individuals? Pairs? Groups? Whole class?)
- What materials will students need?
- How should students record and report their work?

- What different strategies can I anticipate they might use?
- What questions can I ask to encourage student conversation, thinking, and learning?
- What questions can I ask to focus their thinking if they become frustrated or off-task?
- What questions can I ask to challenge students if the initial question is "answered"?

Summarize. The summarize phase of instruction begins when most students have gathered sufficient data or made sufficient progress toward solving the problem. In this phase, students discuss their solutions as well as the strategies they used to approach the problem, organize the data, and find the solution. During the discussion, the teacher helps students enhance their understanding of the mathematics in the problem and guides them in refining their strategies into efficient, effective problem-solving techniques.

Although the summary discussion is led by the teacher, students play a significant role. Ideally, they should pose conjectures, question one another, offer alternatives, provide reasons, refine their strategies and conjectures, and make connections. As a result of the discussion, students should become more skillful at using the ideas and techniques that come out of the experience with the problem.

During the summarize phase, content goals of the problem, investigation, and unit can be addressed, allowing the teacher to assess the degree to which students are developing their mathematical knowledge. At this time, teachers can make additional instructional decisions that will enable all students to reach the mathematical goals of the activities. The following questions can help the teacher prepare for the summary:

- How can I help the students make sense of and appreciate the variety of methods that may be used?
- How can I orchestrate the discussion so students summarize their thinking about the problem?
- What concepts or strategies need to be emphasized?
- What ideas do not need closure at this time?
- What definitions or strategies do we need to generalize?
- What connections and extensions can be made?
- What new questions might arise and how do I handle them?
- What will I do to follow up, practice, or apply the ideas after the summary?

Microteaching

In addition to lab experiences focusing on particular areas of mathematics, CTSE 4030 incorporates an extended microteaching experience, in which the preservice teachers teach lessons to their peers. This creates a simplified environment in which the participants can feel safe in trying out various instructional methods without the complexities of running a classroom. They can also receive detailed feedback from their peers, a highly valued feature of the microteaching experience (Benton-Kupper, 2001). To maximize the benefits of the experience, lessons are drawn from an exemplary high school textbook series, The Interactive Mathematics Project (IMP). This approach has a number of benefits:

- Many students have not experienced instruction that is focused on the development of mathematical problem solving and sense making. While the lab experiences within the methods courses give them a taste of what this might look like, working through a complete unit designed to promote mathematical habits of mind gives them a better sense of how such instruction might play out over time in the classroom.
- Rather than having students pick potentially unrelated topics to teach, using a full unit provides a "coherent sequencing of core mathematical ideas" that "pose[s] problems that promote conceptual understanding, problem solving, and reasoning and are drawn from contexts in everyday life and other subjects" (NCTM, 2014, p. 72).
- Use of exemplary curriculum materials has the potential to enhance teacher learning if curriculum enactment is addressed in the supporting materials (Ball & Cohen, 1996). The IMP materials include information on student thinking, useful questions to ask, and tips on organizing the activity that may inform preservice teachers' thinking about the task being proposed.
- Having an exemplary curriculum to draw on simplifies aspects of the planning process, such as task selection, allowing the preservice teachers to focus on their instructional approaches. The IMP materials also provide useful guidance to inform lesson planning.

The instructor launches the microteaching experience by teaching the first several days of the unit; this allows the instructor to establish effective classroom procedures and norms for participation and the preservice teachers to become familiar with the general approach used in the curriculum materials. As routines are established, members of the class begin taking turns teaching.

In contrast to many microteaching experiences, the preservice teachers were asked to prepare a full lesson and, both for the sake of time and to increase their sense of safety in carrying out the lesson, they are allowed to plan and teach their lesson in pairs.

One of the important norms established in the initial days of the experience is that the participants can only draw on the prerequisite mathematical knowledge that a high school mathematics student studying that unit would have; this is characterized as wearing their "student hats." Following the lesson, a transition occurs; participants put on their "teacher hats," which gives them permission to discuss the mathematics from the perspective of a teacher, how students might respond to the lesson, and the efficacy of the instructional approaches used. Note that this debriefing session begins during the initial days of the unit, while the course instructor is teaching, in order to establish norms for participation. The class collaboratively develops "ground rules" for the debriefing; typically, rules address the need for constructive criticism, maintaining a respectful tone, and including positive observations. The goal is to create a safe environment in which preservice teachers can exchange perspectives about critical aspects of instruction that promote mathematical problem solving.

Field Experiences That Foster Preservice Teachers' Facility With Effective Instruction

Each of the methods courses includes an early field experience, in which preservice teachers are required to spend time working in mathematics classrooms, as follows:

- CTSE 5040, Technology and Applications in Secondary Mathematics. Six three-hour observations are required in a middle or high school mathematics class that incorporates extensive use of technology, assigned in pairs. Preservice teachers are asked to inventory available technology and teach a sample activity focusing on the use of mathematical action technology (Dick & Hollebrands, 2011).
- CTMD 4010, Teaching Mathematics in the Middle School. Seven three-hour sessions are required in a middle school class where the preservice teachers teach in small groups and assist the cooperating teacher with lessons.
- CTSE 4030, Curriculum and Teaching in Secondary Mathematics. Twelve three-hour observations are required in a high school mathematics class, assigned in pairs. This includes three lessons that are designed and taught by the pair.

In addition, preservice teachers complete a semester-long, full-time internship in a middle or high school mathematics class. These experiences are critical in helping students develop their ability to support mathematical problem solving and sense making as they plan lessons, implement them, and then reflect on the success of their lessons and how they might be improved.

Middle school Pi Day. As a part of CTMD 4010, preservice secondary mathematics teachers write lesson plans that focus on a nonroutine problem-solving activity that may require the use of manipulatives to solve. The activities usually involve pi or circles in some way. The preservice teachers create tri-boards to simulate a fair-like atmosphere. The preservice teachers facilitate this activity at a middle school during the school's Pi Day, typically held around March 14 (or 3/14), since 3.14 is a common approximation for pi. Preservice teachers may end up facilitating the same activity three or four times during the day. Thus, they see a variety of responses and thought processes. They reflect on the experience in the form of a written report. This report describes the conditions under which the activity took place, students' thought processes, and examples of students' solution strategies. The preservice teachers enjoy the opportunity to teach multiple groups of students. Their lessons are based on the *Common Core* and NCTM's (2014) *Principles to Actions.*

Middle school small-group lessons. During their practicum experience for CTMD 4010 (the middle school methods class), preservice teachers are required to teach lessons to small mixed-ability groups of students in order to understand students' thought processes. The preservice teachers are required to write at least one lesson and teach their peers' lessons as well. They are required to reflect on how well the lessons were taught and how well the student understood the content. The preservice teachers assist their mentor when they are not teaching by tutoring students. By working with a small group, they are able to ask more questions and focus more on teaching, rather than on having to deal with classroom management issues. Ideally, the preservice teachers will be able to work with the same group of students throughout the semester so that they can see how their students have grown mathematically. Each of the mentor teachers from the school works with two to four preservice teachers, and each of the preservice teachers teach the same lesson to the groups of students within the same class period. Preservice teachers are then able to debrief at the end of the lessons about how well the students understood the lessons and the strengths and weaknesses of the lessons. Oftentimes, a university supervisor (usually the professor of the course) is able to observe the preservice teachers' lessons in their small groups and provide feedback.

The preservice teachers are encouraged to use *Connected Mathematics* (CMP) textbooks as resources to write their lessons. CMP is a problem-centered curriculum promoting an inquiry-based teaching-learning classroom environment. For example, in a lesson related to volume and surface area, the preservice teachers used the following problem:

> ABC Toy Company is planning to market a set of children's alphabet blocks. Each block is a cube with 1-inch edges, so each block has a volume of 1 cubic inch. The company wants to arrange 24 blocks in the shape of a rectangular prism and then package them in a box that exactly fits the prism.
>
> 1. Find all the ways 24 cubes can be arranged into a rectangular prism. Make a sketch of each arrangement you find, and give its dimensions and surface area. It may help to organize your findings into a table.
> 2. Which of your arrangements requires the box made with the least material? Which requires the box made with the most material?

Students use 1-inch cubes to create and find the surface area and volume of different rectangular solids that can be made with 24 cubes. Students see that the volume is always 24 cubic inches, but the surface area changes with the shape. This problem solidifies student understanding of volume and surface area, and it is connected to an authentic problem. The preservice teachers ask students questions and provide scaffolding for the students as they complete the tasks.

The lessons must cover objectives that are included in the Alabama Course of Study and emphasize problem solving and critical thinking. The preservice teachers spend three hours in the schools for six sessions for three weeks at two days per week. The lessons are graded and approved by the professor of the course. The preservice teachers teach at least four different lessons to students.

Full-group instruction. The focus of the field experiences in CTSE 4030 (the high school methods class) is on full-group instruction using problems that promote problem solving and sense making. Students are assigned in pairs to a high school mathematics classroom to conduct 12 three-hour visits. The trajectory of experiences over the course of the semester builds from observing for the first two to three visits to familiarize themselves with the context, to assisting with small-group instruction or segments of full-class discussion over the next four to five visits, to actually planning and teaching three lessons. The first lesson is co-taught by the pair in order to create a nonthreatening experience; each member of the pair takes the lead for one of the remaining lessons, with the other member assisting. Prior to teaching each lesson, they prepare a lesson plan following the format for the program, which must be approved by both their course instructor and their cooperating teacher. Lessons must promote mathematical problem solving and sense making, including attention to the mathematical teaching practices (NCTM, 2014). Following each lesson, both members of the pair prepare a reflection on the lesson. For the individually taught lessons, the lead preservice teacher must prepare a professional work sample in which they provide detailed commentary on the lesson—including the decisions made in planning the lesson, how the lesson was implemented, and support for student learning with a focus on problem-based instruction. In addition, the students keep a journal in which they reflect on their experiences and how they can better support students' problem solving and sense making.

Internship

The internship is an extension of the total program experience. Preservice teachers continue learning content and pedagogical skills during their internship. The internship lasts for 15 weeks. The preservice teachers gradually take on teaching and end up teaching for 20 full days and gradually give the courses back. Three facets of this experience are designed to help preservice teachers increase their ability to support mathematical problem solving and sense making: focus on the craft of teaching, continuous reflection on practice, and collaboration.

Craft of teaching. The craft of teaching is the ability to design lessons that involve important mathematical ideas, to design tasks that help students access those ideas, and then to successfully teach the lesson, which entails effectively launching the lesson, facilitating student engagement with the task, orchestrating meaningful mathematical discussions, and helping to make explicit the mathematical understanding students are constructing (Peterson & Leatham, 2009). Designing tasks that are accessible to students requires consideration of how students think mathematically. This focus on the craft of teaching brings together many aspects of their experiences in the methods courses related to supporting mathematical problem solving and sense making.

Reflecting on practice. During the internship, preservice teachers are required to reflect on their daily interactions with students and teachers. They keep a daily journal, and they have other reflections that are specific to lessons, which they teach. We ask them to reflect on the learning environment, the type of questions they or their cooperating teachers ask, student learning, and so forth. This consistent focus on reflection supports our goal of helping them to become facilitators of learning in a problem-based setting.

Collaboration with teachers. It is important that preservice teachers learn how to communicate effectively with their cooperating teacher, administrators, and others. We have found that placing students in pairs during their internship experience helps them to become more reflective, collaborative, and focused on student learning. Whether placed in pairs or as singletons, this focus on collaboration with their peers, their cooperating teacher, and others in the educational environment sets a foundation for a career-long trajectory focusing on promoting mathematics problem solving and sense making (NCTM, 2014).

Conclusion

Given that most preservice secondary mathematics teachers have been largely taught in an instrumental way, they typically have limited relational understanding of mathematics and a narrow view of what it means to teach mathematics, with little awareness of mathematical problem solving and sense making. Moreover, they are generally the "success stories" of traditional mathematics instruction; that is, they have been recognized as doing well in mathematics and thus may not recognize the need to change. Helping them to reconsider their views of what it means to be an effective mathematics teacher may be challenging, requiring them to face their limitations in what they had always perceived to be an area of strength. To help them build knowledge, dispositions, and skills to support the development of mathematical problem solving in each student requires a long-term, multisemester, multidimensional approach. In this chapter, we have outlined some of the approaches we have used across our program to ensure that our graduates are well prepared to integrate mathematical problem solving and sense making into instructional activities they design for their future classrooms.

References

Ball, D. L., & Cohen, D. K. (1996). Reform by the book: What is—or might be—the role of curriculum materials in teacher learning and instructional reform? *Educational Researcher, 25*(9), 6–8, 14.

Banks, C. A. M., & Banks, J. A. (1995). Equity pedagogy: An essential component of multicultural education. *Theory Into Practice, 34*(3), 152–158.

Benton-Kupper, J. (2001). The microteaching experience: Student perspectives. *Education, 121*(4), 830–835.

Black, P., Harrison, C., Lee, C., Marshall, B., & Wiliam, D. (2004). Working inside the black box: Assessment for learning in the classroom. *Phi Delta Kappan, 86*(1), 9–21.

Boaler, J. (2006). How a detracked mathematics approach promoted respect, responsibility, and high achievement. *Theory Into Practice, 45*(1), 40–46.

Boaler, J. (2008). *What's math got to do with it? Helping children learn to love their least favorite subject—and why it's important for America*. New York, NY: Penguin.

Boaler, J., & Staples, M. (2008). Creating mathematical futures through an equitable teaching approach: The case of Railside School. *Teachers College Record, 110*(3), 608–645.

Charles, R. I., & Lester, F. K. (1984). An evaluation of a process-oriented mathematical problem-solving instructional program in grades five and seven. *Journal for Research in Mathematics Education, 15*(1), 15–34.

Civil, M. (2007). Building on community knowledge: An avenue to equity in mathematics education. In N. Nasir & P. Cobb (Eds.), *Improving access to mathematics: Diversity and equity in the classroom* (pp. 105–117). New York, NY: Teachers College Press.

Cohen, E. G., Lotan, R. A., Scarloss, B. A., & Arellano, A. R. (1999). Complex instruction: Equity in cooperative learning classrooms. *Theory into Practice, 38*(2), 80–86.

Conference Board of the Mathematical Sciences. (2012). *The mathematical education of teachers II*. Providence, RI, and Washington, DC: American Mathematical Society and Mathematical Association of America.

Confrey, J., Maloney, A. P., & Corley, A. K. (2014). Learning trajectories: A framework for connecting standards with curriculum. *International Journal on Mathematics Education, 46*(5), 719–733.

Cuoco, A., Goldenberg, P., & Mark, J. (2010). Organizing a curriculum around mathematical habits of mind. *Mathematics Teacher, 103*(9), 682–688.

Daro, P., Mosher, F., & Corcoran, T. (2011). *Learning trajectories in mathematics: A foundation for standards, curriculum, assessment, and instruction.* CPRE Research Report #RR-68. Philadelphia, PA: Consortium for Policy Research in Education.

Dick, T. P., & Hollebrands, K. F. (2011). *Focus in high school mathematics: Technology to support reasoning and sense making.* Reston, VA: National Council of Teachers of Mathematics.

Dweck, C. (2008). *Mindsets and math/science achievement.* New York, NY: Carnegie Corporation of New York Institute for Advanced Study.

Goldin, G. A., & McClintock, C. E. (Eds.). (1984). *Task variables in mathematical problem solving.* Philadelphia, PA: Franklin Institute Press.

Gutiérrez, R. (2007). (Re)defining equity: The importance of a critical perspective. In N. Nasir N. & P. Cobb (Eds.), *Diversity, equity, and access to mathematical ideas* (pp. 37–50). New York, NY: Teachers College Press.

Gutstein, E. (2003). Teaching and learning mathematics for social justice in an urban Latino school. *Journal for Research in Mathematics Education, 34*(1), 37–73.

Herbel-Eisenmann, B. A., & Breyfogle, M. L. (2005). Questioning our patterns of questioning. *Mathematics Teaching in the Middle School, 10*(9), 484–489.

Kilpatrick, J., Swafford, J., & Findell, B. (2001). *Adding it up: Helping children learn mathematics.* Washington, DC: National Academy Press.

Kujansivu, A., & Rosell, J.-A. (2000, May). Complex instruction as a tool for developing the role of the teacher: A workshop presented at the Intercultural Education and Co-operative Learning conference in Ghent, *Intercultural Education, 11*(Suppl), S21–S26.

Lappan, G., Fey, J. T., Fitzgerald, W. M., & Friel, S. N. (2014). *Moving straight ahead: Linear relationships* (Connected Mathematics 2, Grade 7). Upper Saddle River, NJ: Prentice Hall.

Lipman, P. (2004). *High stakes education: Inequality, globalization, and urban school reform.* New York, NY: Routledge.

Mark, J., Cuoco, A., Goldenberg, E. P., & Sword, S. (2010). Contemporary curriculum issues: Developing mathematical habits of mind. *Mathematics Teaching in the Middle School, 15*(9), 505–509.

Martin, W. G. (2009). The NCTM High School Curriculum Project: Why it matters to you. *Mathematics Teacher, 103*(3), 164–166.

Moschkovich, J. (2007). Examining mathematical discourse practices. *For the Learning of Mathematics, 27*(1), 24–30.

National Council of Teachers of Mathematics. (1980). *An agenda for action.* Reston, VA: Author.

National Council of Teachers of Mathematics. (1989). *Curriculum and evaluation standards for school mathematics.* Reston, VA: Author.

National Council of Teachers of Mathematics. (1991). *Professional standards for teaching mathematics.* Reston, VA: Author.

National Council of Teachers of Mathematics. (1995). *Assessment standards for school mathematics.* Reston, VA: Author.

National Council of Teachers of Mathematics. (2000). *Principles and standards for school mathematics.* Reston, VA: Author.

National Council of Teachers of Mathematics. (2006). *Curriculum focal points for prekindergarten through grade 8 mathematics: A quest for coherence.* Reston, VA: Author.

National Council of Teachers of Mathematics. (2009). *Focus in high school mathematics: Reasoning and sense making.* Reston, VA: Author.

National Council of Teachers of Mathematics. (2014). *Principles to actions: Ensuring mathematical success for all.* Reston, VA: Author.

National Council of Supervisors of Mathematics and TODOS: Mathematics for All. (2016). *Mathematics education through the lens of social justice: Acknowledgment, actions, and accountability* (Joint Position Statement). Retrieved from https://www.mathedleadership.org/member/docs/resources/positionpapers/NCSMPositionPaper16.pdf

National Governors Association Center for Best Practices & Council of Chief State School Officers. (2010). *Common core state standards for mathematics.* Washington, DC: Authors.

Pesek, D. D., & Kirshner, D. (2000). Interference of instrumental instruction in subsequent relational learning. *Journal for Research in Mathematics Education, 31*(5), 524–540.

Peterson, B. E., & Leatham, K. R. (2009). Learning to use students' mathematical thinking to orchestrate a class discussion. In L. Knott (Ed.), *The role of mathematics discourse in producing leaders of discourse* (pp. 99–128). Charlotte, NC: Information Age Publishing.

Schoenfeld, A. (1985). *Mathematical problem solving.* New York, NY: Academic Press.

Schroeder, T. L., & Lester, F. K. (1989). Understanding mathematics via problem solving. In P. Trafton (Ed.), *New directions for elementary school mathematics* (pp. 31–42). Reston, VA: National Council of Teachers of Mathematics.

Skemp, R. R. (1976/2006). Relational understanding and instrumental understanding.

Mathematics Teaching in the Middle School, 12, 88–95. (Originally published in *Mathematics Teaching.*)

Small, M. (2009). *Good questions: Great ways to differentiate mathematics instruction.* Amsterdam, NY: Teachers College Press.

Smith, M. S. (2014). *Exploring exponential relationships: The case of Ms. Culver.* Reston, VA: NCTM. Retrieved from http://www.nctm.org/Conferences-and-Professional-Development/Principles-to-Actions-Toolkit/Resources/PayItForward-Narrative Case/

Smith, M. S., & Stein, M. K. (2011). *Five practices for orchestrating productive mathematics discussions.* Thousand Oaks, CA: Corwin.

Solomon, Y. (2007). Not belonging? What makes a functional learner identity in undergraduate mathematics? *Studies in Higher Education, 32*(1), 79–96.

Strutchens, M. E. (2000). Confronting beliefs and stereotypes that impede the mathematical empowerment of African American students. In M. E. Strutchens, M. Johnson, & W. Tate, (Eds.), *Changing the faces of mathematics: Perspectives on African Americans* (pp. 7–14). Reston, VA: National Council of Teachers of Mathematics.

Tate, W. (1995). Mathematics communication: Creating opportunities to learn. *Teaching Children Mathematics, 1*(6), 344–349, 369.

Teaching Channel. (n.d.). My favorite no: Learning from mistakes. Retrieved from https://www.teachingchannel.org/videos/class-warm-up-routine

Tomlinson, C. A. (2000). *Differentiation of instruction in the elementary grades.* Champaign, IL: ERIC Clearinghouse on Elementary and Early Childhood Education.

APPENDIX
Sample Lesson Plan: S-Pattern Task

Audience: Algebra II With Trigonometry students

Content Objectives

- Quadratic functions can model relationship between figures in a sequence.
- Two quadratic functions are equivalent if each can be rewritten using the distributive property and combining like terms.
- Second-order differences of quadratic functions are constant.

Alabama Course of Study (Algebra II With Trigonometry)

- #12. Interpret expressions that represent a quantity in terms of its context.[1] [A-SSE1]
- #12a. Interpret parts of an expression such as terms, factors, and coefficients. [A-SSE1a]
- #21. Create equations in two or more variables to represent relationships between quantities; graph equations on coordinate axes with labels and scales. [A-CED2]

Behavioral Objectives

The students will

- observe patterns in a set of figures,
- sketch and describe figures based on the patterns they observe,
- write a function rule for a pattern that is growing quadratically and relate the rule to the diagram of figures, and
- explain why the relationship between the figure number and the number of tiles is not linear.

Prerequisites

- The students should be familiar with the differences between linear and quadratic functions.

Materials

- "S-Pattern Task" handout

[1]Standard is a mathematics modeling standard.

- Calculators (if desired)
- Square tiles

Procedure

1. Warm-up (small groups)

Warm-up on the screen—figures from "S-Pattern Task."

Directions: In your small groups, talk about the figures below. Write down at least two patterns that you notice in the set of figures.

- Have you noticed any patterns yet?
- What do you notice about the figures?
- How many tiles are in the first figure?
- What about the second figure?
- What about the fifth figure?
- How are the figures growing?
- What is changing?
- What is staying the same?
- Can you think of any other patterns?

Transition: All right, everyone! Let's talk about the warm-up.

2. Discussion of warm-up and launch of today's investigation (full group)

Call on several groups for the patterns they identified. Continue asking until no groups have additional patterns to add.

- What was one pattern you identified?
- Did anyone else find this pattern?
- Did anyone notice a different pattern?
- What other patterns did you notice?

Say, "For the rest of today's class, we will be investigating this pattern further." Pass out the task sheet.

- Before we get started, what do you notice about problem 1? (It's the warm-up.)

Read through the task together.

- What kinds of things are you trying to find when solving the problems in this task?
- Does anyone have any questions about the activity?

Stress that they will have to explain how their function relates to the diagram.

Transition: Let's get to work. Focus on #2–4. If you finish early, move on to #5 and #6.

3. Investigation of "S-Pattern Task" (small groups)
Circulate and monitor groups as they work on "S-Pattern Task."

- How did you know how to construct the sixth figure?
- Did you use any of the patterns you identified in the warm-up?
- What changes between the sixth and seventh figures?
- How can you determine a function rule for the total number of tiles in any figure?
- What should your input values be? (Figure number)
- What should your output values be? (Total number of tiles)
- What patterns did you see in the figure that relate to the number of tiles?

For different formulas, have students relate them to the picture.

- What does each term represent in your picture?
- Can you simplify your expression?
- Can you relate your simplified expression to the picture?

If they rely on a table:

- How did you get the values in your table?
- What pattern did you find in the table?
- How can you represent the pattern you found algebraically?
- How does this relate to the explorations we did with tables in the *Meaningful Math* textbooks?
- What was the term for what you looked at? (Second differences)

Transition: Okay, everyone. Let's share what we found!

4. Discussion of "S-Pattern Task" (full group)
Call on a group to present #2.

- Does anyone have any questions for this group?
- Can someone else explain what they did?
- How does this relate to the patterns we talked about in the warm-up?

Call on a group to present their function.

- Can someone else explain what they did?
- How do you know that their solution is correct?
- Will your function tell us how many square tiles are in the 100th figure?
- How does your function relate to the pictures?

- What does each term in the function represent in the picture?

Call on another group to present their function.

- How is what they did different from the first group?
- Can both solutions be correct?
- Why or why not?
- If we use the same input in both functions, will we get the same output?

Call on a group to present their function. (Save a group who used a table for last)

- What pattern did they discover in the table?
- What is the term for what they looked at?
- How did that help them figure out their function?
- How do we know this relationship isn't linear?

Putting it all together:

- Now we've seen several different functions. Are they all correct?
- How do we know that they are equivalent?
- What can we do to transform one of these equations into one of the others?
- Can functions that look different actually be equivalent?

Transition: Okay! Let's sum things up.

5. Wrap-up (full group)

Call on students to wrap up the lesson.

- How did we come up with our functions?
- Why did we have multiple functions to represent the same thing?
- How did we know it was quadratic and not linear?
- Does anyone have anything to add? Does anyone have any questions?

Instruct students to answer a question for their exit slip.

- How many tiles would be in the 10th figure? (101)

Transition: Good work today, everyone! Have a great day!

Homework: The students should reflect on the lesson.

Evaluation

- Observe whether students can identify patterns in the sequence of figures.
- Observe whether students can use patterns to sketch or describe undrawn figures.
- Observe whether students can generate a function to describe the relationship between the number of tiles in the figure and the figure number.

- Observe whether students can explain why different functions are equivalent.
- Observe whether students can explain why their functions are quadratic.

Key References

Alabama State Department of Education. (2013). *Alabama course of study: Mathematics.* Montgomery, AL: Author.

National Council of Teachers of Mathematics. (n.d.). The case of Jeffrey Ziegler and the S-Pattern Task. Retrieved from http://www.nctm.org/Conferences-and-Professional-Development/Principles-to-Actions-Toolkit/The-Case-of-Jeffrey-Ziegler-and-the-S-Pattern-Task/

Marilyn E. Strutchens is the Emily R. and Gerald S. Leischuck Endowed Professor for Critical Needs and the Mildred Cheshire Fraley Distinguished Professor of Mathematics Education in the Department of Curriculum and Teaching at Auburn University and coordinator of secondary mathematics education. She is also the director of the Professional Mathematics Learning Communities Project between TEAM-Math and the Alabama Mathematics, Science, and Technology Initiative and teaches courses in mathematics education. Strutchens is a member of the Board of Directors for the National Council of Teachers of Mathematics and serves on the Advisory Committee for the Education and Human Resource Directorate for the National Science Foundation. She has held positions at the University of Maryland at College Park and the University of Kentucky. Her research interests include mathematics teacher preparation, equity issues in mathematics education, and teacher leader development.

W. Gary Martin is the Emily R. and Gerald S. Leischuck Endowed Professor for Critical Needs in Education in the Department of Curriculum and Teaching at Auburn University and is co-director of the Mathematics Teacher Education Partnership (mte-partnership.org). He teaches courses in mathematics education. Prior to coming to Auburn in 2000, Martin served as the director of research for the National Council of Teachers of Mathematics and also held positions at the University of Hawai'i and Northern Illinois University. He began his career as a high school mathematics teacher. His research interests include mathematics teacher preparation, mathematics curriculum, and teacher leader development.

2

CONEXIONES: FOSTERING SOCIOSCIENTIFIC INQUIRY IN GRADUATE TEACHER PREPARATION

Krista D. Glazewski, Michèle I. Shuster, Thomas Brush, and Andrea Ellis

Introduction

The use of socioscientific inquiry (SSI) has been advocated for at least the past decade in order to foster the development of a variety of skills among students (Sadler, 2004; Sadler & Zeidler, 2005). Despite the growing body of evidence that supports SSI as an effective approach in a variety of contexts, there are still challenges that hinder the large-scale adoption and implementation of SSI, such as difficulty transitioning learners to greater independence and supporting them to be successful given the challenges (Sadler, 2011). The purpose of this investigation is to explore the experience of teachers taking graduate-level courses that have been explicitly redesigned to support the implementation of SSI. We explore teacher change through science content learning gains, instructional process, teaching practice, and action research. We are motivated in part by an unacceptably high proportion of fourth, eighth, and twelfth grade students in the United States who are at or below the basic level in science on the National Assessment of Educational Progress (National Center for Education Statistics, 2012). Twenty-eight percent of fourth grade students, 36% of eighth grade students, and 40% of twelfth grade students were at or below the basic level of scientific proficiency. These results are discouraging as *basic* indicates incomplete mastery of science skills and content. Conversely, when looking at the percentage of U.S. students scoring at or above proficient, only 34%

of fourth grade students, 33% of eighth grade students, and a mere 21% of twelfth grade students were at or above proficient in science (National Center for Education Statistics, 2012). This situation requires continued attention, and SSI is an approach that may contribute to positive outcomes in science education.

Socioscientific Inquiry

In SSI, students consider scientific issues that have social implications and comprise a range of trade-offs, concepts, and considerations in order to arrive at informed conclusions (Sadler, 2004). Such issues can range from cloning to environmental challenges to land use decisions (Sadler & Zeidler, 2005). Engaging students in these issues reflects a *science as citizenship* emphasis (Kolstø, 2001) and prioritizes the critical personal context of learning (Bransford, Brown, & Cocking, 2000). Socioscientific reasoning involves four elements: (1) complexity, (2) incorporation and recognition of diverse perspectives, (3) reliance on continuing exploration, and (4) an ability to view information critically, recognizing potential bias (Sadler, Barab, & Scott, 2007). This approach therefore provides valuable opportunities not only for science reinforcement but also for an interdisciplinary and contextual approach to science education, including literacy, social studies, and mathematical skill reinforcement.

SSI has resulted in positive science outcomes in both secondary and postsecondary levels. Klosterman and Sadler (2010) showed that high school students who worked through a global warming SSI unit showed statistically significant pre- to posttest improvements on two different assessments—one more closely aligned with the SSI unit and one aligned with the state content standards. This indicates that SSI instruction can be used to successfully address content standards. Furthermore, SSI approaches address national curriculum reform initiatives for students to engage in meaningful problem solving that incorporates the practice of science and using the language of the discipline (i.e., *Benchmarks for Science Literacy*, American Association for the Advancement of Science, 1993; *National Science Education Standards*, National Research Council, 1996). SSI has also been investigated at the undergraduate level. One study of biology majors compared a four-year SSI program with a lecture-based one. SSI was shown to be as effective as traditional instruction on a measure of undergraduate biology majors' understanding of scientific inquiry (Eastwood, Sadler, Sherwood, & Schlegel, 2013).

How is SSI being adopted, and what are the associated challenges? As reviewed by Zeidler and Nichols (2009), teachers may not be experienced or comfortable with becoming classroom facilitators, rather than instructors who transmit expert knowledge. This challenge of managing classroom activities such as discussions and debates was also highlighted by preservice high school biology teachers who took a course that emphasized SSI (Kara, 2012). These preservice teachers also perceived challenges related to having the time to develop SSI instructional materials (as there are not readily available collections of such materials) and concerns of using SSI and adequately covering the mandated biology curriculum (Kara, 2012). Inservice teachers have expressed similar concerns. While interviewing middle and high school teachers about SSI (and particularly ethics in SSI), several teachers noted challenges to adopting SSI that included insufficient time, insufficient training, and the need to cover the science standards (Sadler, Amirshokoohi, Kazempour, & Allspaw, 2006). Furthermore, in order to facilitate discussions of SSI, the teachers themselves must have a certain level of content knowledge about the specific topic, as well as its current relevance.

In a study by Ekborg, Ottander, Silfver, and Simon (2013), secondary teachers could choose from among six pre-prepared SSI units to teach in their classes. While the teachers used the SSI cases to engage student interest, and had positive opinions about the level of student engagement, the authors raised concerns that the SSIs were not being used to their full potential. Specifically, ethical issues and the complex relationships that can exist between science and society, and that are valued by SSI researchers, were not being emphasized in the way that the teachers were implementing the SSIs.

Lee and Witz (2009) presented in-depth case studies of four high school science teachers and their use of SSI. These teachers appeared to be lone adopters, using SSI because of individual internal motivations without necessarily being aware of reform efforts promoting the use of SSI. While this is encouraging in terms of the use of SSI, it also raises the question of whether their implementation of SSI is consistent with the view of SSI researchers.

While SSI can be used to teach and address ethics that reflect values and global perspectives (e.g., Lee, Chang, Choi, Kim, & Zeidler, 2012; Saunders & Rennie, 2011), the teaching and inclusion of ethics in science instruction is another barrier to maximizing the potential of SSI. As described in Sadler et al. (2006), while researchers value the inclusion of ethics in SSI (and indeed regard this as a strength of SSI), many teachers are reluctant to infuse ethics into objective science courses. The models presented by Saunders and Rennie (2011) may provide support to teachers in this regard. Another example of using a formal model, or scaffold, to assist teachers in implementing SSI is described in France, Mora, and Bay (2012). In this case, high school teachers used two specific models in order to facilitate effective classroom discussions during a controversial SSI. This study was also notable in that it involved extensive teacher professional development and collaborative action research involving the researchers and the teachers, which led to increased confidence for the teachers.

In a study of graduate biology lab instructors, it was clear that these instructors (who generally do not have formal pedagogical training) had a great deal of knowledge about the SSI related to genetically modified crops and a deep appreciation for the relevance of this topic for students' lives. However, this latter aspect—the strong beliefs about the societal importance of the SSI—was generally not emphasized in their teaching (Gardner & Jones, 2012). This again highlights the importance of having skills and knowledge in both the content and in student-centered teaching practices in order to maximize the potential of SSIs in classrooms.

Specific challenges for elementary teachers. At the elementary level, teachers often have little background in sciences, and they tend to place instructional emphasis on reading and mathematics (Griffith & Scharmann, 2008; Rentner et al., 2006). One example of limited science background is provided by Krall, Lott, and Wymer (2009), in which elementary and middle school teachers were surveyed about their content knowledge of photosynthesis and respiration (key science topics in the elementary curriculum). Teachers (particularly in low-performance groups) did not do well and tended to select distracters based on recognized misconceptions of students.

Forbes and Davis (2008) investigated preservice elementary teachers as they evaluated an SSI lesson plan. Because of their limited knowledge of some of the content in the SSI, the indications were that their implementation of the unit would focus more of the content that they felt familiar with, and that they may shy away from discussing the broader issues that required integration of topics that they were not familiar with. The authors concluded that elementary teachers may be constrained by their (limited) content knowledge when implementing SSI.

In another survey, Marshall, Horton, Igo, and Switzer (2009) surveyed 1,222 K–12 teachers about their practices and beliefs with respect to inquiry in math and science, and found that elementary science teachers had the highest reported usage of inquiry but that this usage was less than what they considered to be ideal. There was no assessment of the efficacy of inquiry approaches, or of the content knowledge or pedagogical content knowledge of the teachers. Thus, while teachers may appear to value inquiry, its application specific to content knowledge, pedagogy, and assessment of student-centered outcomes is not well understood.

The lack of science and inquiry emphasis may be due in part to a shortage of time and scientific knowledge on the part of teachers, but recent research indicates it may also be an unintended consequence of the No Child Left Behind Act, which has been shown to result in a narrowing of the curriculum to the emphasized content areas of mathematics and literacy. A recent report indicated that the increased focus on math and reading has resulted in both budgetary and time reductions for science instruction (Griffith & Scharmann, 2008).

Consequently, observations of the narrowed curriculum in elementary schools coupled with limited teacher science knowledges underscores room for improvement of elementary science education, including improvements to teacher practice. Elementary teachers in general exhibit low confidence in teaching science as well as a general lack of ability to communicate about scientific concepts. In a report of preservice teachers' beliefs about science teaching, the researchers found a positive correlation between confidence in teaching science and the number of science content courses taken (Yilmaz-Tuzun, 2007). This indicates that an increase in science experiences at the undergraduate level may increase preservice teachers' confidence for science instruction, which has been supported by other researchers (Bleicher, 2006; Jarrett, 1999). However, confidence is not enough when it comes to quality science instruction; another key factor is the ability to communicate about scientific concepts. In a study among preservice elementary teachers, it was found that this group benefited from explicit and contextualized instruction regarding the nature of science and complex decision making (Matkins & Bell, 2007). In particular, their knowledge and capacity for communicating about science increased through discussions within issues-based experiences (i.e., global climate change) and about the nature of scientific knowledge. In general, the trend toward positively impacting future science elementary teachers tends to favor experiences that promote confidence building and science knowledge.

There are some bright instances, however. A successful elementary implementation of SSI has been described by Dolan, Nichols, and Zeidler (2009), in which students participated in discussions, expanded their content knowledge, and also began to express concerns related to social justice. Additionally, as noted by Zeidler and Nichols (2009), SSI is ideal for elementary instruction, as many aspects of the elementary curriculum come into play (e.g., reading, writing, mathematics) during an SSI unit. Given such encouraging examples and the critical need, it is worth investing effort into considering how to help elementary teachers successfully implement SSI in their classrooms.

Supporting Teacher SSI Practice: Collaborative Action Research

As teacher confidence in teaching science has been noted as a barrier to adopting innovative science curricula (e.g., see Appleton, 2008), it is critical to provide quality teacher preparation in science content knowledge and assessment of student-centered outcomes. Providing this support as part of a cohesive curriculum may have advantages over independent professional development workshops that require an investment of teacher time above and beyond existing professional responsibilities (e.g., James et al., 2006), and over time-intensive one-on-one mentoring programs as described by Appleton (2008).

While SSI is a key focus of this project, as noted previously, inquiry tasks in general and SSI projects in particular tend to exhibit low adoption rates in K–12 settings, despite strong beliefs among teachers that these types of activities are valuable (Marshall et al., 2009). This may stem from a number of sources, but most can be classified under two broad categories: (1) minimal support and resources that would lead toward confidence building and conceptual understanding (described previously), and (2) lack of opportunity to reflect on the inquiry teaching process in a collaborative setting that would elicit valuable input and alternative perspectives. We address these barriers through the collaborative action research model.

When it comes to understanding teacher practice, action research is a valuable tool for meaningful reflection and informed instructional decision making. Within this approach, the researcher (teacher) identifies a problem or question, develops a critical self-study research plan, and systematically collects data in order to arrive at a path of action or deeper understanding regarding the question of inquiry (Capobianco & Joyal, 2008). A key consideration is the quality of the action research method, which Capobianco and Feldman (2006) addressed with science education teachers and discussed as "a coherent body of goals, objectives, and methods ... that originate from inquiring, testing out and reflecting upon practical, personal or political issues" (pp. 498–499). They further emphasize the importance of collaborative discourse, conversation, and exchange, and emphasize the importance of socially constructed knowledge and understanding.

An important dimension of action research is the purposeful, iterative nature of the work, which has been used at length to help science education students integrate pedagogical and content knowledge. In one study, the teacher used action research to understand how her students were articulating complex chemistry concepts and uncovered numerous misconceptions and inaccurate representations (Valanides, Nicolaidou, & Eilks, 2003). The action research work not only uncovered these phenomena but also provided important insight into how she should adjust and improve her practice. In another study, a university science educator worked with three high school teachers to understand and articulate the impact that ongoing action research projects have had on their teaching (Capobianco, Lincoln, Canuel-Browne, & Trimarchi, 2006). They found that each teacher sought different pathways in her approaches to the research, including gaining new knowledge, increasing confidence in science, and inventing curricular approaches when the textbook did not suffice. The authors highlighted the fact that while each found different value in the process, all felt empowered to take risks and understand the outcomes within their teaching as a result of engaging in action research (Capobianco et al., 2006). Another university science educator echoed this feeling of empowerment in her description of conducting action research projects as a way to understand learning interactions within science classrooms (Marin-Dunlop, 2006). Empowerment translated into confidence for teachers in successfully facilitating classroom discussions during a controversial SSI within the collaborative action research project described earlier by France and colleagues (2012). In other words, action research results in very different experiences for each researcher but is consistently described as empowering teachers to understand and move forward in their practice.

Research Purpose

We sought to leverage the examples of teacher empowerment through collaborative action research within our intervention and investigation. Action research connects theoretical models behind SSI with actual classroom practice. In other words, action research represents an important process for helping teachers to reflect on and identify areas for improvement within their SSI approaches. We drew from the recommendations of previous science education professionals, who recommend self-study action research coupled with professional community discussions in order to maximize insight and generate a wide range of solution paths, in much the same way that scientists collaborate with one another in research settings (Lynd-Balta, Erklenz-Watts, Freeman, & Westbay, 2006). Broadly speaking, our investigation explored the experience of graduate teachers within our curricular model that supports teacher change toward SSI approaches through mentoring, modeling, content development, and collaborative action research. In this context, our purpose was to investigate teacher change through science content learning gains, instructional process, teaching practice, and action research.

Methods

Research design and context. We used an evaluative case study approach (Merriam, 1997) to examine teacher practice and teacher change in the context of our curricular model: a two-course bundle for graduate teacher education students that was redesigned and implemented through the partnership of a teacher educator and biologist. Within this context, data were used to examine and evaluate the experiences and practices of the teachers who participated in the new courses. Each data source and its analysis are described in more detail in the following sections.

Redesigning the courses and defining the case. Our case investigation consisted of a redesigned six-credit, two-course graduate bundle for master's-level teachers co-taught through the collaborative effort of a teacher education faculty member and a biology faculty member. The bundle met two different course requirements for a master's degree in education: Technology and Pedagogy, and Research as Praxis I (which typically teaches the action research model of inquiry). The goal of the course was for the participants to develop and implement an SSI project within a classroom setting. Furthermore, participants were directed to ask a question of their teaching practice that connected to their SSI implementation. They proceeded to investigate this question through action research with collaborative input from their peers (this marks a key distinction between action research and collaborative action research).

Course content consisted of modeling technology-enhanced science instruction and inquiry approaches in the context of an SSI unit titled "Is My Food Safe?" We developed a series of six online tutorials to model how we planned and addressed each component of developing the unit: developing the driving question, making decisions about teachable topics, narrowing and defining the learning goals (and connecting them to standards), developing the learning objectives, creating the assessment, and planning lessons. In-class activities consisted of instruction, modeling, and workshop formats as relevant: modeling biology content experiences; modeling the inquiry process; modeling uses of technology tools, manipulatives, and biology equipment for learner investigations; delivering mini-lectures, performing biology labs, describing or discussing applications to classroom teaching; discussing participant ideas for classroom implementations; developing action research plans; and discussing the implementation and role of action research in understanding personal teaching practice. We investigated the case through examining the learning outcomes, teaching practice, and experiences of the graduate teachers.

Participants. Prior to the beginning of the semester, we recruited graduate teachers through graduate email listservs, local school announcements and flyers, and word-of-mouth. Data were collected from among seven students enrolled in the redesigned two-course bundle that met requirements for a master's degree of education program in a large, southwestern university. We use the term *graduate teachers* throughout this chapter to capture the fact that these students were enrolled in master's degree courses intended for K–12 licensed, practicing teachers (though only five of the graduate teachers were licensed at the time of the study). The two-course bundle was developed to model and emphasize SSI teaching approaches and was paired with a requirement for collaborative action research to enable the graduate teachers to simultaneously and systematically examine their SSI practice. The students had different course choices that could have met the degree requirements; in other words, participation in our model was one of several choices.

Of the seven graduate teachers, three were practicing K–12 teachers at the time of the study: one high school biology, one kindergarten, and one second grade. Two were licensed but not currently practicing in the classroom: one was a recent graduate of secondary mathematics education and one was a former special education teacher providing district-level mathematics support for K–8 teachers. Of the remaining two participants, one was an astronomy teacher at the community college and one was a doctoral student in curriculum and instruction.

Data Sources and Analysis

Pre- and post-content test. Graduate teachers were invited to complete the pretest on the first day of class and the posttest on the last day of class. The content test consisted of 18 items and covered biology content we expected students to learn as they participated in the activities designed to model SSI approaches and engage the participants in meaningful experiences. Sixteen of the items were multiple choice, closed response questions and two items were open ended. One open-ended item dealt with the concept of evolution by natural selection and one dealt with photosynthesis and photosynthetic organisms. The multiple choice/closed response items were worth one point each, and each open-ended item was scored out of two possible points, awarded for completeness and accuracy. The major themes of the content test included the scientific process, genotype-phenotype relationships, natural selection, and energy flow in ecosystems. Three sample items are as follows:

1. Can you draw a conclusion from an experiment before you have collected and analyzed the data?
   a. yes, your predictions are the same as conclusions
   b. yes, the experiment only serves to verify what you already know is going to occur
   c. no, the conclusion can only be drawn after the data have been found to support your hypothesis
   d. no, the conclusion must be based on the data
2. What is the impact of natural selection on allele frequencies in a population?
   a. it can cause the allele frequencies to change in unpredictable ways
   b. it has no effect on allele frequencies
   c. it causes specific types of changes in allele frequencies, depending on the selective pressure
   d. natural selection only acts on phenotypes; therefore, it has nothing to do with allele frequencies
3. What is the ultimate source of energy entering almost all ecosystems?
   a. fats
   b. carbohydrates
   c. heat
   d. sunlight

We evaluated the outcomes of the posttest with descriptive statistics and a paired-samples t-test. While our low sample size ($n = 7$) makes it difficult to draw strong inferences or have high confidence these results would be replicated, we feel it is important to evaluate the strength of SSI for conveying a positive learner experience (something that has been well documented in the prior research) *and* learning gains (which has not been well documented, particularly for teachers).

Pre- and post-understanding SSI scenario survey. As with the content test, graduate teachers were invited to complete the pre-survey on the first day of class and the post-survey on the last day of class. The *Understanding SSI Scenario Survey* was developed to document change in participant ideas and beliefs regarding how they approach science in the classroom. This measure was based on an instrument developed by Brush and Saye (2014) to capture similar perceptions in problem-based historical inquiry. We first provided students with an image and medical case summary of an individual who developed a systemic infection from a piercing. The graduate teachers were asked to describe the relevant science concepts as well as potential ideas for teaching this content in the classroom. The second section consisted of four items related to the infection scenario that required graduate teachers to rank potential classroom practices in order of instructional importance. Each practice represented either an inquiry or noninquiry approach and related to one of the following four categories: (1) learning objectives, (2) introductory activities, (3) instructional activities, and (4) assessment activities. Figure 2.1 is an example of the item requiring graduate teachers to rank learning objectives and provide a justification. In order to evaluate the changes in curricular decisions made by participants, we examined the differences in the ways in which the participants ranked choices between the pre- and post-survey responses through a descriptive trend analysis (Saye, Kohlmeier, Brush, Howell, & Maddox, 2009–2010). Numerical data from the survey were analyzed using descriptive statistics. Participants' initial responses to the survey were compared to their responses as they were completing the graduate courses. In addition, participants' responses to open-ended questions were analyzed qualitatively for further explanation of their rankings and selection of survey items.

Post-course focus group. During the final class session of the semester, graduate teachers were invited to participate in a focus group designed to elicit strengths, weaknesses, and experiences of the courses. An outside researcher with no connection to the courses or the university conducted the focus group based on a semistructured protocol developed by the researcher in concert with the instructors. They were asked about their overall experiences in the course, their specific processes developing their SSI units and accompanying action research projects, the implementation of their projects, and any suggestions for

21. When developing a socioscientific inquiry unit related to the material presented in question 20 for your students, rank order the following learning objectives in terms of the importance of each for accomplishing your goals for this unit by placing a number corresponding to the item's importance in the right column.

Item Number	Learning Objective	Item Rank (1–6)
1	Students will describe the two major types of cells in living organisms, and give examples of organisms with each type of cell.	
2	Students will explain why antibiotics can kill bacteria, but are harmless to humans.	
3	Students will explain how the use of antibiotics contributes to the emergence of antibiotic-resistant bacteria.	
4	When accessing popular media reports of outbreaks of infectious disease, students will be able to infer the type of infectious agent, the source of infection, and make recommendations about preventing further infections.	
5	Students will be able to argue either side in a debate about regulations governing parlors that create body art (including piercings and tattoos).	
6	Students will describe the adaptations that allow some bacteria to live on skin, and explain why intestinal bacteria wouldn't be likely to survive on skin.	

22. Consider only your top three ranked choices from item 21. In the space provided, briefly explain why you ordered them in this way and why these three choices are preferable to the other possible selections.

Figure 2.1 Learning objective rank order and justification.

improving the experience (see the Appendix for the full interview protocol). The focus group lasted almost one hour.

We analyzed the focus group data with an interpretive framework that we preestablished to understand more about the strengths, weaknesses, and participant experiences within the course (Erickson, 1986).

Action research projects. The graduate teachers submitted an action research project to document their progress and implementation of their SSI instructional units. Graduate teachers were initially introduced to action research through readings from the course textbook (Mills, 2006), presentations by the instructors, and in-class discussions. As practice, graduate teachers were asked to think about action research questions that could accompany each class meeting. Graduate teachers were then introduced to important concepts necessary for action research, including prior literature, assessment, types of data, and aligning the assessment methods with the action research question. The graduate teachers also had several opportunities to share their action research question with their peers, so that they could receive peer feedback. They submitted an action research proposal before initiating their action research projects, so that the instructors could provide preimplementation feedback. Our analysis consisted of project review for insight into the meaning of SSI as it specifically relates to the participants' current and intended teaching practices.

Results and Interpretations

Pre- and Post-Content Test

The maximum score graduate teachers could have achieved on the content test was 19. The mean for the pretest was fairly low, $M_{pre} = 9.7$, SD = 4.3, and there was a marked increase for the posttest, $M_{post} = 12.6$, SD = 2.8. A paired-samples t-test revealed the gains were significant, $p = .02$, $t(6) = -2.9$, and the effect size was moderately strong, $r = .37$. However, as noted earlier, our low sample size ($n = 7$) makes it difficult to draw strong inferences or have high confidence these results would be replicated.

Understanding SSI Scenario Survey

With the scenario survey, we performed a descriptive trend analysis for each item to evaluate change in rankings from pre- to post-survey for each of the four categories: (1) learning objectives, (2) introductory activities, (3) instructional activities, and (4) assessment activities. We found no discernable trend of change in rankings from pre- to post-survey for introductory activities, instructional activities, or assessment activities; that is, in general, the participants' responses trended toward more of an inquiry orientation toward both the beginning and the end of the course. For the learning objectives category, we found a trend that indicated change in rankings for two of the items, as displayed in Figure 2.2.

This graph displays a ranking change trend from pre- to post-survey for between objectives three and four. In other words, on the post-survey, most students ranked objective three lower (more important) and ranked objective four higher (less important) than they had on the pre-survey. These two objectives are as follows:

> *Objective 3:* Students will explain how the use of antibiotics contributes to the emergence of antibiotic-resistant bacteria.

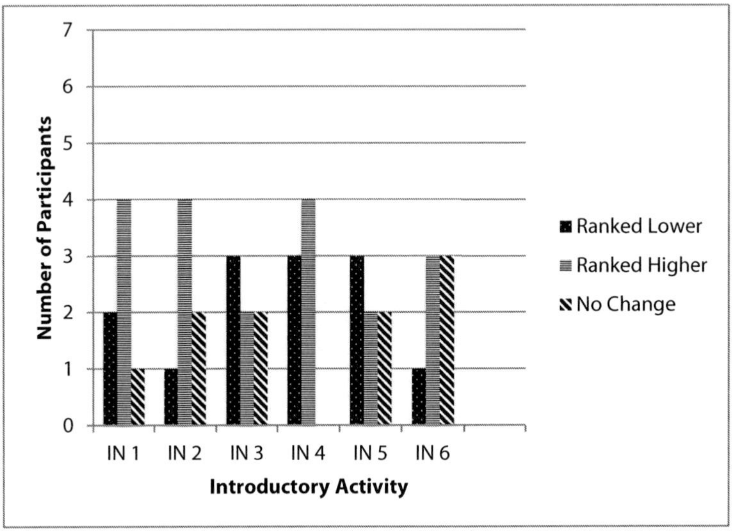

Figure 2.2 Pre- and post-rank order for learning objectives. Note: Lower rankings indicate higher importance for classroom instruction.

> *Objective 4:* When accessing popular media reports of outbreaks of infectious disease, students will be able to infer the type of infectious agent, the source of infection, and make recommendations about preventing further infections.

For the post-course survey, the trend was to rank the more inquiry-oriented learning objective as less important and the more knowledge-based objective as more important. This represents a curious finding. In order to gain insight regarding this shift, we turned to graduate teachers' justifications for their rankings both pre- and post-survey:

Key pre-survey comments. In order to fully comprehend the topic, the students must understand how these antibiotics work—and sometimes, don't. This, of course, then begs the question of how bacteria work. That leads to an understanding of cellular biology in general, but the top priority should be understanding diseases. Tattoo parlors can wait a bit—they won't hurt you if you don't go in.

I ranked item 4 first because it allows and promotes the greatest amount of creativity and critical thinking. Item 5 allows a fair amount of creativity and a large amount of research because the students have to defend one side. Items 6 and 3 involve little creativity but a fair amount of critical thinking. Lastly, items 1 and 2 are generic textbook problems with little creativity.

> #4 I was torn between these—I have no particular reason.

Key post-survey comments. I chose 1–3 as my top choice b/c these seemed to have the most general forms of information that could be applied to many situations. I find it important to pick a RELEVANT topic for an SSI in order to make the most impact on student learning and comprehension of a topic(s).

> #1–3 provided essential general information that can be adapted to fit other areas of bacteria-related studies.

> #4 would be an intro to #5, and they would play hand in hand. #5 is important because it allows the students to realize that infection can happen from piercing and enables them to look for a prevention plan. #6 will force the students to argue on each side about the policies for parlors and body art shops. It allows them to think about the situation and debate about it.

> #3 is open ended and also has great potential for a hands-on activity.

I chose identification of the two types of cells as the most important because all the other discussions/investigations would need to be based on this knowledge. The second idea, understanding why antibiotics kill bacteria but not humans, seems to be the next step in moving to the third, which is actually extremely important to human survival.

I believe it is important for students to know that there are different cell types in living organisms. Students have to be able to apply scientific concepts to societal application. Students should be globally aware and able to point out scientific concepts when they arise in society.

When comparing the pre- and post-survey comments, we noted much richer justifications for their rankings following the course as opposed to before the course. However, we did not expect to observe ranking trends that prioritized knowledge-based over inquiry-based instructional objectives. In the post-survey, graduate teacher comments primarily centered on the importance of content knowledge. We hypothesize this stemmed from the fact that for most of the graduate teachers (with the exception of the high school biology teacher), exposure to and expectation to learn the content was new and unexpected. When they struggled with the concepts or ideas, it possibly highlighted a gap in their own foundational knowledge and led them to wonder how they could teach this content without a deep understanding. It is possible this translated into a pattern of wanting students to know the content deeply as well. This is not a bad trend, and it points to one of our instructional assertions in the course: that deep content learning most effectively happens in inquiry-based settings. Furthermore, while we interpret this outcome as representative of the graduate teachers' value for deep content learning, we are not convinced they attributed this to the inquiry instruction they experienced. However, we do not assume that this finding means inquiry diminished in value for these participants, only that it diminished in importance as compared to knowledge.

Focus Group Summary

During the focus group, we sought to elicit students' perspectives regarding strengths, weaknesses, and experiences within the SSI courses. We found that graduate teachers spoke to three general themes: the integrated nature of our curricular approach, the impact on their teaching, and recommendations for future iterations. Each of these is discussed in more detail in the following sections.

The integrated approach. Because we purposefully and intentionally modeled the SSI approach, made explicit that we expected content learning, and demonstrated technology as a resource, we asked specifically about graduate teachers' impressions of these facets of the course. Most were generally positive and one aspect they particularly liked was the intersecting methods of biology content and technology to support learning. For example, when asked about useful resources and support, one graduate teacher stated, "Most definitely the technology aspect. I understood what was going on with science so it was easy for me, but the technology aspects were all new to me and I loved it. Prezi, webquests, etc." Another concurred: "I agree with technology. I didn't like technology [before], but it was great for this. I was able to incorporate technology in my SSI units. I have done it before but not as focused previously. Technology and having models of SSI were most helpful."

However, some graduate teachers had difficulty framing how the integrated pieces came together, and they seemed to privilege one useful aspect over the others. Here are three different respondents discussing the value of the integrated approach:

> Most beneficial, I would say would be definitely the technology, the technology aspect for myself, because I felt that I guess she (the biology professor) was

> teaching some biology, but she really didn't have time to completely finish the topic. It was just like bits and pieces.... I understood what was going on, so it was beneficial for me the whole time, the science concepts that were presented, but the technology pieces of just different websites to use, different resources to use, the Prezi was a big thing for me. I really liked that, and I have my kids use that in class already, pretty much like that next day, "OK. You [kids] are gonna do this." And WebQuests. Stuff like that that I've never used in class. I think it's just that for me, [it] was the most beneficial.

> See, I love biology. So, and I had a lot of biology in high school and early on. So, it was like a reminder for me, and I was totally engaged and interested in it, but what can I do with bacteria with my kindergarteners? Nothing. You know. So, it was like the model overall.... This is the process. This is what you can do. That was awesome, but the topic of bacteria in my classroom? No.

> My problem is, I am even a math person, but I am trying to figure out how I am supposed to present the data. So, maybe one of the classes can focus on that part a little more, a little harder, something. I mean, I get what data means, but it's just, in this paper, what's [it] supposed to look like[?] I am sort of lost there.

These responses indicate a general appreciation for the approach but also an attempt to separate all the integrated pieces and pull out the meaningful aspects from there.

Impact on teaching. All of the graduate teachers expressed that this experience had a positive impact on their teaching, though only the practicing teachers were able to experience this in an authentic manner directly related to their current practice.

> *Biology teacher:* I only taught [my unit to] one section of genetics, and I think in general I know that I am going to redesign all of my courses to follow sort of this format, because it organizes me in my day today and in my unit. I felt through the incorporation of driving questions that [students were] really engage[d] in a way that I don't think I have seen before. It's almost like [a] constructivist sort of way of doing things. As in, "This is what we're gonna do, but I am not gonna tell you how exactly we are gonna get there. It is your job to make sure we get there. And we are going to construct some of your

own knowledge and I will be there to help you along the way." And I really felt that it enhanced my teaching method.

Second grade teacher: In our classroom, my unit was on recycling and pollution in [the] environment, and we are down from three full trashcans to a half can of trash and two bins of recycling goods. And I hear parents say their kids are forcing them. They [students] come to school and say 'I told my mom she had to get a plastic recycling bin for [our] house.' Parents are actually going out and putting more effort towards their [students'] learning because kids are coming home and sharing why they need to do this and [the] reason behind things. The societal impact that this is having, I am hoping this is gonna be huge.... Like we pointed out [earlier], in elementary school 'oh, there's no time for science.' Well, it is very important to do science in lower grades. This course made me want to make time to teach science. I enjoy teaching science. I feel more confident.

Kindergarten teacher: I think with me I liked going into [the] process of whole action research projects learning how to do a[n] action research project and having the end goal in mind. Along with what [we] said about the driving questions, we pretty much established that in class we will have the driving questions, which were yearlong questions, and then we have a smaller version of our question each week. We always continually revert back to our main driving question over, over, and over, and kids started seeing a connection that all the stuff we talked about science is all connected somehow. I really liked the driving question idea and I liked the idea of how to do action research, even if I don't formally do action research. It's in my class now. If there's an idea, I will go through and review the literature first of all and try to come up with what other people did. And then, I really liked the idea of [an] SSI unit where it [is] socially relevant. It is socially relevant learning and it's not just making them have higher test scores or do better on standardized assessments. I am making an impact, something in their lives that's important, like life skills in academic fashion. I like that.... You know, if you go to any of my district meetings or anything, it's like, "No, there's no time for science, no time for science." They are not supportive. So, this class gave me more confidence to want to teach it more, and knowing that there is a lot of support for science in elementary school.

Community college instructor: I am actually planning a course now, if I can get permission to teach it, where it's astronomy and biology that's dual taught. I see myself using these methods a lot.

Each elementary and secondary teacher's comments demonstrate a deep and nuanced understanding of the "how" and "why" related to SSI. Not unexpectedly, however, those not currently practicing had a more difficult time expressing similar impact on their teaching:

> *Math teacher:* I am secondary math. I am seeing through this class more possibilities to spread into biology. You know, interdisciplinary. They talk about exponential growth. They cover it a little, but I think there's a lot more that could be tied in.
>
> *District resource teacher:* For me, the driving question and then presenting the driving question was valuable. I mean, I am really thinking about "Well, OK. I don't know what really do with [the] science part," and then I got the science part without really thinking about doing science. So, I think that was the important part for me. The driving question that I know that I am gonna use here and now.
>
> *Doctoral student:* Yeah, probably the most useful [thing] that I garnered from [this class] was how to start a website and I doubled biology knowledge in the first day, so, biology was good, and website startup was good.

The math teacher expressed a desire to integrate interdisciplinary approaches but did not have an immediate context for this discussion. The doctoral student, who was previously a health educator, did not have a context for longer-range curriculum planning or integrated delivery of instruction, so it is not surprising that she discussed some of the more surface benefits (yet highly relevant to her). For the district resource teacher, she discussed using the driving question approach to curriculum "here and now," which we interpreted to mean she intends to encourage this approach among the teachers she supports.

Participant recommendations. While all of the graduate teachers expressed value in the course experience, they suggested a number of ideas to improve the course. Graduate teachers had a difficult time with the action research project. An idea that took hold early in the course was that the driving question for the SSI unit was the same as the overarching question for the action research project. No matter how we tried to reframe the separate but connected aspects of these two requirements, participant misunderstandings persisted *even after* submission of the action research project:

> The definitions are extremely vague. 'What is SSI? What is action research?' These are not definable concepts.

> Well, I didn't have any confusion on what they were. But I did feel like when I tried to plan what my SSI was gonna be, I also had, in my mind—I needed to put them together. They told me that ... they are two separate things. So, I guess my feeling would be, my recommendation would be to recognize that some people have a big picture at the end and they need to work backward to it: how these two pieces are gonna fit together to make a picture.

> I wasn't able to separate them, yeah.

> An example or two of what exactly they are talking about [SSI and AR] would be kinda handy. I like to work from examples. It's just a vague concept.

> [Action research is] something that I will never ... use in my classroom, not because it's not useful but because there's no time for me to do it.

> [Action Research] is not something I will use in my classroom because of time, but I know the process now.

Only one graduate teacher expressed a deep understanding of the connections between trying something new in teaching and systematically investigating a question of relevance regarding the new approach: "I really liked the driving question idea and I liked the idea of how to do action research even if I don't formally do action research. It's in my class now. If there's an idea, I will go through and review the literature first of all and try to come up with what other people did."

Other ideas centered on the logistics of the course, such as posting scoring rubrics or putting systems into place regarding the availability of the equipment and resources we modeled during the course. We mentioned these resources were available for use during the course or after but failed to implement a reliable system for check-out, as one participant noted: "[I] liked the availability of the resources. The other stuff was available and it was a good thing, but I'm not sure how they were used." Another individual similarly discussed this: "I had to make a special trip to get [the clickers], and it was difficult logistically. More would have been borrowed if they were easier to access."

Participant Action Research Projects

Table 2.1 summarizes each participant's SSI project approach by detailing the SSI question, the action research question of investigation, and the implementation summary. Because we emphasized the SSI model, it was an important goal for the projects to incorporate science in a meaningful way. Because only four participants were practicing teachers, those not actively practicing (e.g., the education doctoral student and the district-level math specialist) sought partner teachers for their implementations, though it was the participants who delivered the primary instruction, not the partner teachers. Two of the graduate teachers collaborated on the co-planning and co-teaching of their SSI unit ("Should I Leave That Light On?").

Participants asked a wide range of questions about their practice for the focus of their action research projects. When we examined their action research narrative reports, we were especially interested in signals of change in the graduate teachers' practice and indicators of intention to sustain practice when it came to the use of SSI, as described in more detail in the following section.

Signals of change. Several teachers highlighted changes to their practice. Two of the teachers spoke of their change explicitly and used the metaphor of *vehicle* to discuss their change: the biology teacher and the district specialist.

> Change is never an easy undertaking. The way we have always done things tends to get easier and easier, so as creatures of habit, change is taboo. This semester I had the opportunity to become a social scientist and my classroom was the arena in which my experiment took place. I have been teaching science education for 14 years; this semester my journey into the realm of change was challenging on several levels. I had to put myself and my methods under the microscope, and my self-examination can at times be crucial as I am my toughest critic. (biology teacher, AR report, p. 2)

She then went on to describe SSI as a method that facilitated change in her practice and action research as "the vehicle" (biology teacher, AR report, p. 2) used to examine her change. The district math specialist was a former special education teacher, so she was used to trying new things and working within a cross-disciplinary manner in her practice. She said that inquiry was a natural component of her teaching. Her action research project focused on wanting to

Table 2.1 *SSI project and implementation summary.*

Participant	SSI Project	Action Research Project Title	Implementation Summary
High School Biology Teacher	Who owns your DNA?	"Two Heads Are Better Than One": An Evaluation of Group Assessment	One-week implementation with three biology classes
Special Education Teacher (district-level math specialist)	What's in your brain?	How Does Teaching Style Affect a Learner?	Three-day implementation with an honors biology class
Education Doctoral Student (nonlicensed community educator)	Why is diabetes prevalent in our community?	A Socioscientific Inquiry Unit of Culturally Relevant Approaches to Teaching the Native American Student the Issues of Diabetes in Their Community	Multigrade high school science class at a pueblo high school over the course of one week
Community College Astronomy Instructor	What do high-energy objects tell us?	Team-Based Learning in a Community College Class	Implementation in one three-hour class session
Kindergarten Teacher	What does the environment mean to us?	Environmental Education and Its Effect of Pro-Environmental Behaviors at Home	Semester-long implementation with kindergarten course
Second Grade Teacher	Should I leave that light on?	Preoperational Stage and Content and Scientific and Social Awareness	One-week collaborative implementation with a second-grade class
Secondary Mathematics Teacher (certified, full-time graduate student)	Should I leave that light on? (taught in collaboration with the second grade teacher)	Should I Leave That Light On?: Perceptions of Electricity and Its Conservation	One-week collaborative implementation with a second-grade class

know more about learning styles. She noted that she had more than 20 years' experience teaching, and that she consistently valued trying new things. In fact, hers was the only report to include a heading titled "Change of Practice." One outcome for her project was a deeper understanding of the role of technology and its role as a vehicle for change in her practice:

> One of the things [that is] important to the children of these times is teaching with technologies. The students of today are headed into a futuristic world. The power point, clickers, and video technology used here may, in the next decade, be seen as relics of a simpler time. Those of us who are middle aged will never respond to technological inventions with the same fearlessness as the young do today.... I would hate to see the gap between mature teachers and their students widen. We need to be flexible because we are preparing students for jobs that have not been created in the marketplace that has not yet been invented. This point became clear to me while conducting this research project. (District specialist, AR report, pp. 10–11)

Three graduate teachers undertook investigations to understand how their SSI classroom practices might impact behaviors at home: the kindergarten teacher and the second grade teacher working in collaboration with the secondary math teacher, each noting that they had never tried anything like this before. All three reported the type of outcomes they had hoped to observe when they interpreted the results from the student self-report of home behaviors and activities, which represented a "risk" and "something never tried before." The kindergarten teacher compared her results to those of the three other non-SSI kindergarten classroom outcomes on the same measures. For example, she reported "a 16% increase in pro-environmental behaviors at home" when comparing her results to the other kindergarten respondents. She also noted that 19 out of 20 of her students met kindergarten benchmarks in reading and math, though it is unfortunate she did not indicate the benchmark rates for the comparison class. She reflected on her observed outcomes stating, "These assessment pieces were critical to my research because they demonstrate a high percentage of proficiency in reading and math while I simultaneously focused my instruction on science" (kindergarten teacher, action research report, p. 16).

It is important to note that not every graduate teacher signaled change in his or her practice through the action research projects. The full-time education doctoral student was formerly a community educator without any prior teaching experience in formal settings. It is likely that she did not signal any changes to her teaching practice because she did not have prior practice to compare it against. The community college instructor did not implement a true SSI unit in his classroom; rather, he changed one content topic and added a team-based component to it. The result was a change in one aspect of his practice, but nothing he noted as significant in his action research narrative.

Indicators of sustained SSI practice. Almost every graduate teacher indicated that the changes in their practice as a result of this experience would be sustained over time. As the district support individual noted, "it leads to the conclusion that *all* lessons should include tasks [like these]" (district specialist, AR report, p. 12). Similarly, the high school biology teacher outlined a future plan that included restructuring all her courses to include SSI, assisting other teachers with course changes, integrating more technology, and developing a website that will include "the driving question for each of the units that we will be covering in the class" (biology teacher, AR report, p. 14). She further wrote, "As stated before change is never easy, however I believe that I underwent a change in teaching style and method which was positive. Action research provided the vehicle to induce this change. The development of the socio-scientific unit as a means of action research was extremely interesting and gave me a different outlook on lesson delivery and teaching methods" (biology teacher, AR report, p. 14).

The three teachers of elementary students (second grade and kindergarten) indicated they experienced tremendous value in this experience, primarily based on the learning gains and student outcomes as a result of the SSI approaches they tried. The second grade teacher stated, "I am satisfied with the results of my research. I was able to answer the questions I had. [My] students are as capable as other students to be responsible energy users. They are also capable of becoming more environmental[ly] aware and they can transfer content knowledge to their personal lives" (second grade teacher, AR report, p. 10). Similarly, her collaborating partner teacher wrote, "This unit was very successful in its purpose of modifying the attitudes and behaviors of students. In summary, this action research project indicated that energy (in our case electricity) education and energy conservation education played a part in the attitudinal and behavioral modifications in students" (secondary mathematics teacher, AR report, p. 17). The kindergarten teacher spoke about not only the need to continue her SSI work but to potentially convince the other kindergarten teacher to adopt these methods: "My research encouraged me to persuade others to adopt this teaching method as well" (kindergarten teacher, AR report, p. 16).

While the education doctoral student did not indicate changes to her practice (as we discussed previously), we did note signs of her promoting SSI methods when given future opportunity to do so, and she spoke about the importance of her project because of the gap that exists in understanding the types of approaches that work best with Native American learners. She wrote,

> The action research project that was implemented through a socioscientific inquiry unit was primarily integrating science and culture in the classroom. I had a difficult time with this project because I couldn't find much published literature specifically on science education, science performance, and health knowledge of Native American students. Although I didn't have the literature as a foreground, I was fortunate enough to find a school and a class that was willing to implement the action research plan in the classroom. Based on the data and the results we find that student interest increased. The surveys were a great tool for gaining insight from the students. Although this was a well-thought-out project, I fell [*sic*] that there is room for improvement. Time seemed to be a big issue for me. This was my first time teaching a class but also my first time trying to change something in someone else's classroom. I am fortunate that the teacher I was working with was receptive to the project and the findings. I would definitely like to assist other teachers in implementing culturally based curriculum in their classrooms." (Education doctoral student, AR report, pp. 12–13)

Discussion

In this investigation, we sought to understand the learning experiences of graduate teachers within the case of redesigned courses aimed at preparing teachers to implement SSI approaches in the classroom. The data informed our understanding of changes in science content knowledge, perceptions of SSI instruction, strengths of the experience, and recommendations for future refinements of the approach to teacher development.

With regard to changes in graduate teachers' knowledge of biology content, not only were the scores significantly higher following their experience in the course, but every teacher demonstrated improvement from pre- to posttest.

This represents an important first step in understanding both how we prepare teachers for SSI methods and how we boost content understanding in the process. One limitation of the current body of research on SSI methods is that researchers have generally prioritized investigations of student inquiry, problem solving, argumentation, and reasoning (see, e.g., Sadler, 2009; Sadler, Barab, & Scott, 2007; Walker & Zeidler, 2007). Furthermore, researchers have not typically acknowledged the role of teacher content knowledge in this context. Our approach suggests that within the current models for teacher education, teachers with a weak knowledge base can achieve important learning gains. However, we acknowledge that our model emphasized only the content area of biology, which is a limitation for teachers needing broader experiences in other content domains.

As we further consider the role of the content knowledge in our model, we also noted that teachers tended to prioritize content over inquiry-focused objectives in the pre- and post-scenario survey. Furthermore, we did not observe any other discernable trends of rankings for the other types of instructional activities. Because the content was new for most of the teachers, we hypothesized that teachers felt both uncomfortable with their lack of knowledge and, within this position, prioritized knowledge integration over inquiry investigations. This underscores the notion that teacher change is difficult and does not happen easily or within a defined time frame of a semester. For example, Brush and Saye (Chapter 3, this volume) found differences in preservice teacher prioritization of inquiry-based activities when compared to more traditional ones, but these changes occurred over a two-year period. These results suggest that teacher change is involved, lengthy, and impacted by a variety of influences.

In our case, we noted that most teachers likely felt pressure to develop expertise with previously unknown content, and only one teacher had previous expertise in our modeled SSI topic as a high school biology teacher. While we were encouraged to find significant knowledge gains on the pre- to posttest comparison, we also hypothesize that the shift in emphasis on something different from the teachers' own expertise likely highlighted their own lack of knowledge and amplified the importance of deep content knowledge. Thirty years ago, Shulman (1986) began to explore this relationship between content knowledge and pedagogical approaches, which is when he coined the term *pedagogical content knowledge* (PCK). Using the PCK framework as a guide for interpretation, we might consider that it is not likely that graduate teachers can enact complex pedagogical approaches such as SSI when they lack deep knowledge that would enable them to understand the disciplinary organization that includes both substantive and syntactic structures.

However, Shulman's (1986) framework does not reflect other primary findings in this study: most teachers signaled changes in their practice and communicated intent to sustain those changes, which we see as an indicator of perceived value for inquiry. In fact, when we consider the full range of outcomes in this study, we observed indicators for both the value of content and the value of inquiry. The fact that the graduate teachers demonstrated knowledge gains and detailed positive perceptions of their SSI experiences confirms both that these types of experiences are valuable in professional development and can also lead to knowledge gains. We cannot know from this study if the graduate teachers sustained their SSI practices, but the model we have presented reflects an important first step. We attribute this to the modeling, online tutorials, and workshop experiences that fostered opportunities for the teachers to learn both content and SSI approaches from us. We contrast our findings with those of Sadler and colleagues (2006), in which participants noted several challenges toward SSI implementation, including resources and training. Providing a wider range of experiences and input may be a key to sustainable changes in practice.

We also consider the outcomes of the action research investigations that provided the platform for teachers to systematically examine their practice of SSI. However, we acknowledge that deeper expressions of understanding regarding and intentions toward using SSI approaches in the future came from those teachers currently practicing in the classroom. Connected to this, it is worth noting that teachers expressed some degree of frustration with the action research requirement, suggesting that it did not fully serve to support their pedagogical risk taking as we had hoped. We consider that their experience demanded a lot of them when it came to learning both new content and a new pedagogical approach, perhaps too much than could be expected within the span of one semester.

Recommendations

As a result of this work, our recommendations fall into two primary categories: making explicit the connection between SSI and content knowledge building, and maximizing use of collaborative action research for SSI professional development.

Making Explicit the Connection Between SSI and Content Knowledge Building

While the teachers gained significant biology content knowledge as a result of their participation in our program and experienced success with their SSI implementations, we were left with questions regarding their actual capacity for sustained SSI use over time. The teachers expressed more value in their participation as students of SSI over their participation as teachers utilizing SSI methods. We suggest that in these types of settings, SSI facilitators can do more to engage teachers in the process of reflection as they are modeling the techniques. Krajcik and colleagues (1994) suggested that it is the modeling accompanied by time for reflection and feedback that yield the most meaningful kind of experience for teachers.

We also observed that modeling, while tremendously effective, cannot do the work of demonstrating actual classroom practice and the range of associated techniques with a given innovation or approach. Additionally, our success with the six online tutorials toward SSI development was encouraging, but not likely enough to sustain changes in practice. The goal of sustaining practice in SSI has also been noted by other teacher educators as a persistent concern (Eastwood et al., 2013 Ekborg et al., 2013; Kara, 2012). We suggest that online community building and videocase modeling holds tremendous promise for promoting the SSI model as well as common practices as within actual classrooms. While a videocase library does not yet exist for SSI practice, we note other successful videocase libraries in other domains. For example, the *Persistent Issues in History Wise-Practice Case Database* (Brush & Saye, 2014) consists of a library of cases spanning upper elementary through secondary classrooms, representing a wide range of content topics, and capturing the practices of more than 20 teachers. Each case is indexed according to distinct and specific practices (e.g., "attention grabbers" or persuasive presentations), and users can access video demonstrations as well as classroom materials developed by the teacher to accompany the cases.

Maximizing Use of Collaborative Action Research for SSI Professional Development

While we observed that the teachers' project narratives were deep, meaningful, and reflective of important instructional practices in SSI, the teachers questioned the value of the action research projects in contributing to their overall success with SSI approaches. We hypothesize that they likely felt overwhelmed by new content and new pedagogy at once. When we reflect on other researchers' use of collaborative action research, we note that common to their success was a setting in which teachers selected their own topics for investigation out of their *own current practices*. In other words, the teachers' goals for taking risks and making changes to their practices were prioritized over our defined projects' goals, an observation not unique to our project (see Capobianco & Feldman, 2006; Capobianco et al., 2006; Capobianco & Joyal, 2008; Valanides et al., 2003). Teacher voice and choice may need to be made more central throughout the SSI process.

In addition, we suggest that time was a factor hindering the effectiveness of collaborative action research in the development toward sustained SSI practices. The two-course sequence in this case was bundled within the same semester, though there would be no reason why it could not be divided over the course of two semesters. Doing so would alleviate the burden placed on the teachers during the simultaneous learning of content, SSI approaches, and action research models. A two-semester model may lose participants to attrition, but it may make it more manageable for teachers to focus on content learning, SSI approaches, and planning in semester one, and research planning, SSI implementation, and collaborative action research investigation in semester two. In this way, the courses would stay coupled, but not bundled, within the same semester. This would likely yield a more meaningful experience sustained by greater mentoring and support as well as more time to reflect on new practices and more time for development.

Implications for Research

In this study, we have documented three key findings: (1) the ability of SSI to promote increased content knowledge among teachers, (2) change in teacher practice toward SSI, and (3) the successful implementations of SSI in a wide range of settings. However, the strength of these findings are curbed by the low number of participants, which not only diminished the power of our research model but also changed the nature of the interaction between the instructors and the participants. The low student-to-instructor ratio meant each student received significant input and individualized attention, which is not always possible in larger courses. Therefore, we suggest that future research investigate if these types of changes occur in other settings and with larger numbers of participants. Furthermore, future research should follow up with teachers beyond the course or workshop experience to investigate structures that support sustained SSI. We have also mentioned the need for more examples of SSI in practice, different examples in other content areas, and videocase modeling that would capture the work and practice of teachers. Finally, we need greater mechanisms for supporting the increase of teacher science knowledge within the elementary school grades.

Conclusion

As teachers begin to prioritize the Next Generation Science Standards (NGSS Lead States, 2013) in their classrooms, there is a need for the integrated and synthetic teaching of science that is supported by SSI. Curriculum designers, organizers of professional development workshops, and science resource specialists have the opportunity to support teachers to fully leverage the NGSS to improve student learning of science. Incorporating and sustaining SSI practice seem to rely on the capacity to form durable teams of teachers who can cooperatively reflect on and discuss their teaching. What we have documented with this study reflects a range of approaches that may lead to sustained SSI practice and success.

Acknowledgments

This chapter is an updated version of an article previously published in the *Interdisciplinary Journal of Problem-based Learning.* Original citation: Glazewski, K., Shuster, M. I., Brush, T., & Ellis, A. (2014). *Conexiones:* Fostering socioscientific inquiry in graduate teacher preparation. *Interdisciplinary Journal of Problem-based Learning, 8*(1), 21–38.

This project was supported in part by FIPSE Grant #P116V090037. However, the contents do not necessarily represent the policy of the U.S. Department of Education, and you should not assume endorsement by the federal government.

References

American Association for the Advancement of Science. (1993). *Benchmarks for science literacy.* New York, NY: Oxford University Press.

Appleton, K. (2008). Developing science pedagogical content knowledge through mentoring elementary teachers. *Journal of Science Teacher Education, 19*(6), 523–545. http://dx.doi.org/10.1007/s10972-008-9109-4

Bleicher, R. E. (2006). Nurturing confidence in preservice elementary science teachers. *Journal of Science Teacher Education, 17,* 165–187. http://dx.doi.org/10.1007/s10972-006-9016-5

Bransford, J. D., Brown, A. L., & Cocking, R. R. (2000). *How people learn: Brain, mind, experience, and school committee on developments in the science of learning.* Washington, DC: National Academy Press.

Brush, T., & Saye, J. (2014). An instructional model to support problem-based historical inquiry: The Persistent Issues in History Network. *Interdisciplinary Journal of Problem-based Learning, 8*(1), 39–50. http://dx.doi.org/10.7771/1541-5015.1409

Capobianco, B. M., & Feldman, A. (2006). Promoting quality for teacher action research: Lessons learned from science teachers' action research. *Educational Action Research, 14*(4), 497–512. http://dx.doi.org/10.1080/09650790600975668

Capobianco, B. M., & Joyal, H. (2008). Action research meets engineering design: Practical strategies for incorporating professional development experiences in the classroom. *Science and Children, 45*(8), 22–26.

Capobianco, B. M., Lincoln, S., Canuel-Browne, D., & Trimarchi, R. (2006). Examining the experience of three generations of teacher researchers through collaborative science teachers' inquiry. *Teacher Education Quarterly, 33*(3), 61–78.

Dolan, T. J., Nichols, B. H., & Zeidler, D. L. (2009). Using socioscientific issues in primary classrooms. *Journal of Elementary Science Education, 21*(3), 1–12. http://dx.doi.org/10.1007/BF03174719

Eastwood, J. L., Sadler, T. D., Sherwood, R. D., & Schlegel, W. M. (2013). Students' participation in an interdisciplinary, socioscientific issues based undergraduate human biology major and their understanding of scientific inquiry. *Research in Science Education, 43*(3), 1051–1078. http://dx.doi.org/10.1007/s11165-012-9298-x

Ekborg, M., Ottander, C., Silfver, E., & Simon, S. (2013). Teachers' experience of working with socio-scientific issues: A large scale and in depth study. *Research in Science Education, 43*(2), 599–617. http://dx.doi.org/10.1007/s11165-011-9279-5

Erickson, F. (1986). Qualitative methods in research on teaching. In M. C. Wittrock (Ed.), *Handbook of research on teaching* (3rd ed.). New York, NY: Macmillan.

France, B., Mora, H. A., & Bay, J. L. (2012). Changing perspectives: Exploring a pedagogy to examine other perspectives about stem cell research. *International Journal of Science Education, 34*(5), 803–824. http://dx.doi.org/10.1080/09500693.2011.630427

Forbes, C. T., & Davis, E. A. (2008). Exploring preservice elementary teachers' critique and adaptation of science curriculum materials in respect to socioscientific issues.

Science and Education, 17(8), 829–854. http://dx.doi.org/10.1007/s11191-007-9080-z

Gardner, G., & Jones, G. (2012). Perceptions and practices: Biology graduate teaching assistants' framing of a controversial socioscientific issue. *International Journal of Science Education, 33*(8), 1031–1054. http://dx.doi.org/10.1080/09500691003743244

Griffith, G., & Scharmann, L. (2008). Initial impacts of No Child Left Behind on elementary science education. *Journal of Elementary Science Education, 20*(3), 35–48. http://dx.doi.org/10.1007/BF03174707

Jarrett, O. S. (1999). Science interest and confidence among preservice teachers. *Journal of Elementary Science Education, 11*(1), 49–59. http://dx.doi.org/10.1007/BF03173790

James, L. E., Laatsch, S., Boss Bossé, M. J., Rider, R., Lee, T., & Anderson, C. J. (2006). Science center partnership: Outreach to students and teachers. *The Rural Educator, 28*(1), 33–38.

Kara, Y. (2012). Pre-service biology teachers' perceptions on the instruction of socio-scientific issues in the curriculum. *European Journal of Teacher Education, 35*(1), 111–129. http://dx.doi.org/10.1080/02619768.2011.633999

Klosterman, M. L., & Sadler, T. D. (2010). Multi-level assessment of scientific content knowledge gains associated with socioscientific issues–based instruction. *International Journal of Science Education, 32*(8), 1017–1043. http://dx.doi.org/10.1080/09500690902894512

Kolstø, S. D. (2001). Scientific literacy for citizenship: Tools for dealing with the science dimension of controversial socioscientific issues. *Science Education, 85,* 291–310. http://dx.doi.org/10.1002/sce.1011

Krall, R., Lott, K., & Wymer, C. (2009). Inservice elementary and middle school teachers' conceptions of photosynthesis and respiration. *Journal of Science Teacher Education, 20*(1), 41–55. http://dx.doi.org/10.1007/s10972-008-9117-4

Krajcik, J. S., Blumenfled, P. C., Marx, R. W., & Soloway, E. (1994). A collaborative model for helping middle grade science teachers learn project-based instruction. *The Elementary School Journal, 94*(5), 483–497. http://dx.doi.org/10.1086/461779

Lee, H., Chang, H., Choi, K., Kim, S. W., & Zeidler, D. L. (2012). Developing character and values for global citizens: Analysis of pre-service science teachers' moral reasoning on socioscientific issues. *International Journal of Science Education, 34*(6), 925–953. http://dx.doi.org/10.1080/09500693.2011.625505

Lee, H., & Witz, K. G. (2009). Science teachers' inspiration for teaching socio-scientific issues: Disconnection with reform efforts. *International Journal of Science Education, 31*(7), 931–960. http://dx.doi.org/10.1080/09500690801898903

Lynd-Balta, E., Erklenz-Watts, M., Freeman, C., & Westbay, T. D. (2006). Professional development using an interdisciplinary learning circle: Linking pedagogical theory to practice. *Journal of College Science Teaching, 35*(4), 18–24.

Marin-Dunlop, C. (2006). Science learning environments and action research. *Science Scope, 30*(1), 44–47.

Marshall, J. C., Horton, R., Igo, B. L., & Switzer, D. M. (2009). K–12 science and mathematics teachers' beliefs about and use of inquiry in the classroom. *International Journal of Science and Mathematics Education, 7*(3), 575–596. http://dx.doi.org/10.1007/s10763-007-9122-7

Matkins, J. J., & Bell, R. L. (2007). Awakening the scientist inside: Global climate change and the nature of science in an elementary science methods course. *Journal of Science Teacher Education, 18*(2), 137–163. http://dx.doi.org/10.1007/s10972-006-9033-4

Merriam, S. B. (1997). *Qualitative research and case study: Applications in education.* San Francisco, CA: Jossey-Bass.

Mills, G. E. (2006). *Action research: A guide for the teacher researcher* (3rd ed.). Upper Saddle River, NJ: Merrill.

National Center for Education Statistics. (2012). *The nation's report card: Science 2011 (NCES 2012-465).* Washington, DC: Institute of Education Sciences, U.S. Department of Education.

National Research Council. (1996). *National science education standards.* Darby, PA: Diane Publishing Company.

NGSS Lead States. (2013). *Next generation science standards: For states, by states.* Washington, DC: The National Academies Press.

Rentner, D. S., Scott, C., Kober, N., Chudowsky, N., Chudowsky, V., Joftus, S., & Zabala, D. (2006). *From the capital to the classroom: Year 4 of the No Child Left Behind Act.* Washington, DC: Center on Education Policy. Retrieved from http://www.cep-dc.org/displayDocument.cfm?DocumentID=301

Sadler, T. D. (2004). Informal reasoning regarding socioscientific issues: A critical review of research. *Journal of Research in Science Teaching, 41*(5), 513–536. http://dx.doi.org/10.1002/tea.20009

Sadler, T. D. (2009). Situated learning in science education: Socio-scientific issues as contexts for practice. *Studies in Science Education, 45*(1), 1–42. http://dx.doi.org/10.1080/03057260802681839

Sadler, T. D. (2011). Socio-scientific issues-based education: What we know about science education in the context of SSI. In T. D. Sadler (Ed.), *Socio-scientific issues in the classroom* (pp. 355–369). Netherlands: Springer.

Sadler, T. D., Amirshokoohi, A., Kazempour, M., & Allspaw, K. M. (2006). Socioscience and ethics in science classrooms: Teacher perspectives and strategies. *Journal of Research in Science Teaching, 43*(4), 353–376. http://dx.doi.org/10.1002/tea.20142

Sadler, T. D., Barab, S. A., & Scott, B. (2007). What do students gain by engaging in socioscientific inquiry? *Research in Science Education, 37*(4), 371–391. http://dx.doi.org/10.1007/s11165-006-9030-9

Sadler, T. D., & Zeidler, D. L. (2005). Patterns of informal reasoning in the context of socioscientific decision making. *Journal of Research in Science Teaching, 42*(1), 112–138. http://dx.doi.org/10.1002/tea.20042

Saunders, K. J., & Rennie, L. J. (2011). A pedagogical model for ethical inquiry into socioscientific issues in science. *Research in Science Education, 43*(1), 253–274. http://dx.doi.org/10.1007/s11165-011-9248-z

Saye, J., Kohlmeier, J., Brush, T., Howell, J., & Maddox, L. (2009–2010). Assessing the effects of a teacher education program on pre-service secondary social studies teachers' instructional decision-making. *The International Journal of Social Education, 24*(2), 35–76.

Shulman, L. S. (1986). Those who understand: Knowledge growth in teaching. *Educational Researcher, 15*(2), 4–14. http://dx.doi.org/10.3102/0013189X015002004

Walker, K. A., & Zeidler, D. L. (2007). Promoting discourse about socioscientific issues through scaffolded inquiry. *International Journal of Science Education, 29*(11), 1387–1410. http://dx.doi.org/10.1080/09500690601068095

Valanides, N., Nicolaidou, A., & Eilks, I. (2003). Twelfth grade students' understanding of oxidation and combustion: Using action research to improve teachers' practical knowledge and teaching practice. *Research in Science and Technological Education, 21*(2), 159–174. http://dx.doi.org/10.1080/02635140320001272111

Yilmaz-Tuzun, O. (2007). Preservice elementary teachers' beliefs about science teaching. *Journal of Science Teacher Education, 19*(2), 183–204. http://dx.doi.org/10.1007/s10972-007-9084-1

Zeidler, D. L., & Nichols, B. H. (2009). Socioscientific issues: Theory and practice. *Journal of Elementary Science Education, 21*(2), 49–58. http://dx.doi.org/10.1007/BF03173684

APPENDIX
Focus Group Questions for Teachers

1. Discuss the types of curriculum projects you have been developing and implementing for your classes through your participation in this class.
   a. What topics/content are you covering in these projects? How did you go about selecting these topics?
   b. What new things did you try in your instruction as a result of this course? What risks did you take?
   c. Have you been able to implement all (or part) of your projects with your students? If so, what has been the reaction of your students toward your projects?
   d. If you have been able to implement your projects, what evidence do you have that the projects have been effective in terms of positive student learning outcomes?
2. Discuss the process you went through in developing the curriculum projects for your class.
   a. What types of resources/instructional support did you find most (and least) useful as you developed your projects?
   b. If you have been able to implement your projects with your students, what aspects of the class have you found most beneficial in helping prepare you to actually teach your units?
   c. What advice/suggestions would you give to the course instructor(s) to improve the overall effectiveness of the class itself?
3. Discuss how the development and implementation of your projects have impacted your knowledge of science.
   a. Do you believe that participation in this class has positively impacted your overall knowledge of science content? If so, how?
   b. Do you believe that participation in this class has helped you feel more confident to teach science to your own students? If so, how?
   c. Do you believe that participation in this project will influence the amount of science content you include in your curriculum in the future? If so, how?
4. Are there any other comments/suggestions you would like to provide to the instructors/project staff?

Krista D. Glazewski is an associate professor of instructional systems technology at Indiana University, Bloomington. Her work and interests are centered primarily on problem-based and inquiry-based learning within K–12 contexts with teachers and students. She has more than 15 years' experience in public education, first as a middle school teacher and later as a teacher educator.

Michèle I. Shuster is an associate professor in the biology department at New Mexico State University. She was trained as a molecular biologist but currently focuses on biology education, working on a variety of projects that emphasize case study and issues-based approaches at both the K–8 and undergraduate levels. She is also involved in training graduate students and postdoctoral fellows in scientific teaching.

Thomas Brush is the Barbara B. Jacobs Chair in Education and Technology as well as the chair of the Department of Instructional Systems Technology within the School of Education at Indiana University, Bloomington. His research interests focus on developing methods and strategies to promote inquiry-oriented learning, particularly with more open-ended instruction. This involves studying methods for integrating tools to promote collaborative problem-based learning strategies into the learning environment itself and developing alternative techniques to deliver instruction to students.

Andrea Ellis received her PhD in biology at New Mexico State University. Her research interests are in the regulation of mitotic cell division. She has been a scientific teaching fellow and preparing future faculty fellow at New Mexico State University, and currently teaches eighth grade science.

3

AN INSTRUCTIONAL MODEL TO SUPPORT PROBLEM-BASED HISTORICAL INQUIRY: THE PERSISTENT ISSUES IN HISTORY NETWORK

Thomas Brush and John Saye

Introduction

Problem-based learning (PBL) represents an innovative instructional strategy that is receiving increasing attention in K–12 educational settings (Means, Padilla, DeBarger, & Bakia, 2009; Patrick, 2008). PBL provides learners with authentic ill-structured problems without a clear solution path. Using this student-centered approach, the teacher guides students through the problem-solving process (Barrows, 2002). There is a growing body of research that suggests PBL to be more effective than traditional instruction in increased student achievement (Hmelo-Silver, 2004; Ravitz, 2009; Strobel & van Barneveld, 2009; Walker & Leary, 2009; Wirkala & Kuhn, 2011). For example, in a recent study examining of the effectiveness of PBL with middle school students, Wirkala and Kuhn (2011) found that students performed significantly better on a multitude of outcome measures when they engaged in PBL instruction versus lecture-based instruction. Similarly, Strobel and van Barneveld (2009) found that "PBL was superior when it comes to long-term retention, skill development and satisfaction of students and teachers, while traditional approaches were more effective for short term retention as measured by standardized board exams" (p. 44).

Based on the demonstrated effectiveness of PBL, more K–12 schools are integrating technology-supported PBL into their curriculum, including

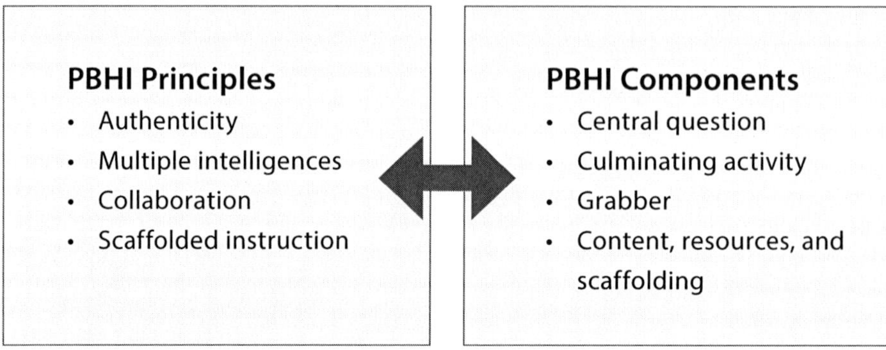

Figure 3.1 Overview of PBHI model.

whole-school integration such as the New Tech High model, currently in place in numerous high schools across the country. In most secondary history classrooms, however, problem-based curriculum reform has not been widely accepted and adopted by teachers (Onosko, 1991; Saye & SSIRC, 2013; Shaver, 1996; Shaver, Davis, & Helburn, 1979; Zukas, 2000). This is despite the fact that social educators have advocated that history instruction move away from the goal of mere retention of historical information.

In order to increase the integration of problem-based inquiry into classroom practice, we have collaborated on an evolving line of inquiry that applies propositions emerging from this research literature to the design and testing of a PBL framework—known as the Persistent Issues in History Network (http://pihnet.org)—that includes a set of digital resources and video-based wise practice cases that represent a professional teaching knowledge base for implementing a particular model of instruction, problem-based historical inquiry (PBHI). PBHI focuses instructional activities on the examination of persistent societal problems in a particular historical context (Callahan, Saye, & Brush, 2009–2010; Saye & Brush, 2004).

The PBHI curricular design we have adopted incorporates specific research-based practices and components that are necessary for successful implementation of PBHI units and activities (see Figure 3.1). These include authenticity of experience, incorporation of multiple intelligences, effective collaboration, and scaffolded supports throughout the experience (Saye & Brush, 2004).

Researchers suggest that the authenticity of the learning experience can have a major positive influence on student engagement (Land, 2000; Newmann, Wehlage, & Lamborn, 1992; VanSickle, 1996). Research also suggests that students may fail to become engaged when placed in circumstances that do not provide them with reasonable opportunities to be successful (Doyle, 1983). Often, school-based tasks are viewed by learners as utilizing skills and knowledge that are not needed in the "real world." In addition, school-based tasks tend to reward only those learners who can demonstrate their knowledge either linguistically or logically. Gardner's (1999) theory of multiple intelligences proposed that learners should be provided with opportunities to demonstrate their knowledge in alternative ways (other than linguistically or logically). Thus, learners need to be provided with a variety of authentic assessments that require collaborative effort and call for a wide array of student abilities in order to produce a successful final product.

In addition, researchers believe that implementing collaborative tasks in classrooms encourages broader engagement and healthier classroom environments, and may help students succeed in developing richer and more complex models of reality than they might do individually (Cohen & Benton, 1988). Thus, learners need to be engaged in collaborative tasks that promote authenticity. These types of authentic collaborative tasks may involve role-playing activities in which students assume the perspectives of historical figures, analyzing and utilizing primary-source documents to support an historical perspective and using those sources as evidence to defend a position regarding a controversial historic event.

Finally, our PBHI model integrates additional aids, or *scaffolds*, to assist students and teachers engaged in PBHI (Brush & Saye, 2002; Saye & Brush, 2002). Scaffolds are tools, strategies, and guides that support students in attaining a higher level of understanding, one that would be impossible if students worked on their own (Hannafin, Land, & Oliver, 1999). In our curriculum development efforts, we have conceptualized two forms of support: hard and soft scaffolds (Brush & Saye, 2002; Saye & Brush, 2002). Hard scaffolds are static supports that can be anticipated and planned in advance based on typical student difficulties with a task. Soft scaffolds are dynamic, situation-specific aids provided by a teacher or peer to help with the learning process.

Integrating PBHI Into Preservice Teacher Education

One major barrier to effective implementation of PBHI in secondary social studies classrooms is the lack of integration of PBHI teaching strategies into secondary social studies teacher education programs. This lack of integration exacerbates the issue of having teachers even prepared to implement PBHI curriculum into their future classrooms (Brush & Saye, 2009). This is not an issue exclusive to preservice social studies programs. In fact, most teacher education programs still approach preservice classrooms with conventional practices (Feiman-Nemser, 2008; Kiggins & Cambourne, 2007), and few preservice teachers have clear conceptions of designing and implementing PBL instruction (So & Kim, 2009). However, more teacher education programs are beginning to recognize the potential for PBL and the need for support in order to integrate PBL into their programs (Edwards & Hammer, 2006; Murray-Harvey & Slee, 2000).

The Auburn University social studies teacher education program emphasizes the development of civic competence as the central purpose for teaching social studies. Although the social studies include numerous social science disciplines, history courses dominate most states' curricula for grades 6–12 (Dye & Huffman, 2003). In Alabama, history courses make up 71% of the 6–12 curriculum. Although our program addresses the other disciplines, we focus our teacher preparation on a civic-oriented approach to teaching history: PBHI.

Over the course of four consecutive semesters, students in the Auburn program work in methods classes and in lengthy field experiences in PBHI-based classrooms to explore, test, and reflect on PBHI principles. Our expectation is that this set of carefully sequenced professional experiences will develop in teacher candidates a nuanced understanding of the professional teaching knowledge on which the program is based.

Our principles for planning and implementing PBHI instruction focus on engaging learners with rich historical content framed around inquiry into essential societal issues. To establish relevance, we build instruction around persisting ethical questions that apply to contemporary society, for instance: "When are citizens justified in resisting governmental authority?" In studying a particular topic in the curriculum—for example, the American Civil War—that broad persisting question might be made more specific: "Was the South justified in seceding from the Union?" Once a framing question is established, we encourage preservice teachers to support disciplined inquiry and ethical reasoning by providing multiple ways of encountering content and actively supporting student thinking. As preservice teachers progress through the four-semester course sequence, they address essential questions about social studies and the preparation of democratic citizens. In each course, students engage in extended field experiences in PBHI-based classrooms and utilize an array of web-based planning guides, digital curriculum materials, tools to facilitate PBL curriculum design and implementation, and wise practice models available via our

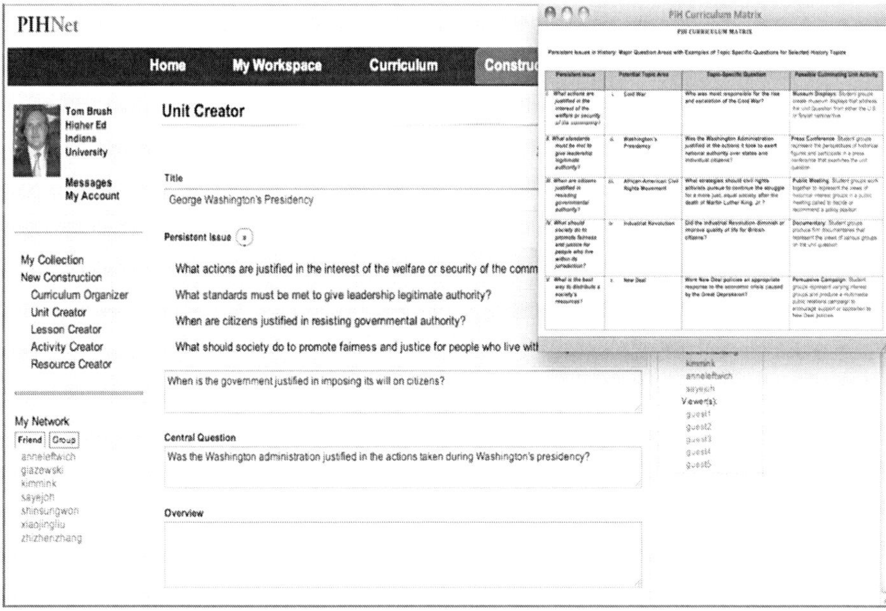

Figure 3.2 PIHNet online PBHI unit scaffold.

project website (http://pihnet.org) that reflect the program's core principles (Brush & Saye, 2009). For example, students use digital unit construction scaffolds to conceptualize and design their PBL units. These scaffolds incorporate key components of our PBHI model in order to facilitate students' inclusion of those components into the units they design in their courses (see Figure 3.2).

Assessing Preservice Teachers' Knowledge of PBHI

Assisting preservice teachers with conceptualizing PBHI strategies and implementing those strategies in classrooms poses numerous challenges to teacher educators. Designing PBHI activities requires teachers to think differently about introductory unit activities, student assessments, and classroom activities that engage learners and provide them with the foundational knowledge necessary to successfully complete the assessment activities (Saye & Brush, 2004). For preservice teachers, there are potentially multiple aspects of the PBHI curricular design that are difficult for them to grasp. To this point, though, we have had little data to assist us with determining the knowledge level of preservice teachers regarding PBHI and no measurement devices for acquiring those data. In addition, we currently lack the tools to determine the effectiveness of curricular practices within our preservice teacher education programs, designed to provide future teachers with skills and experiences that will assist them in conceptualizing PBHI teaching practices, and potentially implement those practices in their future classrooms.

By developing an instrument that attempts to measure knowledge of PBHI curricular practices, we may be better able to customize the activities we implement in our teaching methods courses while at the same time providing an assessment tool that other researchers may be able to use to determine the effectiveness of PBHI curricular interventions in a variety of history and social studies contexts. But developing an instrument to measure an individual's knowledge of problem-based inquiry is more difficult than developing more standard instruments such as attitudinal surveys or observation forms. For measuring this type of knowledge, researchers have recommended assessments that provide content-specific scenarios and ask participants to complete a task based on the scenario. This form of assessment has been successfully implemented in fields such as science (Cooper, Shepardson, & Harber, 2002), business (Callanan & Perri, 2006), ethics (Snow & Bloom, 1996), and even computer security procedures (Barrett, Garrety, & Seberry, 2006). However, the use of scenario-based instruments to measure learners' knowledge of problem-based inquiry strategies (particularly in social studies) appears to be limited.

Purpose of Study

The purpose of this study was to utilize data obtained from implementation of a scenario-based assessment instrument to assess the degree to which preservice teachers integrated PBHI principles into their pedagogical thinking. The instrument was designed to measure specific PBHI strategies emphasized in the Auburn University secondary social studies teacher education program. Preservice teachers completed the survey instrument at the beginning of their teacher education program and again at the end of their student teaching experience.

Specifically, this chapter presents an overview of the scenario-based instrument, findings from implementation of the instrument with multiple cohorts of preservice teachers, and a discussion of participant responses from their initial completion of the survey to their final completion of the survey prior to the end of the program. Finally, implications of these results for preparing preservice teachers to integrate problem-based inquiry strategies in their teaching is discussed.

Method

Participants and Setting

Participants included 120 students completing the secondary social studies teacher education program at Auburn University. Fifty-three percent of participants were female, and all but five participants were 25 years of age or younger. In terms of ethnicity, 92% of the participants classified themselves as "white (other than Latino)," with 4% indicating that they were African American. All participants stated that they used a computer every day.

Participants were enrolled in Auburn's two-year residential teacher education program, which, in addition to 45 hours of prerequisite social studies content courses, included 11 hours of teaching methods/practicum courses and 12 hours of student teaching. All participants completed the program between 2008 and 2012.

Design and Data Sources

The design of this study can generally be considered a cohort survey research design, in which the same participants complete a survey instrument on multiple occasions in order to determine differences in responses to various items over the course of an intervention (Fowler, 2002). Participants were asked to complete the survey instrument at the beginning of their teacher education program (their initial activity in the program), and then to complete the same survey at the completion of their culminating student teaching experience. The data source for this study included participants' responses to the survey items on those two occasions.

Survey instrument. The instrument itself had two sections. The first section (containing 11 items) asked participants to provide background information, including age, gender, ethnicity, academic progress, and computer experience.

The second section of the survey included questions based on the scenario of teaching a 10th grade U.S. history class focusing on the Reconstruction period following the Civil War. Respondents were asked to make instructional decisions in three areas common in planning units of instruction: identifying learning objectives, introducing the unit, and assessing student learning outcomes. The various options available on the survey were included based on both traditional classroom practices and classroom practices consistent with the PBHI curricular framework. We included several options in each survey section that are indicative of the assumptions of the PIH program model. For example:

- We included *learning objectives* that required the analysis and synthesis of foundational knowledge to support ethical decision making.
- We included *introductory activities* that established relevance by connecting to students' experiences and established a purpose for learning the content through a central question that was the focus of instruction.
- We included *collaborative and individual assessments* that required students to publicly present and defend a position related to the issue posed by the central unit question.

In addition, open-ended questions included at the end of each section of the survey asked participants to provide rationales for their ranking and/or selection of items in the scenario.

Validity of instrument. Content and concurrent validity for the instrument were established via a review of the instrument by a panel of three social studies education experts knowledgeable of the Auburn University teacher preparation program and its PBHI principles. These experts reviewed the survey to assess whether the survey items selected as best reflecting PBHI principles were in their judgment valid indicators of the program's goals and instructional philosophy. After independently reviewing the survey, all members of the panel concluded that it accurately assessed PBHI knowledge advocated by the program. Refer to Saye and colleagues (2009–2010) for more detail regarding reliability and validity of the survey instrument.

Procedure

Approximately one week prior to the first class meeting of their initial course in the teacher education program, participants were sent an email by the instructor of their class requesting that they complete the survey. The email contained a link to the survey instrument. Participants were asked to complete the survey prior to their first class.

Approximately one week prior to the end of their student teaching experience, participants were sent an email requesting that they complete the survey again. Once again, the email contained a link to the online survey instrument. Participants were asked to complete the survey prior to their completion of student teaching.

Data Analysis and Results

Numerical data from the survey were analyzed using descriptive and inferential statistical procedures. Participants' initial responses to the survey were compared to their responses as they were completing their student teaching experiences via the nonparametric Wilcoxon rank-order test. The Wilcoxon test is a nonparametric analysis applicable to a repeated-measure design with an intervention, particularly when dealing with data in which participants are asked to rank-order alternatives (Green & Salkind, 2008). The Wilcoxon test provides a means for determining the extent to which participants alter their responses to ranked data between initial responses to items and final responses to items. Since there were multiple inferential tests conducted, Bonferroni correction was used to reduce the likelihood of type I error ($\alpha = .05/23 = .002$; $.01/23 = .0004$; $.001/23 = .00004$).

In addition, participants' responses to open-ended questions were analyzed qualitatively for further explanation of their rankings and/or selection of survey items. The open-ended items were analyzed using constant comparative coding to establish a general overview of the reasons participants indicated for their rankings (Fram, 2013; Straus & Corbin, 1998). Using directed content analysis techniques (Hsieh & Shannon, 2005), open-ended responses in each section of the survey were independently analyzed by the two researchers in order to generate an initial set of codes, which were then used for further analysis. After the independent analyses of each section were completed, the researchers compared their results and noted areas of discrepancy in the coding of the data set. Each discrepancy was discussed and resolved in order to obtain agreement of 100%.

Comparison of Components of Scenario

The scenario-based component of the survey asked participants to rank various aspects of a unit focusing on the Reconstruction period following the Civil War. Participants were asked to provide views on four specific components of the lesson: the objectives for the lesson, the introductory activity for the lesson, methods for ensuring active student involvement in the lesson, and culminating assessment activities for the lesson.

Objectives. Participants were asked to rank six learning objectives in order of importance. These learning objectives included:

1. Students will explain the influence the Reconstruction period had on today's political structure
2. Students will use primary documents to identify major controversies surrounding Reconstruction policies
3. Students will describe the relationship between the Reconstruction period and the Civil War
4. Students will construct an argument that reflects the perspective of a figure from the Reconstruction period
5. Students will explain the reasons for the federal initiatives implemented during Reconstruction
6. Students will use historical evidence to defend a position on the desirability and effectiveness of Reconstruction policies

A summary of responses is provided in Table 3.1. Figure 3.3 presents the results of the inferential statistical analysis.

These data suggest that participants modified their rankings of the possible learning objectives from the time they first completed the survey to when they completed the survey at the end of the program. When they initially completed the survey, more than half of the participants selected learning objective 3 as the objective they considered to be most important to include in the Reconstruction unit. Only 23% of participants ranked learning objective 6 as their first or second choice.

In contrast, more than 62% of participants selected learning objective 6 as their first or second choice on the post-survey, with just more than 23%

Table 3.1 *Percentage of participants who ranked each learning objective as first or second.*

Learning Objective	Pre-Survey %	Post-Survey %
LO 1	41.7	42.5
LO 2	24.4	35.0
LO 3	56.7	23.3
LO 4	19.2	25.8
LO 5	35.0	10.8
LO 6*	23.3	62.5

*Indicates objective best aligned with PBHI principles.

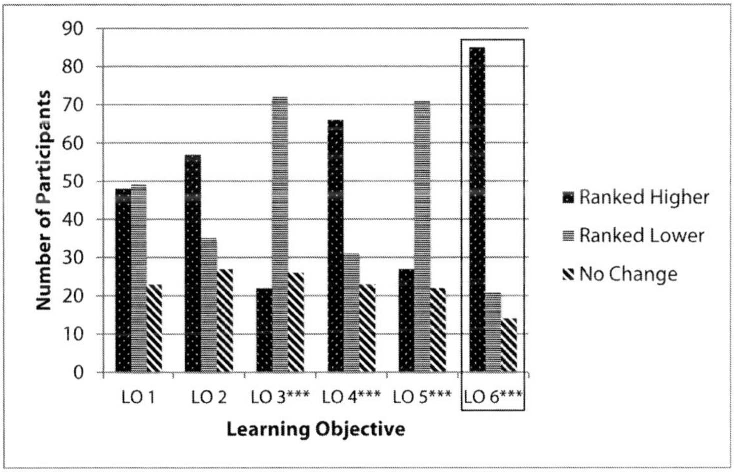

Figure 3.3 Wilcoxon results for learning objectives.

selecting learning objective 3. The changes in rankings for both learning objective 3 (decrease in ranking) and learning objective 6 (increase in ranking) proved to be statistically significant. In addition, it is important to note that learning objective 6 was the objective most closely aligned with PBHI curricular principles integrated into our teacher education program.

Examination of participants' open-ended rationales for the selection of their highest-ranked learning objectives also revealed some differences between the initial survey and the post-survey. On the initial survey, two general themes emerged from the rationale statements. First, participants felt that it was very important for students to understand how past events influenced present-day issues and political structures. More than 40% of participants specifically stated that this should be one of the most important goals of the unit. For example, one participant stated, "I chose [Learning Objective] #1 as most important because I think it is very important to understand and learn how history can affect our lives many years after the fact." Another participant stated, "Looking at the Civil War and the influences that it has on today will help students see how the Civil War can still impact us today."

The second theme related to acquiring broad knowledge about the Reconstruction period. Participants felt it was very important for students to understand "what the Reconstruction period was about and why it took place following the Civil War." More than 50% of participants made reference to the need for students to gain this knowledge. Examples of participant statements included: "10th graders need to first get a solid foundation of information about the Reconstruction period before they can handle [objectives] 4, 5, and 6," "I believe that it is important for the students to know why certain events happened in history and why they came about," and "I think that is the most basic aspect of the Reconstruction period to cover: what Reconstruction was, and how it came about after the war."

On the post-survey, however, different themes emerged from participant responses. The most prevalent theme dealt with the importance of students being able to construct an argument and defend that argument with evidence. More than 60% of participants stated that this should be one of the most important goals of the unit. One participant stated, "I think this is important because it allows students to form their opinions about historical events based on evidence and helps them to develop reasoning skills." Another participant responded, "The first objective [objective 6] would be the central focus of the whole unit. I would want the kids to examine the pros and cons of these policies, assess their value, and defend/criticize from different perspectives."

A second theme focused on the importance of having students use primary sources in order to acquire multiple perspectives on a historical issue. More than 56% of participants stated that this was important. As one participant stated, "I feel that students only understand the controversy of the Reconstruction era by examining the actual documents using historical empathy." Another participant said, "I think it is important to analyze primary documents in order to teach students the importance of firsthand accounts and to explain to students that the further the documents are removed from the time/event the less credible they will be."

Introductory strategy. Participants were asked to rank seven possible introductory strategies in order of how likely they would use them in their Reconstruction unit. These introductory strategies included:

1. Ask students what they know about the Reconstruction period
2. Connect the historical topic to students' own interests and experiences
3. Present a general overview of important events that will be covered in the Reconstruction unit
4. Connect Reconstruction to events studied in the previous unit
5. Have students complete a pretest to determine their general knowledge of the Reconstruction period

6. Connect Reconstruction to broader historical themes or issues
7. Explain to students how their understanding will be assessed at the end of the unit

Responses were aggregated to determine the percentage of participants who selected each introductory strategy as either their first or second choice. A summary of responses is provided in Table 3.2. Figure 3.4 presents the results of the inferential statistical analysis.

As with the learning objectives, participants' responses indicate that the introductory strategies they most preferred changed from the time they first completed the survey at the beginning of their program to when they completed the survey at the end of the program. In the initial survey, participants' preferences regarding the introductory activity seemed to be spread out across many of the possible choices, with 42% of participants selecting Introductory Strategy 3, 48% preferring Introductory Strategy 1, 31% preferring Introductory Strategy 2, 24% choosing Introductory Strategy 4, and 33% choosing Introductory Strategy 5. Only Introductory Strategy 6 and Introductory Strategy 7 were top choices for fewer than 25% of participants.

There were some significant differences in participants' responses on the post-survey. Nearly 70% of participants selected Introductory Strategy 2 as their first or second choice, and more than 50% identified Introductory Strategy 6 as one of their top preferences. Interestingly, only 10% of participants selected Introductory Strategy 3 as one of their top choices—the strategy that was preferred by more than 40% of participants on the initial survey. The changes in rankings for Introductory Strategy 2 (increase in ranking) and Introductory Strategies 1, 3, and 5 (decrease in ranking) proved to be statistically significant.

Table 3.2 *Percentage of participants who ranked each introductory strategy as first or second.*

Introductory Strategy	Pre-Survey %	Post-Survey %
IN 1	48.3	31.7
IN 2	30.8	68.3
IN 3	41.7	10.0
IN 4	25.8	22.5
IN 5	33.3	12.6
IN 6*	14.2	52.5
IN 7	5.9	5.8

*Indicates objective best aligned with PBHI principles.

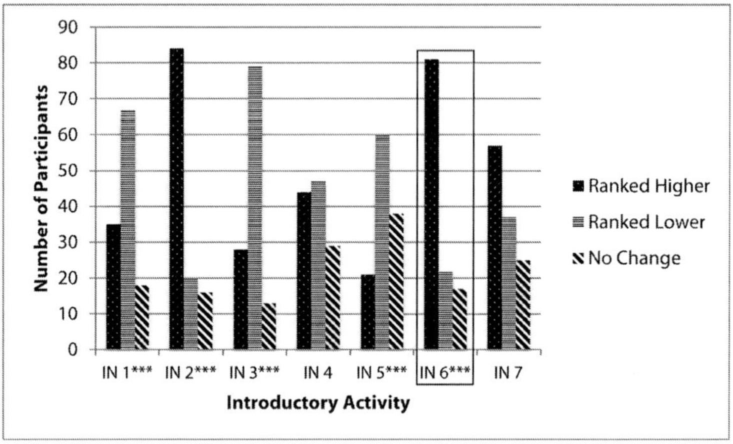

Figure 3.4 Wilcoxon results for introductory strategy.

Introductory Activity 6, the introductory activity most closely aligned with our PBHI curricular principles, also demonstrated a statistically significant increase in ranking.

Examination of participants' rationales for the selection of their preferred introductory strategies once again revealed some differences between the initial survey and the post-survey. As with the overall rankings, the discussions of the reasoning for selecting the introductory strategy tended to be widespread and varied. However, one general theme was present. More than 52% of participants stated that they thought it was important to assess the current knowledge level of their students prior to teaching new content—either informally (by asking students to discuss what they already knew about Reconstruction) or formally (via a pretest). They believed this would assist them in planning and refining their lessons. As one participant stated, "Of the choices given, I would probably give the students a pretest in order to see how much each student knows and to see where I will need to focus my lectures." Similarly, a participant stated, "I think that students should be presented with a pretest in order to determine what they know about Reconstruction and what needs to be taught in further depth." Another participant responded, "Asking students about their current knowledge of Reconstruction would give me a good idea about where to start my introduction about this period."

One very strong theme emerged from responses on the post-survey: the importance of making the information relevant by connecting it to students' experiences. Nearly 70% of participants stressed the importance of finding methods of relating the topic of the unit to students' own experiences while introducing the unit. Their main reasoning for this strategy was that it would potentially increase student interest and engagement in the topic itself, and make the topic more meaningful to students. For example, one participant stated, "It's a good idea to connect historical topics to students' own interests and experiences because it increases the likelihood that they'll get involved and become interested in the topic." Another participant responded, "I think that it is important to connect historical events to students' interests in order to get students fully engaged in the lesson." Finally, one participant posited, "I feel that the only way to grab students' attention is to relate the past to what they're going through today. I think that too many teachers fail to make the subject interesting and therefore lose a lot of the students due to their teaching style." Interestingly, only one participant discussed the use of a pretest to gauge students' preexisting knowledge as one of their preferred introductory activities.

Assessment. In the final section of the survey, participants were asked to select the assessment strategy (or strategies) they would use in their unit. As opposed to ranking the various assessment strategies in order of preference, participants were allowed to select up to three assessment strategies that they felt they would use in their unit. The five possible assessment strategies provided included:

1. An objective test of student knowledge of Reconstruction events and issues
2. An essay test in which students evaluate the desirability and effectiveness of Reconstruction policies
3. An essay test in which students demonstrate understanding of Reconstruction polices and their effects
4. A group project to construct museum displays that reveal the pivotal events of the Reconstruction period
5. A group project to prepare and conduct a mock congressional hearing that debates Reconstruction policies and evaluates their effectiveness
6. A summary of responses is provided in Table 3.3. Figure 3.5 presents the results of the inferential statistical analysis

Results of the initial survey indicated that more than 62% of participants would utilize Assessment Strategy 1 and/or Assessment Strategy 3 in their unit. In contrast, results of the post-survey indicated that more than 75% of participants would include Assessment Strategy 5 in their unit, and that only 30% of participants would select Assessment Strategy 1 and/or Assessment

Table 3.3 ***Percentage of participants who selected each assessment strategy.***

Assessment Strategy	Pre-Survey %	Post-Survey %
AS 1	62.5	30.0
AS 2*	27.5	51.7
AS 3	62.5	29.2
AS 4	22.5	46.7
AS 5*	61.7	75.8

*Indicates assessment strategy best aligned with PBHI principles.

Strategy 3. Participants' decisions to not include both Assessment Strategy 1 and Assessment Strategy 3 in their unit assessments (on the post-survey) proved to be statistically significant changes.

The assessment strategies included on the survey that most closely aligned with PBHI principles (Assessment Strategies 2 and 5) were both selected to be included in the overall unit assessment by a majority of participants on the post-survey. Participants' decisions to include Assessment Strategy 2 in their unit assessments proved to be a statistically significant change, and Assessment Strategy 5 was selected by more participants than any other choice on the post-survey.

In terms of the participants' written rationales for choosing the assessment strategies for their units, there were marked differences between responses made

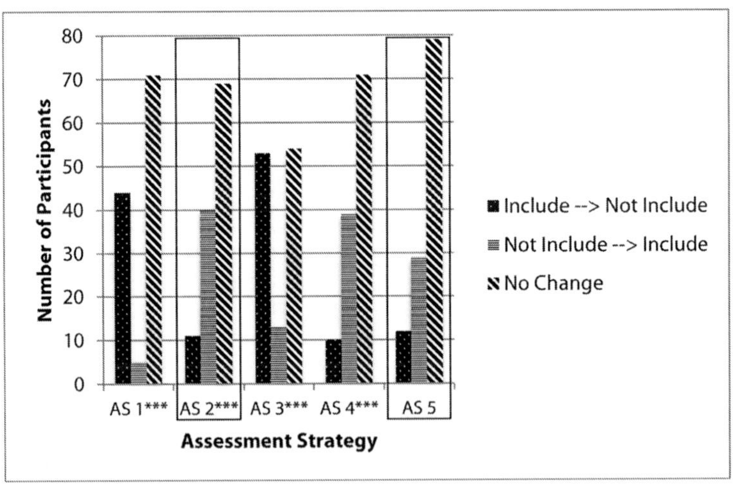

Figure 3.5 Wilcoxon results for assessment strategies.

on the initial survey and responses made on the follow-up survey. On the initial survey, more than 60% of participants stated that they would first use either an objective test or an essay test in which students demonstrate understanding of Reconstruction policies as their initial assessment (in fact, 30% of participants stated that this would be their only form of assessment). The specific reasoning for choosing these types of assessment tended to focus on ensuring mastery and retention of knowledge presented in the unit. Participant comments included: "I would first use an objective assessment for the Reconstruction era so that I can see if the students have learned the solid facts from the Reconstruction era," "I think it is important for students to be able to take an objective test because so many things are covered in a unit that this is a good way to measure what they have retained," and "To me, giving an essay assessment is a good way to determine if the student has mastered the assigned objectives."

Participants' rationales for the assessment strategies they selected on the post-survey tended to focus on providing students with multiple opportunities to demonstrate their understanding. While they did not altogether reject the use of some form of objective assessment (31% specifically stated that they would include some form of objective test as one of their assessment strategies), their overall preference was for more open-ended group assessments such as a mock hearing or museum display. Participants repeatedly stated that providing opportunities to assess students with various learning styles and multiple intelligences was important in their overall assessment strategy. For example, one participant stated, "This [group project] gives students with different learning styles a chance to express themselves and explain what they have learned from the unit." Another student stated, "The group project would be a great assessment method because it'd draw on students' various multiple intelligences [as they] take different roles within their group and present their arguments to class." A fellow participant concurred, stating, "I like the idea of students working together on group projects because it pulls in multiple intelligences and strengths and allows different forms of assessment instead of constantly using written exams—objective or subjective."

Discussion

The purpose of this chapter is twofold. First, we provided an overview of how we have integrated a specific model of problem-based learning—PBHI—into the teacher education program at Auburn University. In addition, we presented one method for providing evaluative information regarding the effectiveness of this model in preparing preservice teachers to implement PBL strategies in their future classrooms. We conducted a study of multiple cohorts of preservice teachers completing Auburn's social studies program and utilized a scenario-based survey instrument to assess their pedagogical understanding and endorsement of PBHI practices. Results suggest substantial changes in preservice teachers' pedagogical thinking from their initial entry into their teacher education program to their completion of the program. In particular, there is some evidence that preservice teachers came to understand and perceive the importance of major aspects of the PBHI curricular framework as it applied to an effective, principle-driven teaching practice: specifically authenticity, multiple intelligences, and collaboration.

In terms of authenticity, there is some evidence in the differences in responses from the initial survey to the post-survey that participants placed great value on incorporating authenticity into the Reconstruction unit they were developing via the survey. For example, when selecting learning objectives for their unit, a vast majority of participants selected learning objectives focusing on analysis and synthesis of evidence, constructing knowledge, and defending arguments in the post-survey. This compares to their responses in the initial survey, where a majority of participants selected learning objectives that focused more on description and explanation of knowledge related to the Reconstruction era. More interestingly, participants' rationales for their selection of learning objectives tended to focus on higher-order thinking (e.g., "constructing their own arguments using historical evidence," "allows students to think critically about the topic," "assess their value and defend/criticize from different perspectives") in the post-survey than the rationales reported in the initial survey (e.g., "understanding what the Reconstruction period was about," "explain the details that were involved [in Reconstruction]," "explain and summarize what happened during Reconstruction").

Participants' choices in terms of introductory activities also provided some evidence that they were concerned about making the unit as authentic and relevant as possible. On the post-survey, nearly 70% of participants stated that they would develop an introductory activity that helped connect the topic to students' own interests—compared to just more than 30% in the initial survey (fewer than the percentage of participants who chose to just give a general overview of the unit). Once again, the reasoning behind the choices provide insight into the selection of choices, with participants focusing on how to engage students and make the content meaningful in the post-survey (e.g., "Connecting to students' interests makes the information more meaningful," "Relevance is the most important thing," "You are grabbing their attention and making the topic relevant to their lives"), as opposed to focusing more on attempting to assess student knowledge in order to better plan for the unit—the predominant rationales presented in the initial survey (e.g., "Give the students a pretest in order to see how much each student knows," "Asking students about their current knowledge ... would give me a good idea about where to start," "Ask students what they knew already ... so that I could decide how much detail I needed to go into").

The assessment activities participants selected provided further evidence that they valued both authenticity (e.g., "These assessments seem most authentic") and how multiple intelligences could be incorporated into assessment. On the post-survey, more than 70% of participants stated that they would utilize some form of group-based assessment activity (either a mock congressional hearing or a museum display), and numerous participants stated that they would use multiple forms of assessment in order to provide learners who may have different strengths and learning styles with opportunities to successfully demonstrate their knowledge of the information presented in the unit. Their justification for selecting their assessment strategies included: "cover as many learning styles as possible," "it'd draw on students various multiple intelligences," "[a] group project will allow students that might not do well on a written test to adequately show what they have learned," and "it incorporates all of the multiple intelligences." In contrast, on the initial survey none of the participants explicitly stated that they would provide students with multiple opportunities to demonstrate their knowledge in different ways as a rationale for their choices of assessment strategies. In fact, although a large percentage of participants chose to include group projects such as the mock congressional hearing in their overall assessment strategies on the initial survey, many made this choice simply because they enjoyed group projects when they were in school (e.g., "I chose the two group projects because I like group projects"), because they thought students would find the projects to be fun ("I chose to do the mock congressional hearing because I felt that it would be a fun experience"), or because they thought it would assist students with retaining information covered in the unit ("I went to the group project to try [to] keep the information interesting and maybe they won't forget it as easily").

Finally, participants' assessment choices on the survey provided some evidence that they not only believed that incorporating collaboration strategies into unit activities was important, but that they understood how collaboration could facilitate overall student learning. As stated previously, more than 70% of participants selected a group project as their preferred assessment strategy on the post-survey, and many indicated that incorporating collaboration would be beneficial to students in multiple ways (e.g., "[they could] take different roles within their group and present their arguments," "the group project would allow all students to participate, and they learn best by participating," and "all students would be engaged and active"). While many of the participants also included a group project as an assessment strategy on the initial survey, none of them specifically described the potential pedagogical benefits of having students work collaboratively, other than in a very general way (e.g., "[It] would allow the students to show their knowledge," "It helps people become more social," or "It is important for students to debate and work as a team").

Conclusion and Implications

Results of our evaluation with multiple cohorts of preservice teachers provides some evidence to suggest that, when provided with opportunities to explore, critique, implement, and evaluate PBHI teaching strategies within their teacher education program, preservice teachers are able to articulate the core curricular framework of PBHI and incorporate that framework into the design of instructional activities. Preservice teachers' selection of various components of a unit on Reconstruction seemed to more closely align with the core principles of PBHI on the post-survey than on the initial survey. More importantly, preservice teachers seemed to be better able to articulate their reasons for making various curricular choices on the post-survey. Their responses suggest the potential of teacher preparation programs unified around a set of core, research-based principles for promoting reflective professional teaching knowledge in their graduates.

This research also provides some promise for using scenario-based surveys as one method for determining how well preservice teachers understand various curriculum frameworks. While this assessment strategy is by no means fully authentic, we believe that it does provide a *more* authentic assessment of preservice teachers' knowledge of PBHI and ability to apply PBHI in teaching situations than other alternatives such as general "belief" surveys or more objective assessments focusing on the specific components of the PBHI framework. Ideally, this assessment can be used to determine (in a more general sense) the effectiveness of a teacher education program's ability to facilitate preservice teachers in understanding various curricular models. Coupled with more authentic assessments, such as evaluation of actual development and implementation of PBHI activities with students, this survey tool could provide valuable information to teacher educators and allow them to better model and guide preservice teachers' mastery of PBHI teaching strategies.

Acknowledgments

This chapter is an updated version of an article previously published in the *Interdisciplinary Journal of Problem-based Learning.* Original citation: Brush, T., & Saye, J. (2014). An instructional model to support problem-based historical inquiry: The persistent issues in history network. *Interdisciplinary Journal of Problem-based Learning, 8*(1), 39–50.

References

Barrett, M., Garrety, K., & Seberry, J. (2006, June). *ICT professionals' perceptions of responsibility for breaches of computer security.* Proceedings of the Australian and New Zealand Academy of Management Conference, Yeppon, Queensland, Australia.

Barrows, H. S. (2002). Is it truly possible to have such a thing as dPBL? *Distance Education, 23*(1), 119–122.

Brush, T., & Saye, J. (2002). A summary of research exploring hard and soft scaffolding for teachers and students using multimedia-supported learning environments. *Journal of Interactive Online Learning.* Retrieved from http://www.ncolr.org/jiol/issues/pdf/1.2.3.pdf

Brush, T., & Saye, J. W. (2009). Strategies for preparing preservice social studies teachers to integrate technology effectively: Models and practices. *Contemporary Issues in Technology and Teacher Education, 9*(1). Retrieved from http://www.citejournal.org/vol9/iss1/socialstudies/article1.cfm

Callahan, C., Saye, J., & Brush, T. (2009–2010). Educative curriculum materials to develop social studies teachers' professional teaching knowledge. *The International Journal of Social Education, 24*(2), 5–33.

Callanan, G., & Perri, D. (2006). Teaching conflict management using a scenario-based approach. *The Journal of Education for Business, 81*(3), 131–139.

Cohen, E. G., & Benton, J. (1988). Making groupwork work. *American Educator, 12*(3), 10–17, 45–56.

Cooper, B., Shepardson, D., & Harber, J. (2002). Assessments as teaching and research tools in an environmental problem-solving program for in-service teachers. *Journal of Geoscience Education, 50*(1), 64–71.

Doyle, W. (1983). Academic work. *Review of Educational Research, 52*(2), 159–199.

Dye, P., & Huffman, L. (2003). *National survey of course offerings in social studies, Kindergarten–Grade 12, 2002–2003 survey.* Council of State Social Studies Specialists. Retrieved from https://higherlogicdownload.s3.amazonaws.com/SOCIALSTUDIES/9c660cd9-d474-45c6-86f2-ea70fd3258a7/UploadedImages/survey2003.pdf

Edwards, S., & Hammer, M. (2006). Laura's story: Using problem based learning in early childhood and primary teacher education. *Teaching and Teacher Educator, 22*(4), 465– 477.

Feiman-Nemser, S. (2008). From preparation to practice: Designing a continuum to strengthen and sustain teaching. *Teachers College Record, 103*(6), 1013–1055.

Fowler Jr., F. (2002). *Survey research methods* (3rd ed.). Thousand Oaks, CA: Sage.

Fram, S. (2013). The constant comparative analysis method outside of grounded theory. *The Qualitative Report, 18*(1), 1–25.

Gardner, H. (1999). *Intelligence reframed: Multiple intelligences for the 21st century.* New York, NY: Basic Books.

Green, S. B., & Salkind, N. J. (2008). *Using SPSS for Windows and Macintosh: Analyzing and understanding data.* Upper Saddle River, NJ: Pearson.

Hannafin, M., Land, S., & Oliver, K. (1999). Open learning environments: Foundations, methods, and models. In C. Reigeluth (Ed.), *Instructional design theories and models* (Vol. II). Mahwah, NJ: Erlbaum.

Hmelo-Silver, C. (2004). Problem-based learning: What and how do students learn? *Educational Psychology Review, 16*(3), 235–266.

Hsieh, H., & Shannon, S. (2005). Three approaches to qualitative content analysis. *Qualitative Health Research, 15*(9), 1277–1288.

Kiggins, J., & Cambourne, B. (2007). The knowledge building community program: A partnership for progress in teacher education. In T. Townsend & R. Bates (Eds.), *Handbook of teacher education* (pp. 365–380). Dordrecht, The Netherlands: Springer.

Land, S. M. (2000). Cognitive requirements for learning with open-ended learning environments. *Educational Technology Research and Development, 48*(3), 61–78.

Means, B., Padilla, C., DeBarger, A., & Bakia, M. (2009). *Implementing data-informed decision making in schools—Teacher access, supports and use.* Report prepared for U.S. Department of Education, Office of Planning, Evaluation and Policy Development. Prepared by SRI International, Menlo Park, CA.

Murray-Harvey, R., & Slee, P. (2000). *Problem based learning in teacher education: Just the beginning!* Paper presented at the Australian Association for Research in Education, Sydney, December 4–6.

National Council for the Social Studies. (2008). *About NCSS*. Retrieved from http://www.ncss.org/about/

Newmann, F. M., Wehlage, G. G., & Lamborn, S. D. (1992). The significance and sources of student engagement. In F. Newmann (Ed.), *Student engagement and achievement in American secondary schools* (pp. 11–39). New York, NY: Teachers College Press.

Onosko, J. (1991). Barriers to the promotion of higher order thinking in social studies. *Theory and Research in Social Education, 19*(4), 341–366.

Patrick, S. (2008). ICT in educational policy in the North American region. In J. Voogt & G. Knezek (Eds.), *International handbook of information technology in primary and secondary education* (pp. 1109–1117). New York, NY: Springer.

Ravitz, J. (2009). Summarizing findings and looking ahead to a new generation of PBL research. *Interdisciplinary Journal of Problem-based Learning, 3*(1), 4–11.

Saye, J., & Brush, T. (2002). Scaffolding critical reasoning about history and social issues in multimedia-supported learning environments. *Educational Technology Research and Development, 50*(3), 77–96.

Saye, J. W., & Brush, T. A. (2004). Promoting civic competence through problem-based history learning experiments. In G. E. Hamot, J. J. Patrick, & R. S. Leming (Eds.), *Civic learning in teacher education: International perspectives on education for democracy in the preparation of teachers* (Vol. 3, pp. 123–145). Bloomington, IN: ERIC Clearinghouse for Social Studies/Social Science Education.

Saye, J., Kohlmeier, J., Brush, T., Howell, J., & Maddox, L. (2009–2010). Assessing the effects of a teacher education program on pre-service secondary social studies teachers' instructional decision-making. *The International Journal of Social Education, 24*(2), 35–76.

Saye, J., & the Social Studies Inquiry Research Collaborative (SSIRC). (2013). Authentic pedagogy: Its presence in social studies classrooms and relationship to student performance on state-mandated tests. *Theory and Research in Social Education, 41*(1), 89–132.

Shaver, J. P. (1996). The prospects of issue-centered education. In D. W. Saxe (Ed.), *Handbook on teaching social issues* (pp. 380–386). Washington, DC: National Council for the Social Studies.

Shaver, J. P., Davis, O. L., & Helburn, S. W. (1979). The status of social studies education: Impressions from three NSF studies. *Social Education, 4*(3), 150–153.

So, H., & Kim, B. (2009). Learning about problem based learning: Student teachers integrating technology, pedagogy and content knowledge. *Australasian Journal of Educational Technology, 25*(1), 101–116.

Snow, R., & Bloom, A. (1996). A survey-based pedagogical approach to ethics in the workplace. *The Journal of Applied Behavioral Science, 32*(1), 89–100.

Strauss, A., & Corbin, J. (1998). *Basics of qualitative research: Techniques and procedures for developing grounded theory* (2nd ed.). Thousand Oaks, CA: Sage.

Strobel, J., & van Barneveld, A. (2009). When is PBL more effective? A meta-synthesis of meta-analyses comparing PBL to conventional classrooms. *Interdisciplinary Journal of Problem-based Learning, 3*(1). Retrieved from http://docs.lib.purdue.edu/ijpbl/vol3/iss1/4

VanSickle, R. L. (1996). *Questions of motivation for achievement in social studies.* In B. G. Massialas & R. F. Allen (Eds.), *Crucial issues in teaching social studies K–12* (pp. 81–105). New York, NY: Wadsworth.

Walker, A., & Leary, H. (2009). A problem based learning meta analysis: Differences across problem types, implementation types, disciplines, and assessment levels. *Interdisciplinary Journal of Problem-based Learning, 3*(1), 12–43.

Wirkala, C., & Kuhn, D. (2011). Problem-based learning in K–12 education: Is it effective and how does it achieve its effects? *American Educational Research Journal, 48*(5), 1157–1186.

Zukas, A. (2000). Active learning, world history, and the Internet: Creating knowledge in the classroom. *International Journal of Social Education, 15*(1), 62–79.

Thomas Brush is the Barbara B. Jacobs Chair in Education and Technology as well as the chair of the Department of Instructional Systems Technology within the School of Education at Indiana University, Bloomington. His research interests focus on developing methods and strategies to promote inquiry-oriented learning, particularly with more open-ended instruction. This involves studying methods for integrating tools to promote collaborative problem-based learning strategies into the learning environment itself and developing alternative techniques to deliver instruction to students.

John Saye is the Mildred Cheshire Fraley Distinguished Professor of Secondary Social Science Education in the Department of Curriculum and Teaching at Auburn University and is director of the Persistent Issues in History Network (pihnet.org). He teaches courses in social studies education. Prior to coming to Auburn in 1994, Saye taught high school social studies for 12 years. His research interests include authentic pedagogy, problem-based inquiry, teacher thinking, and collaborative communities of practice.

4

Preservice Elementary Teachers Learning to Teach PBL Through Science-Integrated Engineering Design

Pamela S. Lottero-Perdue

Introduction

In this chapter, I share the ways in which preservice elementary teachers in my junior-level science teaching internship course have learned to teach children to engineer solutions to a design problem, and in so doing, have learned to teach a form of problem-based learning (PBL). Key features of the internship course to support interns' engagement first as learners, and then as teachers of PBL include: (1) using a science-engineering integrated unit of instruction, which culminates in an engineering design challenge; (2) focusing on the development and use of scaffolds to support instruction; (3) my modeling of lessons and facilitation techniques to interns; (4) giving interns time to develop a facilitator role prior to teaching the engineering design challenge; (5) providing continual feedback to interns; (6) having interns teach small groups of students; and (7) providing peer support through co-teaching. In what follows, I briefly describe the unit and how engineering design within the unit aligns with PBL's essential features. I then discuss the internship course and how it supports interns as they learn to teach science-integrated engineering design PBL.

Unit

Over the past five years, the unit that interns in my course have experienced as learners, and then taught to fourth graders, is Rocks, Minerals, and Materials Engineering (RMME). This is one of six integrated units that is part of the required elementary science curriculum for first through fifth graders in Harford County (Maryland) Public Schools (Lottero-Perdue, 2011). Each of these units engages students in learning scientific and engineering practices and content within the Next Generation Science Standards (NGSS Lead States, 2013), and is a connected blend of science lessons and an Engineering is Elementary (EiE) unit. The EiE program has developed 20 different units, each of which focuses on a particular field of engineering (e.g., agricultural or materials engineering), and has been designed to apply and reinforce science concepts developed prior to engaging in the EiE unit via the teacher's science curriculum. The RMME unit combines science lessons on rocks, minerals, and Earth materials with lessons on materials engineering via the EiE unit, *A Sticky Situation: Designing Walls* (hereafter, *Designing Walls*) (EiE, 2011). The RMME unit takes 15 instructional hours and is one of four units in the fourth grade science curriculum, each of which takes a similar amount of instructional time. This is reflective of the relatively low amount of instructional time allocated for science or engineering instruction across the country (Blank, 2013).

PBL occurs within the EiE *Designing Walls* portion of the RMME unit. There are five lessons within any EiE unit. For *Designing Walls*, these are: (1) the technology lesson, where students learn how technologies solve problems and (in the RMME version of this lesson) that pencils, roads, and rock walls are examples of technologies made with Earth materials; (2) the engineering story, where students read about how two children engineer a wall using Earth materials to solve the problem of a bunny eating vegetables in their school garden (EiE Team, 2008); (3) a materials engineering lesson, where students brainstorm ways that different materials can be used to solve different problems; (4) a lesson where students observe real rock-and-mortar and brick-and-mortar walls in their schools, neighborhoods, and homes, and then create and test different mortars made of single or paired Earth materials (clay, soil, and sand); and (5) the engineering design challenge, where students solve the "wall problem," engineering a strong, small-scale rock-and-mortar wall using the engineering design process (EDP) (Figure 4.1). The first four lessons lay the groundwork for PBL that occurs in the engineering design challenge. Table 4.1 summarizes the EiE EDP that students use for the challenge (EiE, 2016a).

Figure 4.1 Team walls that have dried and are ready for testing.

The EiE program has identified itself as a project-based learning (PjBL) curriculum that engages students in inquiry-based, constructivist learning (EiE, 2016b). PjBL involves learning via "an extended, student-influenced inquiry process structured around complex, authentic questions and carefully designed products and learning tasks" (Hallermann, Larmer, & Mergendoller, 2011, p. 5).

Table 4.1 ***The engineering design process (EDP) steps within the engineering design challenge.***

EDP Step	Students:
Ask	• Identify the problem • Ask questions about the problem • Identify design constraints (limitations) and criteria (requirements) • Consider relevant prior knowledge
Imagine	• Brainstorm design ideas • Draw and label those ideas
Plan	• Pick one idea • Draw and label the idea • Identify needed materials or conditions
Create	• Carry out the plan; create the design • Test the design
Improve	• Reflect on testing results • Plan for, create, and test a new design • Test this new design

From *The Engineering Design Process* by Engineering Is Elementary, 2016, Boston, MA: Author. Reprinted with permission.

<table>
<tr><th colspan="3">RMME Unit</th></tr>
<tr><th>County Science Curriculum</th><th colspan="2">EiE Designing Walls Unit</th></tr>
<tr><td rowspan="3">(Structured) Inquiry-Based Learning</td><td colspan="2">Project-Based Learning (PjBL)</td></tr>
<tr><td>Technology, Storybook, Materials Engineering, Wall Observation, and Mortar Testing</td><td>Engineering Design Challenge/EDP</td></tr>
<tr><td>(Structured) Inquiry-Based Learning</td><td>Problem-Based Learning (PBL)</td></tr>
</table>

Figure 4.2 Learning approaches (shaded) within parts of the RMME unit, including inquiry-based, project-based, and problem-based learning.

The inquiry-based elements of the EiE *Designing Walls* unit are largely seen in the lessons leading up to the engineering design challenge, while the unit's PjBL label captures the cohesive nature of the entire *Designing Walls* unit. Within the PBL literature, PBL and PjBL are unique entities with potential for overlap. PjBL instruction may not be recognized by PBL advocates as PBL unless it is driven by an authentic problem and meets essential criteria for PBL (Barron et al., 1998; Brush & Saye, 2014). Such is the case for the EiE *Designing Walls* unit, where both inquiry-based instruction and PBL approaches are contextualized within PjBL (Figure 4.2).

PBL in ***Designing Walls***

Across the literature, four essential features typify PBL curriculum and instruction: (1) the importance of a complex real-world problem for which there are multiple possible solutions; (2) the need to integrate knowledge from multiple disciplines to define and solve the problem; (3) the students' roles as self-directed learners, supported by the facilitative role of the teacher or tutor; and (4) learning that takes place in collaboration with others (Hmelo-Silver, 2004; Savery, 2015). In what follows, I summarize each of these features, and then describe how the EiE *Designing Walls* unit addresses each. I also more briefly examine the extent to which the unit addresses three additional features of PBL.

The Problem

According to Jonassen and Hung (2015), PBL problems should be: somewhat ill-structured and open ended, complex yet accessible to the students, and authentic. The ill-structured nature of the problem requires that students spend time clarifying and researching the problem itself before moving on to solutions (Savery, 2015). Open-ended problems generate multiple possible solutions (Hmelo-Silver, 2004). Problems should be as complex as possible, emulating the real world, where problems "would not be problems" if they were simple (Savery, 2015, p. 8). Further, problems should be "moderately challenging without being overwhelming" (Hmelo-Silver, 2004, p. 241). With respect to authenticity, problems in PBL must be designed with an awareness of students' background knowledge, interests, or future interests.

Engineering design problems are some of the most ill-structured, open-ended, and complex problems (Jonassen, 2000; Jonassen & Hung, 2015). They may start as ill-structured problems, yet they are structured by engineers or their clients as the problem is defined through problem statements, constraints, and criteria. When developing engineering design solutions, engineers consider multiple variables or factors, trade-offs between variables, and multiple possible design solutions.

The EiE *Designing Walls* unit meets the aforementioned criteria for having a central problem that drives elementary students' learning. The wall problem is first set in the context of the storybook. When students observe walls in the real world, and then test different mortars, they are made aware that they are doing so to apply this knowledge later to the wall problem. These prior-to-design learning opportunities—in addition to relevant prior science learning—are within the "related conceptual space" that surrounds the particular "problem space" of the engineering design challenge (Hmelo-Silver, 2015).

By the time that students begin the engineering design challenge, they are curious and ready to try designing a strong wall for themselves. In the Ask step of the EDP, after being reintroduced to the problem and before being presented with constraints and criteria, students are given an opportunity to ask questions about the problem. They may ask: What can we use to make our mortar? or How will we test the wall? This is part of the important process within PBL of researching and further defining the problem before moving into the solution space. If students were "real engineers" faced with a problem and considering their own questions about the problem, they would conduct research and find answers to these questions from multiple sources. However, for the EiE *Designing Walls* engineering design challenge, it is the teacher who provides answers related to the common constraints and criteria to which all students in the class must abide. Certainly, other questions (e.g., What mixture should we use?) have answers that can only be determined by students working in their teams and are *not* answered by the teacher.

While there are shared constraints and criteria, there is more than one way to solve the wall problem and multiple factors that affect the strength of the wall that students must consider, including: mortar mixture, how well the mortar is mixed, how the rocks are stacked, and the distribution of the mortar. Thus, while the problem is defined by the teacher and curriculum, the solution options are less constrained. Students cannot construct a brick wall or a wooden wall to solve the problem, but they have a variety of options regarding the design of their rock-and-mortar wall.

The design challenge within the EiE *Designing Walls* unit is a case of an engineering design problem that has been "instructionally designed and adjusted to lower ill-structuredness levels" (Jonassen & Hung, 2015, p. 30) via use of a defined problem and shared constraints and criteria. Further, the unit has been designed to be difficult, but not impossible, to solve for elementary learners—allowing for multiple possible solutions and the possibility of design failure and subsequent improvements.

Integrating and Applying Knowledge

One of the defining aspects of a good PBL problem is that it "provide[s] opportunities for students to examine the problem from multiple perspectives or disciplines" (Jonassen & Hung, 2015, p. 25). Engineers draw from all necessary sources of knowledge to define or solve a problem, including scientific knowledge, mathematical knowledge, an understanding of relevant technologies, and knowledge of clients and their needs. Design problems "require a high level of prior knowledge preparation in order for the students to be able to engage in application and transfer" (p. 32).

Students integrate and apply a mix of scientific, experiential, and engineering knowledge as they solve the wall problem. This includes: knowledge about Earth materials; observations of walls in their schools, neighborhoods, and homes; results of mortar testing; and, from the storybook, knowledge of the EDP and what materials engineers do. Students are not, for example, presented with the wall problem, and then left to figure out what they need to know to solve the problem. Instead, after being presented with the problem, constraints, and criteria, students are asked to draw on what they learned that would be appropriate to consider as they go about designing their walls. This prompt is just enough to suggest that students approach the development of their first design in a *reasoned* (not random) direction, but not so much as to direct students' problem solving toward a particular solution.

Student and Teacher Roles and Scaffolds

Barrows (1986) identified the development of self-directed learning (SDL) skills as one of four "educational objectives possible with PBL" (p. 482). Applying PBL to medical training, Barrows saw the utility in future doctors being metacognitive—aware of their "personal learning needs"—and able to locate information they needed to know to diagnose and solve medical problems. SDL remains a prominent feature of PBL. The teacher in PBL is a facilitator of students' knowledge development, rarely providing information and most often offering guidance. Hmelo-Silver (2004) wrote that the PBL facilitator encourages students to justify their thinking to promote the development of higher-order thinking skills and poses questions to students to help them externalize their metacognitive practices. Further, teachers facilitate students' collaborative efforts, inquiring about how group members are or could be working together. Most of these teacher-student interactions are what Saye and Brush (2002) called "soft scaffolds." These are "dynamic and situational," requiring that facilitators "continuously diagnose the understandings of learners and provide timely support based on student responses" (p. 82).

Particularly, as PBL has reached across different learning contexts and down into K–12 learning spaces, PBL researchers have also suggested the importance of the use of hard scaffolds to support student learning. Saye and Brush (2002) described hard scaffolds as "static supports that can be anticipated and planned in advance based on typical student difficulties with a task" (p. 81). These hard scaffolds anticipate students' learning challenges and needs. They may be conceptual, guiding learners toward particular ideas; strategic, suggesting particular ways to approach a problem or task (Hannafin, Lands, & Oliver, 1999); or they may serve as "ritualizing" activities, or processes to be emulated (Kolodner et al., 2003). Examples of hard scaffolds include graphic organizers and strategic guidance from an "expert" in an online environment.

The science and engineering lessons leading up to the engineering design challenge in the EiE *Designing Walls* unit are taught using a structured inquiry-based approach (Anderson, 2002; Banchi & Bell, 2009; National Research Council, 2000). In this approach, the teacher both provides information and facilitates instruction (Savery, 2015), with emphasis on the latter. The engineering design challenge begins with the teacher in an information-providing role as he or she provides the problem, constraints, and criteria for the engineering design challenge in the Ask step of the EDP. After this point, however, the teacher is only a facilitator, and students direct their engagement in the process with the assistance of soft and hard scaffolding. Teachers facilitate student learning in the Imagine, Plan, Create, and Improve steps of the EDP, much the same way as has been described of PBL tutors who interject questions, restate students' ideas, ask students to provide evidence for their decisions, and ensure that teams work in collaborative ways (Hmelo-Silver & Barrows, 2015). The EDP is used as a strategic scaffold throughout this process, and graphic organizers within EiE EDP worksheets are hard scaffolds who serve to organize students' decisions and results throughout the process.

While teachers are facilitators in the Imagine, Plan, Create, and Improve steps, students are engaged in self-directed engineering design, determining how they will go about solving the wall problem. It is they who decide on the mortar components, determine the layout of the rocks, create their walls, test their walls (releasing a demolition ball so that it strikes the wall with light, strong, and even stronger amounts of force), examine their testing results and the testing results of others, use this information to guide the design of a new improved wall, and repeat the process for their second design. All of this occurs with teacher facilitation, soft scaffolding, and hard scaffolding, but the learning process is student directed.

Collaboration

Another key facet of PBL learning environments is that students work together to define and solve problems in collaborative teams. Collaboration "allows students to draw on each other's perspectives and talents in order to more effectively devise solutions for the problem(s) at hand" (Ertmer & Glazewski, 2015, p. 91). The collaborative nature of PBL pushes students to learn how to work together and develop collaborative skills (e.g., communication, negotiation, compromising, coming to consensus) that are important in the real world (Savery, 2015; Hmelo & Silver, 2004).

Students begin to work in teams (of approximately three students) in the Imagine step of the EDP. In this step, students may first brainstorm multiple ways to solve the problem individually, and then come together to discuss those ideas, or they may brainstorm together as a team. Teams continue to work together throughout the rest of the EDP. Children bring different strengths to the team, as some may have greater exposure to the design of real rock-and-mortar walls, be better at drawing the plan, or be more skilled at physically constructing the wall.

The larger group settings of five or more students that seem typical in other PBL contexts contain too many voices and too many hands for elementary teams engaged in engineering design. By "too many voices," I mean that it can be difficult for elementary children to share their ideas, come to consensus, and compromise as they make decisions in the EDP. These collaborative challenges are eased somewhat with fewer voices. Similarly, one of the more motivating and engaging parts of the design challenge is the creation of the wall. Having fewer hands means that each child can contribute more to this creation process. The smaller engineering teams are also in communication with other teams as they learn from one another's testing results and design decisions in large-group or whole-class discussions.

Other Elements of PBL

Two additional, related features of PBL are that students should be: (1) encouraged to reflect on their learning throughout the learning process and (2) assessed on their understanding of the PBL process (Savery, 2015). The metacognitive practice of students reflecting on their own learning enables them to "better understand what they know, what they learned, and how they performed" (p. 9). Whole-class discussions throughout the engineering design challenge (and prompted in the EiE *Designing Walls* teacher guide) routinely engage students in reflection and sharing after the first designs are tested and as students consider how to improve. Here and in small-group discussion, teachers-as-facilitators encourage students to look at where they are, where they have been, and where they are going in the EDP. At the end of the EDP, students reflect on how they moved through each EDP step and made decisions. Final RMME unit assessments ask students to articulate reasoning for design decisions made in the EDP and also ascertain students' understanding of the EDP.

The Internship

In their junior year, all of the elementary education majors at Towson University (TU) enroll in a "math-science" semester, in which the elementary science teaching internship (hereafter, "internship") takes place. Also during this semester, these majors (hereafter, "interns"), take science and/or mathematics content/methods courses and a mathematics teaching internship. At the beginning of the semester, most interns express a combination of excitement and anxiety about teaching science to children, and only a few in each cohort will have taught science in after-school programs or summer camps. Some interns have had negative experiences as science learners. Many have no idea what it might look like to teach engineering to elementary students.

Interns experience the math-science semester in a cohort of between 16 and 20 interns; the number is kept relatively small to accommodate the logistical needs of the internships. Each academic year, there are more than 10 cohorts of the elementary science teaching internship at TU. Each internship cohort requires a single partner school site for the internship; an internship coordinator at TU helps to form and maintain school partnerships.

Hall's Cross Roads Elementary School (HCRES) has been a partner school for the internship experience since 2012. HCRES has approximately 500 students in grades K–5. Student demographics by race/ethnicity are as follows: 43% black or African American, 34% white, 13% two or more race/ethnicity categories, 8% Hispanic or Latino/a, and 2% Asian. A Title I school, 81% of its students are on the Free and Reduced Meals program. Approximately 20% of HCRES students receive special education services, including speech and language services. For TU, this partnership provides a supportive space and welcoming environment for our preservice teachers to learn to teach science and engineering to a diverse group of children while exposing them to the challenges and rewards of teaching in a Title I school.

In the sections that follow, I describe key components of the internship at HCRES. These elements include: unit selection and modification, scheduling, small-group instruction, instructional modeling, lesson plan writing, reflections, and teaching observations. We have used the same internship model containing these elements across our cohorts for more than 10 years (Sandifer, Lising, & Renwick, 2007).

Unit Selection and Modification

Interns teach an enhanced version of the RMME unit at HCRES. We have modified the unit by replacing unit worksheets with science and engineering notebooks, creating a more open-ended, student-driven documentation process for students (Fulton & Campbell, 2014; Gilbert & Kotelman, 2005); adding a field trip to a local quarry (not a part of the unit for other schools in the system);

and adding an intern-created lesson on the rock cycle to complete the science portion of the unit.

Scheduling

The internship is taught once per week at HCRES for a period of 3 hours and 50 minutes. At HCRES, this time period includes: 1 hour and 10 minutes of preparation time, 50 minutes of teaching time, and the remainder of time spent cleaning up after teaching, relocating to a new site for methods instruction, and conducting methods instruction.[1]

Small-Group Instruction

The interns in a cohort are paired, and then co-teaching pairs are spread evenly across the fourth grade classrooms at HCRES. For example, in a year where there were 18 interns and three classrooms, each classroom had three co-teaching pairs of interns.[2] Each co-teaching pair teaches the same group of seven to nine students throughout the semester. Those student groups are created by classroom teachers (hereafter, "mentor teachers"), who group students heterogeneously with respect to academic ability and behavior.

There are many reasons we use small-group instruction, as described by Sandifer, Hermann, Cimino, and Selway (2015), who wrote about this model as it is used in this and other teacher preparation programs at TU. It requires just one partner school per cohort, and thus the instructor is available to see and mentor all students each day. It is less intimidating for interns to teach a small group (as compared to a whole class), and interns learn the value of collaborating with other interns in their classrooms. Importantly, interns get to know their students in their small groups and "are able to focus squarely on the pedagogical issues that are relevant to inquiry-based science teaching (idea development, questioning, etc.)" (p. 134). The downsides of this model are that it can be challenging to set up multiple mini-classrooms in one classroom space, and it can be quite noisy in the classroom.

Instructional Modeling

One primary way the internship helps to prepare interns to teach their students is that I model RMME unit lessons and instructional practices for interns during methods instruction time. In this way, interns experience the unit as

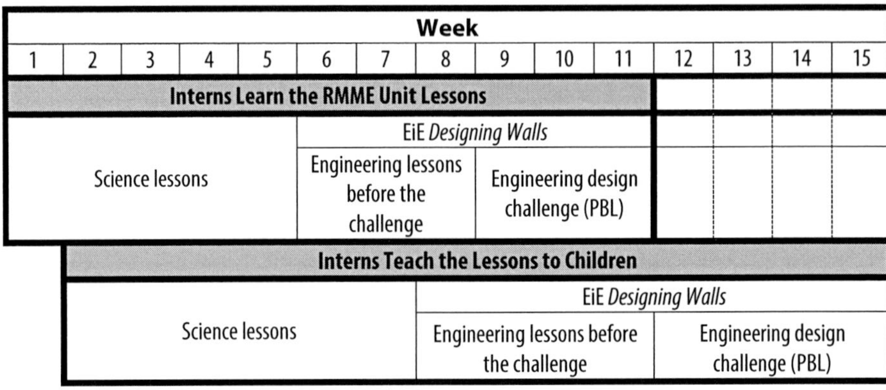

Figure 4.3 Unit schedule for 15 weeks of the internship course.

learners prior to being expected to teach it. Figure 4.3 represents how the 15-week semester unfolds, with interns first experiencing the RMME unit as learners, and then teaching the RMME unit to students at HCRES. Notice that the schedule is somewhat offset, with my modeling of RMME lessons wrapping up by week 11 and interns teaching the unit to students ending in week 15. This enables the interns to complete the engineering design challenge themselves before starting to teach it to their students.

I begin the RMME unit by modeling nearly all aspects of early science lessons—using what I call "robust modeling" of these lessons—including how to structure notebook pages. I then gradually reduce the extent of my modeling, applying a more "selective modeling" approach that focuses on areas of need as my interns gain skill and confidence in teaching science. Toward the end the science portion of the unit, my modeled instruction gives way to showing them the required materials for an activity, directing them to the curriculum for the procedure, and having them try out the activity, asking for help from me as necessary. The rock cycle lesson, a final science lesson added to the existing RMME unit, is designed completely by my interns and is based on their understanding of the rock cycle from the Earth and Space Science course that I also teach to them during the math-science semester.

The modeling I provide in the engineering portion of the unit before the engineering design challenge ranges from robust modeling (e.g., the quarry field trip, where I take my interns before we all take elementary students there) to selective modeling (e.g., the wall observation and mortar-testing lesson, where I model many, but not all, aspects of the observation and testing processes).

I employ a more robust modeling approach with respect to the engineering design challenge since the EDP is new territory for the interns. I carefully take them through the challenge and, along the way, emphasize key teaching strategies, including how to: guide students in asking questions about the problem/goal, resolve disagreements among students when they have to select one idea out of the brainstorming process, allow students to make their own design decisions, remind students of relevant background information, encourage students to explain their design decisions *without* interjecting teacher ideas into the design, lead the wall-testing process, ask students questions to guide their failure analysis, and prompt students to consider their own and other teams' testing results as they plan their second wall. I make suggestions about the components that should be included in their students' notebooks but leave notebook page creation up to the interns.

Lesson Plan Writing

Another way that interns are prepared to teach their students is through their submission, and, if necessary, subsequent revisions of lesson plans each week. Interns in each co-teaching pair co-plan the lesson, meeting with each other and discussing how they will approach instruction. One intern in the pair writes the plan, and interns alternate the writing responsibility each week. Plan writers download a template document, and then add to that document, later submitting it as their plan. The template shows the basic organization of each lesson. Some sections of the plan are written for them; others contain instructions as to what planning details must be included. For example, in the EDP Plan step of the engineering design challenge, interns are asked to explain how they will: elicit from students where they are in the EDP, explain the requirements of the EDP Plan step to their students, and describe what each member of the co-teaching team will do as students work. One intern wrote as a part of this section of the plan: "[We] will facilitate the discussion in each of their groups to make sure students understand the task and are using the information from [mortar] testing. Ultimately [we] will allow students to lead the discussion of their planning." I grade plans using a rubric, provide written feedback on those plans, and return graded, commented plans to interns in time for the interns to make revisions to those plans prior to teaching.

Designing notebook pages becomes part of the interns' planning process approximately halfway through the semester. Prior to the rock cycle science lesson—the final science lesson before moving into the quarry visit and EiE

Designing Walls unit—interns use notebook pages that I designed to go with their science lessons. As part of my instructional modeling, interns copy these notebook pages into their own science and engineering notebooks. From the quarry visit onward, interns design notebook pages to go with the lessons, and they are usually quite ready to apply their own thinking to notebook page layout and design. I share requirements for those pages, but the interns design page layout, write questions, and so forth. I ask interns to create what I call "model notebook pages." These are notebook pages as if completed by the strongest member of their student group. Students do not see the completed version of these pages; rather, the interns complete them so that they carefully plan and prepare notebook pages that consider how students might respond to them. A model notebook page as created by an intern is shown in Figure 4.4. Figure 4.5 shows a corresponding notebook page created by a student in the intern's group.

Reflections

Reflection is an essential teaching practice (Danielson, 2007). It is a particularly important activity within the internship so that interns have a chance to consider what went well in the lesson, what did not go as well, what they would change about the lesson if they were to teach it again, how they could improve their teaching, and what they are learning about themselves as a teacher of science or engineering. Many of these elements are the focus of whole-class discussions after each day of teaching, and together, these are the required elements of written reflections that individual interns write each week. At times, interns are given freedom to respond more openly as they reflect on the lesson, not bound to these particular elements, and other times, interns are asked to reflect on a particular aspect of their teaching as related to an article they read or video they watched.

In addition to grading reflections based on a rubric, I comment on interns' reflections, providing insights, encouragement, and suggestions, as appropriate. Reflections help me understand how interns are responding to their students and grappling with what it means to teach science and engineering. Excerpts from reflections written by one intern, Kira, exemplify a relatively common case of how interns can be transformed by the internship experience.[3] Three aspects of her transformation are evident in Table 4.2:

1. Kira's growth and development as a facilitator rather than an information provider, and the challenges and rewards of this facilitator role;

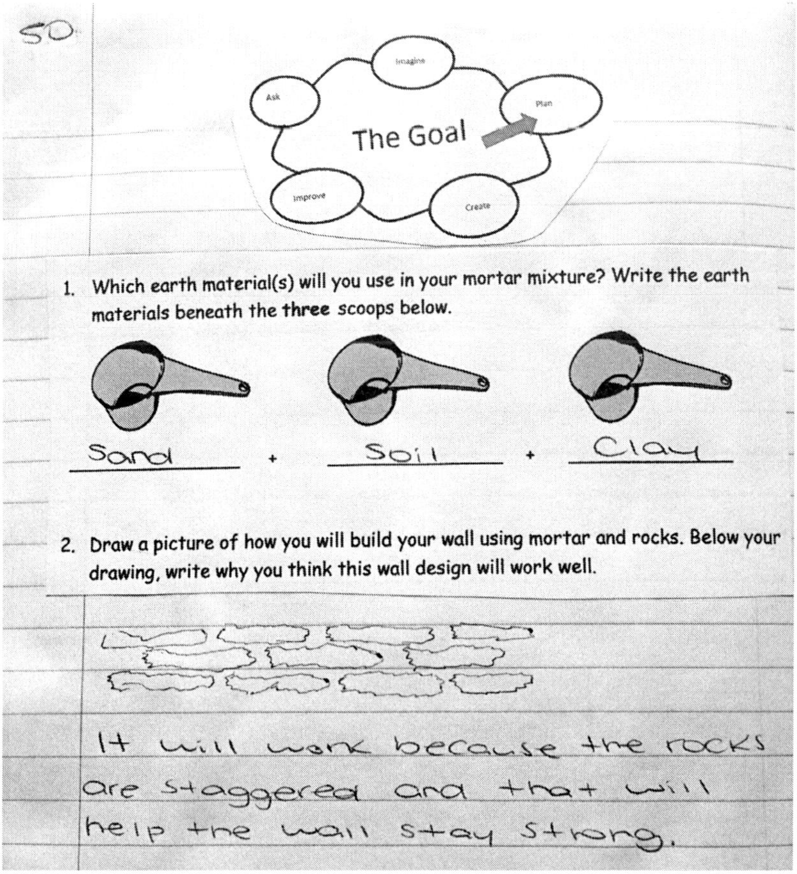

Figure 4.4 The engineering design challenge: Plan section of an intern's model notebook page.

2. the broadening of her reflective thinking to include how students learned to problem solve and apply prior knowledge to their design processes; and
3. her transformation from a future teacher worried about teaching science and engineering to one who has grown (and expects to continue to grow) in confidence and skill in these areas.

Kira's growth was not without struggle, however, but seemed worthwhile. After a semester in the internship, she offered the following insights to my next cohort of interns: "It will be tough, it will be challenging, but it will be so rewarding and so amazing. You will learn so much about yourself this semester and that introspection will be invaluable to your growth as an educator."

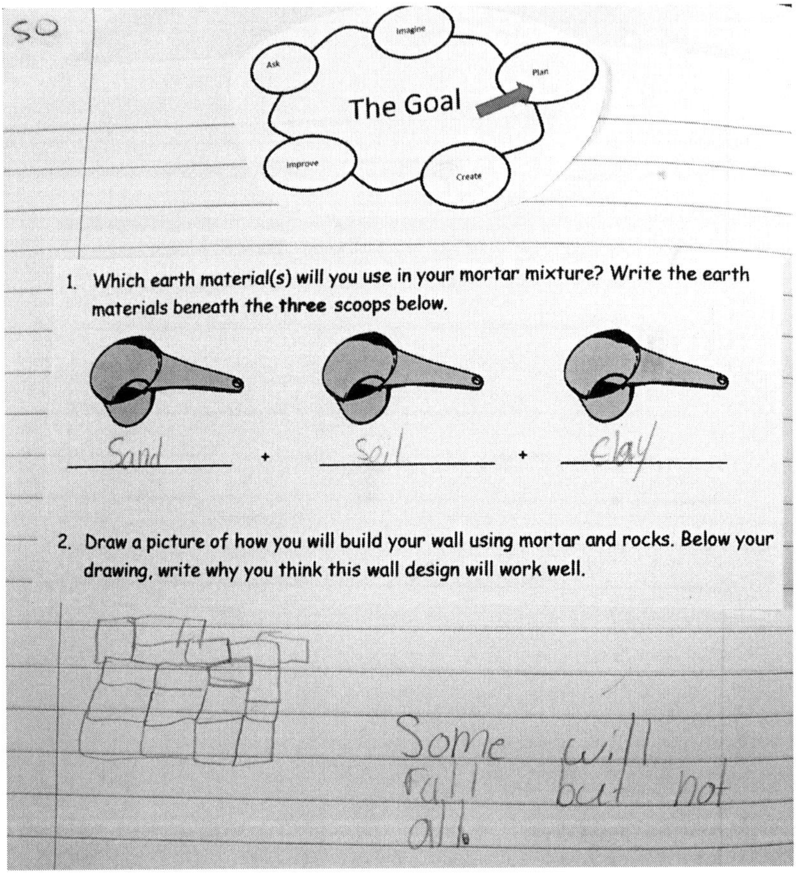

Figure 4.5 The engineering design challenge: Plan section of an intern's model notebook page as completed by a student.

Table 4.2 ***Selected reflections from an intern, Kira, throughout the internship experience.***

Source	Excerpts from and summaries of Kira's reflections
First reflection	"Science never came easily to me in school, and it was never really a subject that I fully enjoyed. When I decided I wanted to become a teacher, I was nervous that this apprehension would subconsciously transfer to my students."
Reflections about science teaching	*Prior to Kira's final reflection on the science portion of the unit, she primarily reflected on the mechanics of teaching (e.g., time management) and on student engagement and behavior. In this final science reflection, she began to articulate her desire to better facilitate instruction for her students through questioning:*

Continued

Table 4.2 ***Continued.***

Source	Excerpts from and summaries of Kira's reflections
Reflections about science teaching (*continued*)	"Sometimes, I'm afraid of giving them too much information and guiding their answers too much that I end up not helping them very much at all. I need to get better at asking questions to guide them in the right direction without explicitly giving them the answers—just getting them to think more critically and generate ideas."
Reflection after the materials engineering lesson	"[Some of my stronger students] offered really good innovative ideas and, [working in pairs], attempted to help their classmates problem solve.... I'm sure that a lot of [the other students] had ideas, but they were so afraid of their ideas not being valid that they chose not to share anything at all."
Reflection after preparation for mortar testing	"One of my girls suggested a good idea [about mortar mixtures].... We let [the students] discuss whether or not they thought this was a good idea and why. I thought it was really awesome to reach this conclusion by themselves, without us telling them anything, and really engage in that higher-level thinking.... I was finally able to start guiding them in the right direction without directly giving them the answers. I was able to pose questions to stimulate their thinking instead of just giving them the answers to their questions."
Reflection after the engineering design challenge lesson (planning)	"It seemed like no matter how many times we went over that a combination of earth materials worked better as a mortar than single Earth materials [from our mortar testing], some of them still wrote 'clay + clay + clay' for their [wall] mortar mixture [in their notebooks]. It was frustrating.... I can only hope that when they work as teams next week, they'll talk to each other and generate ideas and realize why a single material mortar might not be the best to use.... I'm excited to see them interact with the materials and continue to work through the EDP."
Reflection after the engineering design process (wall testing)	"One of the things that struck me the most about this lesson was my own growth as a teacher of science and engineering. I've told most of my peers in the cohort about my 'traumatic' [high school] engineering experience, where I had a project ... that I couldn't complete and felt very embarrassed and not as smart as the others in my class at the time. Ever since then, I've been very wary of most science and engineering processes because I was afraid of failing again and feeling the way I felt then. However, on Tuesday, I was the knowledgeable one. I was able to work through the EDP with my students and aid them in understanding new concepts. Watching them enjoy it made me less hesitant about engineering, and I think that fear that I had at the beginning of the semester about not being able to teach science in a fun way that also teaches them something is gone. I don't feel like a master in my content area, but I feel completely comfortable in it now."

Teaching Observations

I observe each intern twice per semester, and mentor teachers observe each intern in their respective classrooms twice per semester. These four observations of each intern are scheduled throughout the semester. Mentor teachers typically observe throughout the entire teaching period. I have the entire cohort to observe, often making it necessary to shorten observation time per intern to one half of the teaching period. Mentor teachers and I comment on similar topics as we observe, recording notes on a form to share with interns. For example, the mentor teacher is asked to provide qualitative feedback about the extent to which the intern is prepared to teach; encourages students to generate their own ideas, reason, and think critically; listens carefully to students and treats them with respect; and uses questioning and other guidance in useful and appropriate ways.

When I observe co-teaching pairs, each intern receives feedback that combines comments relevant to both interns and comments specific to each intern. Importantly, observations are all intended to be a formative assessment of teaching—providing feedback that is both encouraging, when possible, and constructive, when necessary. Interns are typically nervous enough to be observed when there is no grade associated with the observation; it seems overly onerous to add a summative assessment to this experience.

Other Aspects of the Internship

During methods instruction time, I share articles, videos, and other texts about standards, pedagogical practices, and techniques. Interns learn about the following topics and apply this learning to their instruction: scientific and engineering practices in the NGSS (NGSS Lead States, 2013); notebooking (Gilbert & Kotelman, 2005); co-teaching (Linz, Heater, & Howard, 2011; Villa, Thousand, & Nevin, 2008); evidence-based reasoning (Kirsch & Stetsenko, 2012; Lottero-Perdue, Nealy, Roland, & Ryan, 2011); using prompts and questions to encourage students to share evidence and reasoning with one another (Ferris, 2015; Michaels, Shouse, & Schweingruber, 2008); strategies to support students who live in poverty (Jensen, 2013); and how to differentiate instruction for students with special needs (CAST, 2008; Lottero-Perdue, Lovelidge, & Bowling, 2010; Steele, 2007). Students are sometimes required to address these in sections of their lesson plans and in reflections, as described earlier. Finally, while lesson plans and reflections comprise the bulk of interns' grades in the internship, they are also evaluated on their professionalism as learners and teachers, and have one or two final exam essay(s), including writing an advice letter to the next cohort of interns.

How Interns Learn to Teach PBL

The internship experience at HCRES is designed to help interns learn to be effective facilitators of inquiry-based, practice-based science learning and science-integrated engineering design PBL. Earlier in the chapter, I addressed how the engineering design challenge within the EiE *Designing Walls* unit represents the core of PBL for students and described how the design challenge creates a structured problem for students to solve, allows students working in collaborative teams to direct their own solution generation, encourages students to apply relevant background science and experiential information learned in the science lessons and other EiE lessons in finding solutions of the problem, and so forth. In this final section, I address the ways in which—beyond the support of the RMME and EiE *Designing Walls* curriculum itself—my interns are supported to teach key aspects of PBL. These supports include: (1) interns learning to use hard scaffolds, (2) my modeling of the facilitator role and soft scaffolds, (3) giving interns time to develop their facilitator role prior to the engineering design challenge, (4) my providing continual feedback to interns about the teaching process, (5) having interns teach groups and teams (and not the entire class), and (6) providing peer support through co-teaching.

Interns Learning to Use the EDP and Notebooks as Hard Scaffolds

The complexity that is inherent with PBL can be made more manageable for students—be they preservice teachers or fourth grade students—via the use of preplanned strategic or conceptual hard scaffolds (Saye & Brush, 2002). One such hard scaffold within the engineering design challenge of the EiE *Designing Walls* unit is the EDP itself (see Table 4.1). First addressed in the unit in the storybook, the EDP represents a framework, modeled after EDPs used by real engineers, for engineering design practice. Like their students, interns are introduced to this strategic scaffold in the storybook (EiE Team, 2008), and then learn to use it to solve the wall problem when I facilitate the interns' engineering design challenge. The EDP becomes the primary way for interns to organize the pages of students' notebooks. These notebook pages are another form of hard scaffolding, providing organization for the details that go into each step of the EDP. Students learn how to develop notebook pages after my modeling of notebook pages in the first half of the RMME unit, after their use or (and sometimes dissatisfaction with) my notebook pages with their students, and when they design their "model notebook pages" and receive my feedback about how to improve them. They also know to utilize the RMME and EiE *Designing Walls* teacher guides—available to them throughout the semester—for ideas about how to structure the documentation process throughout the EDP.

Modeling the Facilitator Role and Soft Scaffolds for Interns

I suspect that if I were to hand my interns the teacher guides and wish them well as they prepared to teach the RMME unit, with enough time and dedication they would likely be able to move their students through the basic components of the science and engineering lessons. This would be overwhelming, unfriendly, and unhelpful to my interns, and it would also leave out the important process of my students first experiencing the unit as students before shifting into a mind-set of how to teach the unit. While my interns might figure out how to use the hard scaffolds (e.g., worksheets) and learn many good ideas about facilitation as written in the guides, these novice teachers would not be able to experience what facilitated instruction looks like in the RMME unit. Additionally, they would not be witness to how I use soft scaffolds, those unplanned responses and questions that, for example, may be used to assist teams who are struggling with a design decision or a team dispute (Saye & Brush, 2002).

When I model instruction during our methods instruction time, I not only teach the unit as I want my interns to teach it but also "pause" the lesson at key points to reflect on the facilitative strategies that I just used. For example, after eliciting claims and evidence to support those claims about which Earth material mortars were the strongest, I pause and ask: Did I just look at the class data, and then summarize the results for you? [Eliciting: No.] Who provided the claims and the evidence to support those claims? [Eliciting: We, the students.] I do this in my modeling of the engineering design challenge as well. I demonstrate how I ask each team to explain their design decisions in the Plan step without judgment or influence from me as the teacher. I pause to ask my interns: If a team wants to construct a wall that uses a weak stacked arrangement of rocks, what do you do? [Eliciting: Ask them to explain their design decisions, and if they are firm on those decisions, allow them to design the walls that way.] We discuss that the testing part of the EDP will reveal that such an arrangement would not make for a strong wall, and that the EDP allows for teams' walls to fail and for them to have a chance to improve their walls. In sum, I explicitly teach the interns that teacher direction can actually disrupt the design process for students. As interns work through the EDP in their teams, they experience my soft scaffolds—how I pay attention to their questions and explanations, pose questions to them, and so forth. They may also observe me doing this with other teams. They see that while the students are directing their design process, the teacher still has a role as a facilitator and in-the-moment responder and questioner; he or she does not, however, occupy space as information provider once students begin the problem-solving process.

Interns Having Time and Experience to Develop a Facilitator Role

One of the benefits of having the PBL portion occur at the end of the RMME unit is that students are able to gradually develop their roles as facilitators. Within the science portion of the unit, the interns are engaging students in inquiry-based learning, which blends two teacher roles: facilitator and information provider (Savery, 2015). In the internship and within the RMME unit, the emphasis (through my modeling, our course readings, and discussions) is on teacher facilitation and student-centered instruction; however, the information role is sometimes called upon (e.g., to reveal that the different colors in granite correspond to different minerals). Most of my interns are familiar with learning experiences, prior to the internship, where teachers are information providers; they are less familiar with what it means to facilitate science instruction. When interns begin to teach, they often focus more on what they are doing and saying rather than on (1) how they can do and say less, and (2) how they can encourage their students to do and say more. Through some combination of the interns' experiences as learners and teachers, as interns get deeper into the semester, I see more evidence that they are starting to take on and become more comfortable with this facilitative role.

This transition was evident in Kira's final science reflection on the rock cycle lesson, where she shared: "I'm afraid of giving them too much information and guiding their answers too much that I end up not helping them very much at all" (see Table 4.2 for full quote). Later in her reflection about the mortar-testing investigation prior to the engineering challenge, she commented:

"I was able to pose questions to stimulate [students'] thinking instead of giving them the answers to questions." Although she was somewhat frustrated by one of her team's choices for the mortar mixture for their wall—and had hoped that they would better apply what they learned from the mortar investigation—she was ready by this point in the unit to let the students on the team work it out: "I can only hope that when they work as teams next week, they'll talk to each other and generate ideas and realize why a single material [clay-only] mortar might not be the best one to use." Notice that she did not plan to *tell* them why this was a poor choice but hoped that they would figure it out for themselves. Although I cannot say for sure, I suspect that if the engineering design challenge were earlier in the unit, my interns might not have been ready to let go of the information provider role to let students select their own designs, even if those design decisions were not strong, and to let students' designs fail if they must (trusting that the testing process would inform the team's next wall design, making it stronger and better planned).

Continual Feedback to Interns

This internship course is the most difficult course I teach. This is due in large part to the amount of feedback I must provide every week to my interns prior to their next teaching day. This feedback takes the form of notes that populate the sides of their lesson plans and reflections, or within the one or two pages of typed feedback I provide after observing each intern; it also takes the form of conversations I have with students during their preparation and methods instruction time. On lesson plans—where my written feedback is most frequent and voluminous—my comments are a blend of praise and suggestions for improvement regarding how interns can be better facilitators and more student-centered, and encourage students to think and reason as well as to connect design decisions to prior learning, all of which support PBL instruction. My comments also address more mundane aspects of preparing to teach the lesson (e.g., having appropriate materials, being specific about supportive co-teaching roles). My observations represent just two snapshots of interns' instruction throughout the semester but provide meaningful feedback with regard to PBL techniques. Mentor teachers also provide feedback regarding interns' teaching via two formal observations and many informal observations. Further, when interns co-plan their lessons, they provide feedback to one another regarding how they should approach teaching the engineering design challenge and other parts of the RMME unit.

Interns Teaching Small Groups

The small-group (as compared to whole-class) instructional model that we employ in our internship is ideal for interns learning to teach PBL. The groups of approximately seven to nine students, each taught by a co-teaching pair of interns, are divided into smaller teams for the engineering design challenge. These teams work independently, and then come together for larger group discussions and design testing. In this high teacher-to-student ratio environment, interns can give close attention to students as they work through the design process and try out soft scaffolds throughout the engineering design challenge. In so doing, interns practice the facilitative tutor role of PBL (Barrows, 1986).

Support Through Co-Teaching

Interns work in co-teaching pairs during the HCRES internship, co-planning and working together to teach the lesson. With relatively rare exceptions, co-teaching decreases interns' stress levels, providing a built-in support system. If a co-teacher is unsure about how to respond to a student's question or a team's dilemma, their co-teaching partner may be able to step in to offer a soft scaffold. If behavior issues arise, one co-teacher can continue the lesson as the other handles the issue, something that Kira and her co-teacher, Christine, experienced. And, as Kira noted in her reflection after her students prepared for mortar testing, Kira and Christine fed off one another as they encouraged a student-led discussion that stemmed from one student's idea that mortars made of three materials would be better than those made of just two (see Table 4.2 for more details). This is evidence of not simply co-teaching support but of co-teaching support of the teacher-facilitator role and of letting students direct their own learning.

Concluding Thoughts

In the early PBL literature, Barrows (1986) identified the "understandings and skills of the teacher or tutor" as an "unplanned variable" that can affect educational outcomes for students engaged in PBL experiences. He cautioned that tutors should neither be "overly directive" nor fail to offer guidance as students reason, question what they know, and conduct research (p. 485). Even though the PBL context about which Barrows wrote, medical school, is vastly different than the context of fourth graders at HCRES learning to design within a science-engineering integrated unit, the need for the teacher or tutor to be a facilitator of learning—not too directive yet providing support and guidance—still applies. Through the junior science teaching internship, I have attempted to teach my preservice elementary teachers to become facilitators of learning and teachers of engineering design PBL. Over the past five years, more than 90 interns have learned to teach children to use the EDP to engineer strong rock-and-mortar walls.

Notes

1. At no point do the interns observe mentor teachers in this internship experience.
2. In years with an odd number of interns, a mentor teacher and I organize a small group of two or three children with special needs for one intern to teach.
3. Kira is a pseudonym. Excerpts in this table and elsewhere in the chapter were used with Kira's permission. These excerpts were used to exemplify key aspects of interns' engagement in the internship and were not collected as part of a research study.

References

Anderson, R. (2002). Reforming science teaching: What research says about inquiry. *Journal of Science Teacher Education, 13*(1), 1–12.

Banchi, H., & Bell, R. L. (2008, October). The many levels of inquiry. *Science and Children, 46*(2), 26–29.

Barron, B., Schwartz, D., Vye, N., Moore, A., Petrosino, A., Zech, L., Bransford, J., & The Cognition and Technology Group at Vanderbilt. (1998). Doing with understanding: Lessons from research on problem- and project-based learning. *The Journal of the Learning Sciences, 7*(3/4), 271–311. http://www.jstor.org/stable/1466789

Barrows, H. S. (1986). A taxonomy of problem-based learning methods. *Medical Education, 20*(6), 481–486. http://dx.doi.org/10.1111/j.1365-2923.1986.tb01386.x

Blank, R. (2013). Science instructional time is declining in elementary schools: What are the implications for student achievement and closing the gap? *Science Education, 97*(6), 830–847. http://dx.doi.org/10.1002/sce.21078

Brush, T., & Saye, J. W. (2014). Guest editors' introduction: Special issue on technology-supported problem-based learning in teacher education. *Interdisciplinary*

Journal of Problem-based Learning, 8(1), 1–3. http:/dx.doi.org/10.7771/1541-5015.1480

CAST. (2008). *Universal design for learning guidelines version 1.0.* Wakefield, MA: Author.

Danielson, C. (2008). *Enhancing professional practice: A framework for teaching* (2nd ed.). Alexandria, VA: Association for Supervision and Curriculum Development.

Engineering is Elementary (EiE). (2011). *A sticky situation: Designing walls.* Boston, MA: National Center for Technological Literacy.

EiE. (2016a). *The engineering design process.* Retrieved from http://www.eie.org/overview/engineering-design-process

EiE. (2016b). *Our curricular design process: Design principles.* Retrieved from http://www.eie.org/overview/design-principles

EiE Team. (2008). *Yi Min's great wall.* Boston, MA: National Center for Technological Literacy.

Ertmer, P. A., & Glazewski, K. D. (2015). Essentials for PBL implementation: Fostering collaboration, transforming roles, and scaffolding learning. In A. Walker, H. Leary, C. E. Hmelo-Silver, & P. A. Ertmer (Eds.), *Essential readings in problem-based learning: Exploring and extending the legacy of Howard S. Barrows* (pp. 89–106). West Lafayette, IN: Purdue University Press.

Ferris, S. (2015). Methods and strategies: Making talk productive. *Science and Children, 52*(9), 67–73.

Fulton, L., & Campbell, B. (2014). *Science notebooks: Writing about inquiry* (2nd ed.). Portsmouth, NH: Heinemann.

Gilbert, J., & Kotelman, M. (2005, November/December). Five good reasons to use science notebooks: Key understandings about science notebooks maximize learning for all students. *Science and Children, 43*(3), 28–32.

Hallermann, S., Larmer, J., & Mergendoller, J. R. (2011). *PBL in the elementary grades: Step-by-step guidance, tools and tips for standards-focused K–5 projects.* Novato, CA: Buck Institute for Education.

Hannafin, M., Land, S., & Oliver, K. (1999). Open learning environments: Foundations, methods and models. In C. Reigeluth (Ed.), *Instructional design theories and models* (Vol. 11, pp. 115–140). Mahwah, NJ: Erlbaum.

Hmelo-Silver, C. E. (2004). Problem-based learning: What and how do students learn? *Educational Psychology Review, 16*(3), 235–266. http://dx.doi.org/10.1023/B:EDPR.0000034022.16470.f3

Hmelo-Silver, C. E. (2015). The learning space in problem-based learning. In A. Walker, H. Leary, C. E. Hmelo-Silver, & P. A. Ertmer (Eds.), *Essential readings in problem-based learning: Exploring and extending the legacy of Howard S. Barrows* (pp. 43–56). West Lafayette, IN: Purdue University Press.

Hmelo-Silver, C. E., & Barrows, H. S. (2015). Problem-based learning: Goals for learning and strategies for facilitating. In A. Walker, H. Leary, C. E. Hmelo-Silver, & P. A. Ertmer (Eds.), *Essential readings in problem-based learning: Exploring and extending the legacy of Howard S. Barrows* (pp. 69–84). West Lafayette, IN: Purdue University Press.

Jensen, E. (2013). *Engaging students with poverty in mind: Practical strategies for raising achievement.* Alexandria, VA: ASCD.

Jonassen, D. H. (2000). Toward a design theory of problem solving. *Educational Technology Research and Development, 48*(4), 63–85. http://dx.doi.org/10.1007/BF02300500

Jonassen, D. H., & Hung, W. All problems are not created equal: Implications for problem-based learning. In A. Walker, H. Leary, C. E. Hmelo-Silver, & P. A. Ertmer (Eds.), *Essential readings in problem-based learning: Exploring and extending the legacy of Howard S. Barrows* (pp. 17–41). West Lafayette, IN: Purdue University Press.

Kirsch, S. A., & Stetsenko, A. (2012, Summer). What does it mean to know? Third-grade students research using claims and evidence in science. *Science and Children, 49*(9), 44–49.

Kolodner, J. L., Camp, P. J., Crismond, D., Fasse, B., Gray, J., Holbrook, J., … Ryan, M. (2003). Problem-based learning meets case-based reasoning in the middle-school science classroom: Putting Learning by Design into practice. *Journal of the Learning Sciences, 12*(4), 495–547. http://dx.doi.org/10.1207/S15327809JLS1204_2

Linz, E., Heater, M., Howard, L. A. (2011). *Team teaching science.* Arlington, VA: NSTA Press.

Lottero-Perdue, P. S. (2011, June). *Making elementary engineering work: Lessons from partnerships and practice, the SySTEmic Project, Maryland.* Paper presented at 2011 Annual Conference and Exposition, Vancouver, BC. https://peer.asee.org/18316

Lottero-Perdue, P. S., Lovelidge, S., & Bowling, E. (2010, March). Engineering for all: Strategies for helping all students succeed in the engineering design process. *Science and Children, 47*(7), 24–27.

Lottero-Perdue, P. S., Nealy, J., Roland, C., & Ryan, A. (2011, December). Caught on video! Using handheld digital video cameras to support evidence-based reasoning. *Science and Children, 49*(4), 56–60.

Michaels, S., Shouse, A. W., & Schweingruber, H. A. (2008). *Ready, set, science: Putting research to work in K–8 science classrooms.* Washington, DC: National Academies Press. http://dx.doi.org/10.17226/11882

National Research Council (NRC). (2000). *Inquiry and the National Science Education Standards: A guide for teaching and learning.* Washington, DC: National Academies Press. http://dx.doi.org/10.17226/9596

Next Generation Science Standards (NGSS) Lead States. (2013). *Next Generation Science Standards: For states, by states.* Washington, DC: National Academies Press.

Sandifer, C., Hermann, R. S., Cimino, K., & Selway, J. (2015). Early teaching experiences at Towson University: Challenges, lessons, and innovations. In C. Sandifer & E. Brewe (Eds.), *Recruiting and educating future physics teachers: Case studies and effective practices* (pp. 129–145). College Park, MD: American Physical Society. http://www.phystec.org/webdocs/EffectivePracticesBook.cfm

Sandifer, C., Lising, L., & Renwick, E. (2007). *Towson's PhysTEC course improvement project, Years 1 and 2: Results and lessons learned.* Annual Proceedings of the Association for Science Teacher Education Conference.

Saye, J. W., & Brush, T. (2002). Scaffolding critical reasoning about history and social issues in multimedia-supported learning environments. *Educational Technology Research and Development, 50*(3), 77–96. http://dx.doi.org/10.1007/BF02505026

Savery, J. (2015). Overview of problem-based learning: Definitions and distinctions. In A. Walker, H. Leary, C. E. Hmelo-Silver, & P. A. Ertmer (Eds.), *Essential readings in problem-based learning: Exploring and extending the legacy of Howard S. Barrows* (pp. 5–15). West Lafayette, IN: Purdue University Press.

Steele, M. M. (October, 2007). Science success for students with special needs. *Science and Children, 45*(2), 48–51.

Villa, R. A., Thousand, J. S., & Nevin, A. I. (2008). *A guide to co-teaching: Practical tips for facilitating student learning* (2nd ed.). Thousand Oaks, CA: Corwin Press and Council for Exceptional Children.

Pamela S. Lottero-Perdue is an associate professor of science education in the Department of Physics, Astronomy and Geosciences and director of the integrated STEM Instructional Leadership program at Towson University. She is also chair of the Pre-College Engineering Education Division of the American Society for Engineering Education. Lottero-Perdue includes engineering in her preservice early childhood science methods and elementary science content and internship courses, and has developed engineering education courses for middle school preservice teachers and elementary inservice teachers. Her most recent research focuses on how students respond to engineering design failures, and how teachers respond to students whose designs fail and position what it means to fail in the classroom.

Part II

Problem-Based Learning in K–12 Contexts

5

Teacher as Designer: A Framework for Analysis of Mathematical Model-Eliciting Activities

Margret A. Hjalmarson and Heidi Diefes-Dux

Background

John Dewey (1990) stated, "The fundamental point in the psychology of an occupation is that it maintains a balance between the intellectual and the practical phases of experience" (p. 133). Although many studies have examined the structure of mathematics teachers' knowledge (e.g., Ball, Thames, & Phelps, 2008; Shulman, 1986), and in particular their understanding of problem solving or other methods related to inquiry-based teaching, less investigation has been conducted on the teacher as a designer of tools for practice, or the "practical phases." Some studies of teaching in mathematics education have focused on teacher development, where researchers have an ideal notion of teaching in mind and investigate how teachers carry out that ideal (Carpenter, Fennema, Peterson, Chiang, & Loef, 1989; Romberg, 1997). Other studies have focused on the interactions between teacher professional development facilitators and teachers, and their impact on teaching (Borko & Putnam, 1995; Elliott et al., 2009; Simon & Tzur, 1999; Swafford, Jones, Thornton, Stump, & Miller, 1999). However, the studies do not focus particularly on the products and objects teachers design for their classrooms. Rather, emphasis is placed on teachers' behaviors, teachers' cognition, or particular pedagogical techniques related to their practice and understanding of content. Other investigators described the need for research at multiple stages of instruction, from the ideal curriculum to the implemented curriculum to the experienced curriculum (Clements, 2002, 2007; MacNab, 2000). One interpretation of "curriculum" is what students should know and be able to do as represented in a particular set of instructional materials and the related teaching methods. For problem-based learning, this interpretation means considering learning and instruction from the intentions of the original designers to the teachers' interpretations and implementation of practices to the students' experiences and learning. Teachers often need to design support structures in order to implement curriculum or activities in their classrooms. Gutstein (2003), for example, discussed how he modified and supplemented a reform-based curriculum in order to better serve his urban, Latino student population. Maher (1988) explicitly referred to the teacher as designer and investigated both the tools teachers developed and the teachers' conceptual learning. Two points are important to note: (1) that materials and products, particularly for inquiry-based teaching or problem-based teaching, may be revised, modified, or supplemented by the teachers in order to fit their needs and contexts, and (2) that modification is a cyclical process of design, testing, and revision as teachers learn more about what works and what does not work according to their perceptions of classroom needs.

There is still a need for research on problem-based learning at the K–12 level (Savery, 2006). In addition, a challenge in problem-based mathematics teaching is developing a classroom environment that uses engaging, problem-based activities for students that elicit complex, creative mathematical thinking (Ertmer & Simons, 2006). The study described here focused on how teachers designed tools to support teaching and learning using small-group, mathematical modeling activities, referred to as model-eliciting activities (Doerr & English, 2003; Lesh, Hoover, Hole, Kelly, & Post, 2000). For instance, one task required students to generate a procedure for determining the number of boxes required to pack one million books collected in a school book drive. After the activity, groups presented their work in a whole-class presentation, and sometimes classmates were encouraged to ask questions after the presentation. Such modeling activities are an important part of modeling as a mathematical practice where students make sense of the world via the creation and exploration of mathematical models within the recommendation of the *Common Core State Standards for School Mathematics* (National Governors Association Center for Best Practices and Council of Chief State School Officers, 2010). This study was completed prior to the development of the *Common Core*; however, focus on modeling for students has increased the need for teacher development and the classroom practices to support students' learning of modeling practices and ways of thinking.

The model-eliciting activity and subsequent presentations raised assessment issues for the teachers in terms of what and how to assess what students presented and discussed. As a result, teachers developed products and strategies for orchestrating and assessing the presentations. These products and strategies are referred to here as "presentation tools" and include any tools the teachers designed that were associated with the students' final presentations of their models (e.g., a scoring rubric, presentation outlines). We refer to the products as "tools" to emphasize the functional nature of the objects the teachers designed. Any tool is designed with a particular purpose and function in mind. The most fundamental test of a tool is whether it carried out the function as desired. This leads to a design process as tools are designed and tested multiple times to bring them closer to fulfilling the intended purpose.

The study addressed the following question: What is a framework for analyzing the characteristics of the tools teachers design for implementation with mathematical modeling activities? To answer this question, a design research lens was taken in assembling case studies of teacher practice around middle school mathematics activities. The three teachers designed tools (referred to as presentation tools) related to the students' oral presentations and discussions of their solutions to the problem-solving activities. Each teacher used multiple model-eliciting activities, so the tools were revised and modified over time to meet their intended purposes for implementing the activities. Based on the common characteristics that emerged, a framework was developed to sort, classify, and track the tools over time.

Design Research

Due to the complexity and constraints of teaching mathematics, we draw a parallel to design research in other contexts in order to examine tool development by middle school mathematics teachers and to develop a framework for characterizing such tools. Design research and experiments as initially conceived by Brown (1992) and others (Collins, 1990, 1992; Edelson, 2002) focused on investigating teaching methods in real classroom situations. This represented a shift from laboratory-based research to classroom-based research (Brown, 1992). We focused on presentation tools as one artifact of mathematics teachers' design process associated with complex, problem-based activities. Revision of the tools and processes over time occurred as the teachers used different activities, learned more about how students would solve the given problems, and continued to think about how the presentations were achieving their goals as teachers. Tools were developed by the teachers who solved local problems but with features and characteristics transferable to other, similar situations. The notion of the "best" tool was locally defined by the needs of the designer (in this case, the teacher), and tools were refined over time to become better suited to the teachers' purposes and to accommodate changing needs in the local context.

The design of the tools for teaching is similar to the design of tools in engineering contexts in that multiple variables must be considered, the problems that exist are human problems in a changing environment, and the design situation faces various constraints (Hjalmarson & Lesh, 2008). Design research encompasses both the study of a product and the design process. The design metaphor is related to engineering design, where products are designed to solve human problems within particular contexts. In engineering, problems are identified and engineers need to creatively integrate knowledge from multiple disciplines. Any problem-solving situation (in teaching or in engineering) will face constraints and opportunities. Engineering, like teaching, includes the design of products within constraints where revision is a natural part of the design process.

In the case of mathematics teaching, knowledge about mathematics, students' learning, pedagogy, and the local context are integrated. Teachers engineer, or design, their classrooms in order to optimize students' learning. The classroom environment and tools are open to modification to continuously improve their functioning. The design process becomes more complex as the tasks assigned to students become more complex and teachers work in unfamiliar territory, where students' responses are not always predictable. The lack of predictability is where design becomes useful as a metaphor for teaching. Because the students' solutions to a problem-based task are unknown to a degree, the teacher needs to design tools that are responsive to multiple solutions and ways of thinking. The open-ended nature of the tasks and work in small groups increases the complexity of the analysis and the number of pedagogical decisions to be made by the teacher. Hence, designing tools for a changing context (where teachers learned more about students' thinking and changed their expectations of students) and complex work by students becomes a process of integrating knowledge of teaching and mathematics, determining which variables are important to assess, and developing tools to aid teaching.

Design research was used as a lens to investigate the design of an artifact, examine the underlying assumptions of that artifact, and generate frameworks to facilitate further analysis of teacher-designed tools. Other examples of design research include work in software (Bannan-Ritland, 2003; Kelly, 2014; Oshima et al., 2004), curriculum (Barab & Luehmann, 2003), teaching practice (Shattuck & Anderson, 2013), and other collections of educational products (Bannan-Ritland, 2003; Cobb, Confrey, diSessa, Lehrer, & Schauble, 2003; Gersten, 2005; Gorard, Roberts, & Taylor, 2004; Kelly, 2014). This study is distinct from previous work in design in that the teachers were the principal tool designers. Design research projects often incorporate teachers or other stakeholders as partners in the design process (Anderson & Shattuck, 2012; Penuel, Fishman, Cheng, & Sabelli, 2011). Their role is often to design, implement, or provide feedback about products designed by researchers (Bannan-Ritland, 2003; Edelson, 2002; Gersten, 2005; Jitendra, 2005). The teacher as designer metaphor has been explored previously in mathematics education (Maher, 1988) but not in relationship to design experiments or design research.

Problem-Based Learning and Model-Eliciting Activities

The goal of a model-eliciting activity is for students to develop a model that solves a problem or makes a decision for a client. Models in this sense are procedures, explanations, or processes that are used to interpret a situation, often set in a real-world problem (Lesh & Doerr, 2003). The model-eliciting activities used in this study were developed using six principles for thought-revealing activities for students (Lesh et al., 2000). The principles are designed to describe the types of tasks that will help students develop their own models, interpret situations, and use their own ways of thinking in conjunction with mathematical knowledge. For instance, in the Million-Book Challenge activity, students had to determine a procedure for finding how many boxes would be needed to pack and ship one million books collected in a school-based book drive. The complexity of the task was that the size of the books was unknown and varied. The books collected ranged from elementary picture books to novels to reference books. This variation meant students needed to collect data about typical books, perform estimates about book size and volume, and generate a model for making the estimate for the number of boxes needed. This task is similar to tasks in engineering design and other applied fields where statistical inference is needed to estimate and generate a model for predicting a value.

The task required students to use area, volume, data analyses, and statistics to generate their models.

As a problem-solving process, the students had to draw on their own knowledge and experience with packing and estimation in order to develop a solution. Traditional mathematics teaching proceeds with the teacher demonstrating a concept or topic and the students completing a series of exercises to practice the algorithm or skill that was demonstrated. Model-eliciting activities work in the opposite direction. Previous studies have examined students' solutions to model-eliciting activities where a range of models are developed using multiple mathematical topics (Carmona-Dominguez, 2004; Doerr & English, 2003; Magiera & Zawojewski, 2011). In an interview with Katy, an eighth grade teacher in this study, she described the strength of the activities as

> having to actually just kind of look at a situation and pull from their knowledge base an actual mathematical concept that they could apply to that. Kind of the opposite of what we normally do, where we say, "Ok here's the concept, now apply it to this situation." Giving them the situation and letting them pull out a concept—opposite of the way we usually present the material—which is just so much more valuable. To have them be able to look at the situation and actually come up some mathematical concept that would work.

The students typically spent three to five days on a single activity. The first day was an introduction and orientation to the problem and its context. In the following days, the students worked in small groups to develop their final solution. The final day comprised presentations of students' solutions to the whole class. During the final day, each group presented its solution and explained what they had done to solve the problem. Then, the teacher and the rest of the class had an opportunity to ask questions of the group. Teachers structured and conducted the presentations differently. The differences in structure and emphasis are the focus of this study.

Model-eliciting activities and problem-based learning are related instructional approaches (Chamberlin & Moon, 2008). Both approaches include problems situated in realistic, meaningful contexts that require students to design approaches to solving a task. Both approaches also include the integration of knowledge and skills toward the solution of the task. Model-eliciting activities for middle school are usually designed for students to complete in a few days so students are not required to do as much background research as they might do in a problem-based learning activity. Examples of model-eliciting activities focus on data analysis (Bostic, 2013; Chamberlin & Zawojewski, 2006; Doerr & English, 2003; Magiera, 2013), algebra, and other mathematical constructs (Diefes-Dux, Hjalmarson, Zawojewski, & Bowman, 2006) across a range of grade levels, from elementary school (Coxbill, Chamberlin, & Weatherford, 2013; Lesh, English, Riggs, & Sevis, 2013) to undergraduate (Diefes-Dux, Hjalmarson, Miller, & Lesh, 2008; Diefes-Dux et al., 2006; Hjalmarson, 2007).

The model-eliciting activities in this study were used on their own; however, model-eliciting activities could be used as the introduction to a longer unit (Lesh, Cramer, Doerr, & Zawojewski, 2003). A distinctive characteristic of model-eliciting activities is that students are designing a model as their final product. The model is a procedure or process rather than a single numeric answer (Lesh et al., 2000). The model includes representations of the conceptual systems used to develop a procedure or explanation for a purpose (Lesh, Doerr, Carmona, & Hjalmarson, 2003). Problem-based learning does not necessarily have such an explicit focus on the development of procedures or processes.

Researcher Principles

Design-based research focuses on the creation and analysis of principles that guide the research (Anderson & Shattuck, 2012). Three principles guided the design of this study and its focus on the teacher as designer of the presentation tools. First, the teachers have the most expertise about their classrooms and teaching contexts. Second, the teachers should be the owners and developers of their products. Finally, because the teachers were the owners of the products, Hjalmarson functioned as a consultant, providing suggestions and advice only as requested. The goal was not to be a professional development facilitator intending to teach them about presentations and classroom discourse but rather to provide advice if requested and document their design processes in order to find out how the presentations naturally fit into their goals for their students' learning. The teachers were the primary designers of the tools for their own classrooms.

The first principle, teacher as expert, represents the core of the study. When requesting their participation, teachers were told that the study would investigate tools surrounding the students' presentations. In this instance, the teacher as expert was important because he or she had the most experience in the classroom context. All the teachers had previously used similar activities. We wanted to work with teachers who had reached a point where they wanted to use the activities with some regularity and to integrate them into regular classroom practice.

The second principle, teacher as owner, was critical to understanding the needs teachers naturally had within the context and the types of solutions they deemed appropriate to identified problems. For instance, student work can be assessed as the students present in class. Tools that are designed for this purpose need to be sensitive to the classroom expectations and the nature of assessing oral presentations. The teacher's ownership of the products also meant that she had an authentic interest in revising the tools with successive activities. She could determine what was useful and not useful, even as the operational definition of "useful" might change over time. The teacher was responsible for revisions based on her understanding and analyses.

The final principle, researcher as consultant, was important for Hjalmarson's relationship with the teachers as principal designers of the tools. Hjalmarson did not determine the purpose of the presentation tools and provided input only when requested from the teachers. Part of the rationale was to be able to document the design of tools in as natural an environment as possible when a researcher is present. The study investigated how the teachers designed tools based on their own needs and from their own resources rather than a tool imposed from the outside. This principle depends on the first two in that seeing them as experts and principal designers enabled the role of researcher as consultant.

Methodology for Data Collection and Analysis

Methods

Three middle school teachers in the urban fringe of a large city participated in the study. Two teachers taught sixth grade (Amy and Abby), and the third teacher taught eighth grade (Katy). They were selected based on the following criteria. Each teacher agreed to implement at least three model-eliciting activities over the course of one school year. All three teachers had been using activities for at least two years and had participated in summer institutes or professional development workshops about model-eliciting activities. They agreed to let the first author observe in their classrooms throughout each model-eliciting activity and provided us with copies of the presentation tools. Two teachers' tools are described in more detail in subsequent sections (Amy and Katy).

Data Sources

Four primary sources of data were collected for this study: presentation tools, observation notes throughout the school day, transcripts of classroom interactions, and semistructured interviews. Contact summary sheets and document summary forms were used for observations and tool collection for preliminary analysis as the data were collected (Miles & Huberman, 1994). The forms were designed to provide responses to the research questions about the type of tool used and the purposes for the tool. Hjalmarson completed the data collection and analyses between fall 2002 and spring 2004.

Each teacher completed at least three model-eliciting activities during the course of the study. Because the presentation tools are the focus of this study, they were the most important source of data. The other data supported the interpretation of the presentation tools. Hjalmarson collected the tangible tools each teacher used. Tools were often being designed as the activity was under way (on-the-spot design), so having the tools in advance of the activity or the presentations was sometimes neither possible nor desirable. The questions asked by the teacher of each presentation were noted and audiotaped. Tapes were transcribed, and the transcripts were filed with the field notes for the day. Notes for each tool included when the tool had been implemented, the type of tool it was, and any observations made about student or teacher reactions to the tool using a document summary form (Miles & Huberman, 1994)

In many cases, because Hjalmarson was in the classroom, the teachers discussed the tools with her informally throughout the school day. Daily notes included as much about these spontaneous, informal discussions as possible (Merriam, 2001; Patton, 1990). These spontaneous conversations provided insight into the teachers' on-the-spot decision making and impressions of the activity. They served as short, unstructured interviews within the school day to discuss events as they unfolded (Fontana & Frey, 1998; Patton, 1990).

The study also included one semistructured interview (Merriam, 2001) with each teacher at the end of the data collection in order to document their impressions of the model-eliciting activities in general and of the presentations in particular. Each teacher was asked slightly different questions based on the tools they had implemented and on the observations of the classroom. All of the interviews included questions about what they valued about the model-eliciting activities, their goals for the presentations, unexpected results from the students, and their implementation of the activities and presentations. Specifically, the interviews focused on finding out what the teachers wanted to hear and learn from the students during the presentation and what they expected the students to be doing during the presentations (either as presenters or audience members) to document the purpose behind the presentation tools. Their responses supported later analysis of the transcripts of whole-class discussions, the tools, and other field notes about the presentations in their classrooms. An interview before the start of the activities was not possible because we did not have enough notice from the teachers before the start of the activity to schedule a time to meet. However, the data gathered in the classroom as the teachers worked (in particular, the tools they designed) helped document their purposes for using the activities and their initial purposes for the presentation tools.

Data Analysis

As with the data collection, data analysis was guided by chronologically documenting the presentation tools as they were designed. Consistent with the need to document the design process for developing the case studies of each teacher, data analysis for the study was divided into two major phases: during and after data collection. The analysis during the data collection included all analyses from the first day in the first teacher's classroom until the last day of data collection. Data analysis about the entire set of data collected from all teachers was categorized as occurring after data collection.

Data analysis was also divided into two approaches: within-case and cross-case analysis (Merriam, 2001; Miles & Huberman, 1994). Each teacher in the study covered one case including at least three model-eliciting activities for within-case analysis. A preliminary analysis of the tools occurred as they were collected from each teacher. Transcripts and the field notes supported the analyses of the purpose for each presentation tool. Constant comparison analysis (Merriam, 2001; Strauss & Corbin, 1998) occurred between activities within each teacher case study.

The cross-case analysis built on the results from the within-case analysis. Constant comparison of results for the cross-case analysis aided the analysis for individual cases as well as the models we designed for generating results across teachers (Merriam, 2001; Strauss & Corbin, 1998). Constant comparison for the cross-case analysis during the data collection occurred as data was collected from classroom to classroom. In addition, constant comparison occurred as a larger set of tools was collected and with more experience within the classroom settings. The constant comparison analysis situated the individual teachers' set of tools within the set of all teachers' tools and provided a description of the range and types of presentation tools.

The initial data analysis occurred as the data collection progressed (Merriam, 2001), as is typical for design research studies (Anderson & Shattuck, 2012; Collins, Joseph, & Bielaczyc, 2004). The summary forms captured the preliminary data analysis to record impressions of the tool design and implementation (Miles & Huberman, 1994) and were supported by the field notes for each day. The field notes recorded as much information as possible about what the teacher said about the tools and about how they were used in the classroom. As discussed previously, this data collection included recording comments the teachers made in informal discussions with the first author throughout the school day as well as the use of the tool with their students. The documentation forms noted how the tool had been used in the classroom and any potential changes that the teacher mentioned. Analysis of the current presentation tool, its purposes, and its effectiveness at meeting the purpose supported the analysis of tool revision.

The second phase of data analysis occurred after data collection. First, the tools were organized by type and categorized using the scheme in Table 5.1.

Next, the teachers' purposes for the presentation tool and the presentation itself were identified. The purposes for the presentation tools were triangulated by examining the interview transcripts, field notes, and transcripts from classroom observations. For example, Katy described what each category meant on her scoring guide to the students at the start of the activity. When she used the scoring guide to assess responses, it provided further data about her purposes for the tools and about how well the tool met those purposes. The scoring process revealed how well the guide captured her expectations for student responses and how the scoring guide served to differentiate high-quality and low-quality responses.

Table 5.1 *Tool characteristic categories.*

Characteristics	Description	Example
Structure	What the tool looks like	Scoring guide, presentation outline
Form	How the tool is implemented	Written, verbal
Content	What is included in the tool	Questions about final product
Time of use	When the tool is used or discussed in the classroom	Introduction to activity, presentations

Design Case: Presentation Outline

In order to illustrate the design process, one of the teacher cases is described here in more detail. This example was selected because Amy's purposes were clear, and she designed a unique tool. Unlike the other two teachers, who primarily designed scoring rubrics, Amy designed a presentation outline she revised over time. From the presentation, she wanted to learn about her students' thinking processes for solving the problem. The outline was classified as a presentation tool because Amy had represented a purpose in a tangible way that she shared with students. The outlines facilitated the students' presentations and communicated her expectations for the activity to them. Amy wanted to learn more about her students' solution processes for the activity, so she designed an outline for each activity that consisted of a series of questions or statements that students should respond to in their presentations (Hjalmarson, 2003, 2004). As she stated in the following interview excerpt, she was interested in the path between their first idea for a solution and their final product.

> The reason that I started doing the questions is I just didn't feel I was gettin' enough out of 'em. They would get up and either present their letter or if it was a poster board, they'd get up ... introduce themselves, present their poster board, and I just felt like, "Ok, but how did you get there?" I wasn't finding how they were getting there to be able to make that presentation. That wasn't gettin' shared. And, that's what I was more interested in than anything. Especially since so often the results are not always correct. So, I was more interested in their thinking.

As she stated, the tool was developed to meet a need she identified in order to enrich the experience for her students and to help her learn about their thinking. She had been designing presentation outlines before the start of the study during the previous school year. During this study, she designed four outlines.

Amy was interested in her students' thinking, both as they presented their own solutions and as they responded to presentations by other teams. She reminded them during the question phase that she would ask questions but that she wanted them to ask questions of the group as well. The first outline was for the mini-golf activity. The students had to design a miniature golf course using specified shapes for the holes. The holes were not drawn to scale, and the task required the students to scale up the holes and make them all the same scale in order to determine how to position them in the given area. All of the groups produced a letter and a miniature golf course layout on a poster board. The outline Amy wrote on the board for them to follow included the obstacles the group may have encountered ("Getting started struggles"). She asked about the moment they knew how to solve the problem ("Aha! moment") and the final product (reading the letter and describing the layout). "Who did what" asked them to describe how tasks were divided among the members of the group (e.g., writing the letter, cutting out shapes). Questions came either from Amy or other students in the class.

Amy was interested in how each group solved the activity, from their initial ideas to their final product. Based on her experience, she felt the students had not explained clearly or specifically the solution paths they had followed. She was trying to determine a way to word a question to elicit each group's solution path more clearly. Even though the outlines were improving, she was still not entirely satisfied with their effectiveness in eliciting students' solution processes, even toward the end of the study when we discussed them. She explained:

> [Be]cause some case studies lend [themselves] more to talking about struggles they had getting started. What I would like to hear them do more—and this is another question I haven't figured out exactly how to word—is paths that they started to follow. Like they thought, "Oh, this'll work," and then what caused them to realize that it didn't. And, so then what did they start thinking next or move to next?

For the next activity (Million-Book Challenge described previously), she changed the introduction of the task. The students read the problem individually and wrote about their initial ideas and thoughts about the problem in a notebook. The change to the introduction created a change in the presentation. When each group presented, students spoke about their individual initial ideas before the group started working together. Describing the individual ideas led to a clearer description of the path from initial thoughts to final product when they responded to the first statement in the revised outline in Figure 5.1. The presentation tool was affected by an instructional decision that occurred early in the solution process. The interaction between the tool and instructional decisions illustrates how changes were made to both the tool and the classroom context.

Another change between the two outlines was the addition of "How confident are you about your answer?" as a statement in the outline. This change

Million-Book Presentation Outline

- First thoughts
- How you chose your group
- Troubles
- Plan to solve
- How confident are you about your answer?
- Read your letter
- Questions

Figure 5.1 Million-book presentation outline.

occurred when Amy used the Million-Book Challenge activity first with her advanced class, and then with her other classes. The outline for the presentations in the advanced class did not contain the question, but she asked it to groups after their presentations and found it elicited information about their processes. In answering the question, the groups had to describe the mathematics of their solutions and could compare their mathematical methods with methods from other groups that had presented. They could also describe strengths and weaknesses of their procedures. Such descriptions explained their mathematical thinking related to the task. As a result, Amy added the question to the outline when she used it with the rest of her classes. This change was the shift of an informal question to a formal part of the outline, and it provides another illustration of changes to the tool that were a direct result of classroom practices in situ.

The use of the presentation outlines structured the students' presentations and communicated Amy's expectations to the students. After a few activities, the students knew what to expect from the outline, even before she wrote it on the board for them to follow. They knew the types of questions she was going to ask them about their product and process. From a design perspective, to improve the value of the presentation, Amy's outline facilitated her learning about students' thinking and mathematical solutions. The outline developed as she learned more about her students' interaction with the activities. Amy's design process for her presentation outlines was grounded in her purpose for the presentations (hearing about solution process) and in her classroom practice.

Lawnmower Case Study Scoring Guide

- Which 4 employees should be hired? (3 points)
- Explain the method you used in detail to make this decision. (5 points)
- How did you use the data provided to make your decision? (5 points)
- Is your response in the form of a letter? (2 points)

Figure 5.2 Lawnmower case study scoring guide.

Design Case: Scoring Guides

In contrast to Amy's focus on process, Katy's scoring guide focused exclusively on the final product (i.e., the mathematical model the students developed) rather than on group interaction, metacognition, and so on. Figure 5.2 shows the scoring guide she designed for the Lawnmower activity. In referring to the "method" and how they used the data (the second and third items in the rubric), she intended for them to describe their mathematical model or procedure. Katy's other scoring guides were similar. The task in the Lawnmower activity was to design a procedure for hiring employees based on information about individuals' prior performance mowing lawns. The students needed to aggregate the data statistically and determine which variables were relevant to the hiring question. She used the scoring guide during class as each group presented. She asked the first author to score the presentations using the rubrics as well, and we discussed the scoring after school.

Because the guide needed to be completed in class as Katy was listening to the presentations and monitoring classroom activity, the guide needed to be simple and short. Katy used the task description as a guide for developing the rubric so the task and the assessment would be closely aligned. Time was an important variable because the class periods were only 45 minutes long. If all the groups were going to present, then Katy did not have a lot of time between groups to take notes about their work or to complete a complex rubric or scoring guide. Katy also collected the letters the students wrote (unlike Amy, who did not collect the letters). Katy did not complete an assessment of individual students in the group. She also did not incorporate their problem solving or group interaction as part of the scoring requirement. The central focus of all her rubrics was the group product that had emerged.

Katy's rubrics served a fundamentally different purpose, and the type of product designed to meet that purpose was different from Amy's outlines. Katy was more focused on the quality of the final product and whether the students had created a usable procedure. The changes to Katy's rubrics were not as significant as the changes to Amy's outlines throughout the study, but both teachers did refine their presentation tools over time. The two sets of tools represent different yet equally valid goals for presentation tools. The tools accomplished some goals well but were never intended to meet other goals (e.g., the presentation outline was not intended to quantify student performance on the activity, the scoring rubric was not intended for understanding student process). As a result of the qualitatively different goals represented in the tools designed by each teacher, the framework for tool analysis was developed.

Development of Framework for Presentation Tool Analysis

To support the development of a framework for analyzing the collection of all the presentation tools, the tools were categorized based on the characteristics in Table 5.2.

Table 5.2 *Description of tool characteristics.*

Tool	Structure	Form	Content	Time of Use
Amy				
Mini-Golf Outline	Set of 6 points for an outline	Orally by students	Initial struggles, aha, group interaction, description of final product	Presentation
Million-Book Outline	Set of 6 points for an outline	Orally by students	Impressions, struggles, group interaction, aha, final product	Presentation
Million-Book Outline (Revised)	Set of 7 points for an outline	Orally by students	Impressions, struggles, group interaction, confidence in solution, final product	Presentation
Mini-Golf Outline	Set of 6 points for an outline	Orally by students	Initial struggles, aha, group interaction, description of final product	Presentation
Million-Book Outline	Set of 6 points for an outline	Orally by students	Impressions, struggles, group interaction, aha, final product	Presentation

Continued

Table 5.2 *Continued.*

Tool	Structure	Form	Content	Time of Use
***Amy** (continued)*				
Million-Book Outline (Revised)	Set of 7 points for an outline	Orally by students	Impressions, struggles, group interaction, confidence in solution, final product	Presentation
Snowflake Outline	Set of 5 points for an outline	Orally by students	Impressions, struggles, group interaction, final product	Presentation
Katy				
Summer Reading Scoring Guide	Scoring guide with 3 categories	Written by teacher	System content, usability, letter	Introduction, working, presentation
Departing on Time Scoring Guide	Scoring guide with 3 categories	Written by teacher	Detailed ranking process, ranking, letter	Introduction, working, presentation
Lawnmower Scoring Guide	Scoring guide with 4 categories	Written by teacher	Detailed ranking process, ranking, use of data letter	Introduction, working, presentation
Abby				
Mini-Golf Scoring Guide	Scoring guide with 4 categories	Written by teacher	Group work, work shown, model, letter	Introduction, presentation
Mini-Golf Long Follow-up	Worksheet with 8 categories	Written by students	Construction of scale models, generalizing golf course, problem solving, reflection about methods, group interaction	Post-presentation
Mini-Golf Short Follow-up	Worksheet with 4 categories	Written by students	Reflection about methods, group interaction-	Post-presentation
Quilt Rubric	Scoring guide with 3 categories	Written by teacher	Final product, explanation of process, specific mathematical content	Post-presentation
Snowflake Rubric	Scoring guide with 5 categories	Written by teacher	Explanation, visuals, knowledge, final product, reasonableness of solution	Post-presentation

Table 5.3 *Examples of tools in each quadrant of the framework.*

	Description	Example
Group	Questions in a presentation about how the group came to its conclusions	Rubric analyzing the final solution produced by the group
Individual	Questions in a presentation about individual contributions to the process	Questions in a presentation about individual contributions to the final solution (e.g., What were your initial ideas?)

This analysis resulted in the development of a framework for categorizing the tools designed by the teachers. The function of the framework was to both classify and examine the holistic nature of a set of tools. The framework had two dimensions. The first dimension was between individual and group products. The students worked in groups, but teachers may have asked questions about individual contributions or assigned individual assessment scores. The second dimension was between the process and the product. Each item in the tool was classified according to whether it was focused on the final product (e.g., the letter or solution) or on the students' solution process (e.g., group functioning, reflection on idea development). Table 5.3 shows how tools might fit within each quadrant of the framework.

The dimensions work in concert with each type of focus used by at least one teacher. A single tool may have components that fit within different quadrants of the framework. All quadrants were represented by at least one tool designed by the teachers. The framework is one means of organizing a diverse set of tools designed by teachers and classifying them based on their purpose. Table 5.4 shows how the components of Amy's tools were categorized within the framework. As shown, her focus was largely on the group process with less emphasis on the final product or individual products. In contrast, Katy's tools (shown in Table 5.5) all fall within the group product quadrant. She revised her tools for that purpose.

Where Amy's tools have components distributed across multiple quadrants of the framework, Katy's tools are centralized in one quadrant. The point here is not to say that one teacher's tools are better than the other's but rather to illustrate the diversity of tool purposes and types and how teacher practice can reflect different types of tools to support the same type of activity. The point is also to recognize that teachers may move between multiple purposes for the same type of activity, or they may be more focused on a single purpose given the time constraints of the classroom environment.

Table 5.4 ***Analysis of Amy's presentation outlines on the analysis framework.***

	Process	Product
Group	MG-Outline-1	MG-Outline-4
	MG-Outline-2	MG-Outline-5
	MG-Outline-3	MB1-Outline-6
	MB1-Outline-2	MB2-Outline-5
	MB1-Outline-3	MB2-Outline-6
	MB1-Outline-4	S-Outline-4
	MB1-Outline-5	
	MB2-Outline-2	
	MB2-Outline-3	
	MB2-Outline-4	
	S-Outline-1	
	S-Outline-2	
	S-Outline-3	
Individual	MB1-Outline-1	
	MB2-Outline-1	

MG = Mini-Golf activity
MB1 = Million-Book Challenge activity (version 1)
MB2 = Million-Book Challenge activity (version 2)
S = Snowflake activity

Table 5.5 ***Analysis of Katy's scoring guides on the analysis framework.***

	Process	Product
Group		SR-Rubric-1
		SR-Rubric-2
		SR-Rubric-3
		DOT-Rubric-1
		DOT-Rubric-2
		DOT-Rubric-3
		L-Rubric-1
		L-Rubric-2
		L-Rubric-3
		L-Rubric-4
Individual		

SR = Summer Reading activity rubric
DOT = Departing on Time activity rubric
L = Lawnmower activity rubric

A strong point of the framework is the organization of tools by purpose and function. It does not organize them by quality because quality is a characteristic locally determined by the teacher using and designing the tool. A tool for analyzing problem-solving processes might not be good for analyzing final products, but that determination is up to the teacher who designs the tools. The framework organizes the tools based on what the tools are intended to do rather than an external characterization of what aspects of the model-eliciting activity or the presentation are valuable. For instance, the framework presents two different types of teacher's purposes when Katy's tools and Amy's tools are classified. Realistically, as represented by the placement of components of the tools on the framework, teachers are interested in multiple aspects of the model-eliciting activity (or any other problem-solving activity). The tools represent an interest in both mathematical content and mathematical process. The framework could be used for other types of tools related to complex problem-solving activities.

A second strength of the framework is the documentation of varying units of analysis used by the teacher. The unit of analysis is critical as teachers shift between individual learning, group learning, and whole-class learning. As an example of whole-class analysis, Chamberlin and colleagues studied student-thinking sheets that teachers developed to organize class sets of student work by solution type (Chamberlin, 2002; Zawojewski, Chamberlin, Hjalmarson, & Lewis, 2008). In this project, teachers developed individual, small-group, and whole-class tools. Moving between the three levels is critical for teachers as they plan and analyze instruction. With a different set of tools and further study, teachers' aggregated analyses of whole-class work could be captured. Informally, the teachers in the present study did analyze information about the whole class, but no tools were developed specifically for this purpose. The tools focused on either the individual's work or a group's work. Further work could investigate the whole-class level of analysis.

In terms of analyzing teacher practice and the development of tools, the framework highlights a few characteristics. First, a shifting focus within practice is a natural part of teaching. Sometimes, teachers wanted information about a group as the unit of analysis. Sometimes, they were interested in the individual unit of analysis. More detailed study could examine teachers shifting between individuals, groups, and the whole class. For secondary teachers, there is the added dimension of multiple whole classes divided into block periods that have their own characteristics. The question is not whether a teacher should focus on individuals or groups but when and why the unit of analysis needs to be a group or the individual. The purpose dimension of the framework highlights how the function of a tool varies within an activity and across activities. Some teachers had a constant purpose from activity to activity, and some teachers had purposes that varied across and within activities. Recommendations by the National Council of Teachers of Mathematics (2000) stressed that mathematical processes are part of mathematics standards alongside content. The *Common Core Standards* extend this notion to other mathematical practices such as reasoning and problem solving (National Governors Association Center for Best Practices and Council of Chief State School Officers, 2010). This framework for analysis of teacher tools encompasses both types of standards: process and content. The framework also highlights how purposes change and how teachers' views of their classrooms change. At various points, a teacher is interested in students as individuals, as groups, or as a class, depending on the purpose for the activity at hand. In parallel to the question about the unit of analysis, the question is not whether teachers should focus on process or product but when and how they should focus on either dimension.

Conclusions and Implications

Similar to thought-revealing activities for students, this project was conceived as a thought-revealing activity for teachers by examining the design and development of tools for their classrooms. The products enabled us to see how they perceived the purpose of the model-eliciting activities in the classroom and how they perceived what aspects of the activity were valuable. The study emphasized what the teachers designed in terms of external products rather than their behaviors in the classroom. The "action" of the classroom was not the primary focus of the investigation. Even though the teachers' uses of the tools with students were part of the data collection, the design research lens emphasized the products teachers designed more than their actions in the classroom or what they said. We wanted to know what aspects of their teaching were elicited by the tool design, so data collection was situated around the presentation tools. However, every tool has limitations; no tool can capture all aspects of a classroom activity. The presentation tools demonstrated what kinds of design choices the teachers made for the particular phase of the activity (presentations) and what aspects of the model-eliciting activity were valuable from their perspective.

The primary contribution of this study is the development of a framework for analyzing and examining change in teachers' tools designed to support practice for model-eliciting activities. Problem-based learning activities can also include the assessment of students' final products as well as their problem-solving processes (e.g., group interaction, reflection, problem-solving strategies). Given a greater number of teachers or tools, the framework could be used to investigate the change in teacher focus (individuals or groups) depending on the type of activity. The teachers' unit of analysis could be useful for understanding how and when they analyze their students' learning. Both levels are important for teachers to understand. What is not clear is how, when, and why teachers shift their views from one level to another. A third level not addressed in the tools in this study is the whole class. Mathematics teachers may compare and contrast different classes of students if they teach multiple classes of students in a single day. For the purpose dimension of the framework (product and process), further investigation could focus on how teachers practice changes related to the purposes. In addition, how do teachers relate students' problem-solving processes and cycles to their final products?

This study examined teacher purposes for instruction from the perspective of the tools they designed to support students' presentations of solutions to complex problems. Particularly relevant for modeling as a mathematical practice, the teachers provided an opportunity for students to interpret situations and engage in an iterative process to craft appropriate models. Following this process, they also required students to share and describe their models to other people. Across the three teachers, four separate types of purposes in two dimensions occurred (individual vs. group analysis, focus on product or process). The framework for analyzing the tools could extend beyond the given set of tools to other tools designed by teachers using model-eliciting activities or forms of problem-based learning where students are designing products in a small group within a realistic context.

Acknowledgments

This chapter is an updated version of an article previously published in the *Interdisciplinary Journal of Problem-based Learning.* Original citation: Hjalmarson, M. A., & Diefes-Dux, H. (2008). Teacher as designer: A framework for teacher analysis of mathematical model-eliciting activities. *Interdisciplinary Journal of Problem-based Learning, 2*(1), 57–78.

References

Anderson, T., & Shattuck, J. (2012). Design-based research: A decade of progress in education research? *Educational Researcher, 41*(1), 16–25. http://doi.org/10.3102/0013189X11428813

Ball, D. L., Thames, M. H., & Phelps, G. (2008). Content knowledge for teaching: What makes it special? *Journal of Teacher Education, 59*(5), 389–407. http://doi.org/10.1177/0022487108324554

Bannan-Ritland, B. (2003). The role of design in research: The integrative learning design framework. *Educational Researcher, 32*(1), 21–24. http://doi.org/10.3102/0013189X032001021

Barab, S. A., & Luehmann, A. L. (2003). Building sustainable science curriculum: Acknowledging and accommodating local adaptation. *Science Education, 87*(4), 454–467.

Borko, H., & Putnam, R. T. (1995). Expanding a teacher's knowledge base: A cognitive psychological perspective on professional development. In T. R. Guskey & A. M. Huberman (Eds.), *Professional development in education: New paradigms and practices* (pp. 35–65). New York, NY: Teachers College Press.

Bostic, J. D. (2013). Model-eliciting activities for teaching mathematics. *Mathematics Teaching in the Middle School, 18*(5), 262–266. http://doi.org/10.5951/mathteacmiddscho.18.5.0262

Brown, A. L. (1992). Design experiments: Theoretical and methodological challenges in creating complex interventions in classroom settings. *The Journal of the Learning Sciences, 2*(2), 141 178.

Carmona-Dominguez, G. (2004). *Designing an assessment tool to describe students' mathematical knowledge.* West Lafayette, IN: Purdue University Press.

Carpenter, T. P., Fennema, E., Peterson, P. L., Chiang, C., & Loef, M. (1989). Using knowledge of children's mathematics thinking in classroom teaching: An experimental study. *American Educational Research Journal, 26*(4), 499–531.

Chamberlin, M. (2002). *Teacher investigations of students' Work: The evolution of teachers' social processes and interpretations of students' thinking.* West Lafayette, IN: Purdue University Press.

Chamberlin, M., & Zawojewski, J. (2006). A worthwhile mathematical task for students and their teachers. *Mathematics Teaching in the Middle School, 12*(2), 82 87.

Chamberlin, S. A., & Moon, S. M. (2008). How does the problem based learning approach compare to the model-eliciting activity approach in mathematics? *International Journal of Mathematics Teaching and Learning.* Retrieved from http://www.cimt.org.uk/journal/chamberlin.pdf

Clements, D. H. (2002). Linking research and curriculum development. In L. D. English (Ed.), *Handbook of international research in mathematics education* (pp. 599–630). Mahwah, NJ: Lawrence Erlbaum Associates.

Clements, D. H. (2007). Curriculum research: Toward a framework for "research-based curricula." *Journal for Research in Mathematics Education, 38*(1), 35–70.

Cobb, P., Confrey, J., diSessa, A., Lehrer, R., & Schauble, L. (2003). Design experiments in educational research. *Educational Researcher, 32*(1), 9–13. http://doi.org/10.3102/0013189X032001009

Collins, A. (1990). Toward a design science of education. Technical Report No. 1. Retrieved from http://eric.ed.gov/?id=ED326179

Collins, A. (1992). Toward a design science of education. In E. Scanlon & T. O'Shea (Eds.), *New directions in educational technology* (pp. 15–22). New York, NY: Springer-Verlag.

Collins, A., Joseph, D., & Bielaczyc, K. (2004). Design research: Theoretical and methodological issues. *The Journal of the Learning Sciences, 13*(1), 15–42.

Coxbill, E., Chamberlin, S. A., & Weatherford, J. (2013). Using model-eliciting activities as a tool to identify and develop mathematically creative students. *Journal for the Education of the Gifted, 36*(2), 176–197. http://doi.org/10.1177/0162353213480433

Diefes-Dux, H., Hjalmarson, M., Miller, T., & Lesh, R. (2008). Model-eliciting activities for engineering education. In J. Zawojewski, H. Diefes-Dux, & K. Bowman (Eds.), *Models and modeling in engineering education: Designing experiences for all students* (pp. 17–36). Rotterdam, The Netherlands: Sense Publishers.

Diefes-Dux, H., Hjalmarson, M., Zawojewski, J., & Bowman, K. (2006). Quantifying aluminum crystal size part 1: The model-eliciting activity. *Journal for STEM Education, 7*(1&2), 51–63.

Doerr, H. M., & English, L. D. (2003). A modeling perspective on students' mathematical reasoning about data. *Journal for Research in Mathematics Education, 34*(2), 110–136. http://doi.org/10.2307/30034902

Edelson, D. (2002). Design research: What we learn when we engage in design. *Journal of the Learning Sciences, 11*(1), 105–121.

Elliott, R., Kazemi, E., Lesseig, K., Mumme, J., Carroll, C., & Kelley-Petersen, M. (2009). Conceptualizing the work of leading mathematical tasks in professional development. *Journal of Teacher Education, 60*(4), 364–379. http://doi.org/10.1177/0022487109341150

Ertmer, P., & Simons, K. D. (2006). Jumping the PBL implementation hurdle: Supporting the efforts of K–12 teachers. *Interdisciplinary Journal of Problem-based Learning, 1*(1), 40–54.

Fontana, A., & Frey, J. H. (1998). Interviewing: The art of science. In N. K. Denzin & Y. S. Lincoln (Eds.), *Collecting and interpreting qualitative materials* (pp. 47–78). Thousand Oaks, CA: Sage Publications, Inc.

Gersten, R. (2005). Behind the scenes of an intervention research study. *Learning Disabilities Research and Practice, 20*(4), 200–212.

Gorard, S., Roberts, K., & Taylor, C. (2004). What kind of creature is a design experiment? *British Educational Research Journal, 30*(4), 577–590.

Gutstein, E. (2003). Teaching and learning mathematics for social justice in an urban, Latino school. *Journal for Research in Mathematics Education, 34*(1), 37–73.

Hjalmarson, M. A. (2003). *Designing a discussion: Teacher as designer.* Presented at the Mathematics Education Research Group of Australasia, Geelong, Australia.

Hjalmarson, M. A. (2004). *Designing presentation tools: A window into mathematics teacher practice* (Dissertation). Purdue University, West Lafayette, IN.

Hjalmarson, M. A. (2007). Engineering students designing a statistical procedure for quantifying variability. *The Journal of Mathematical Behavior, 26*(2), 178–188.

Hjalmarson, M. A., & Lesh, R. (2008). Engineering and design research: Intersections for education research and design. In A. Kelly, R. Lesh, & J. Baek (Eds.), *Handbook of design research in education: Innovations in science, technology, engineering and mathematics learning and teaching* (pp. 96–110). New York, NY: Routledge.

Jitendra, A. K. (2005). How design experiments can inform teaching and learning: Teacher-researchers as collaborators in educational research. *Learning Disabilities Research and Practice, 20*(4), 213–217.

Kelly, A. E. (2014). Design-based research in engineering education: Current state and next steps. In A. Johri & B. M. Olds (Eds.), *Cambridge handbook of engineering education research* (pp. 497–418). New York, NY: Cambridge University Press.

Lesh, R., Cramer, K., Doerr, H. M., & Zawojewski, J. (2003). Model-development sequences. In R. A. Lesh & H. M. Doerr (Eds.), *Beyond constructivism: Models and modeling perspectives on mathematics problem solving, learning, and teaching* (pp. 35–58). Mahwah, NJ: Lawrence Erlbaum Associates.

Lesh, R., & Doerr, H. M. (Eds.). (2003). *Beyond constructivism: Models and modeling perspectives on mathematics problem solving, learning, and teaching.* Mahwah, NJ: Lawrence Erlbaum Associates.

Lesh, R., Doerr, H. M., Carmona, G., & Hjalmarson, M. (2003). Beyond constructivism. *Mathematical Thinking and Learning, 5*(2–3), 211–233. http://doi.org/10.1080/10986065.2003.9680000

Lesh, R., English, L., Riggs, C., & Sevis, S. (2013). Problem solving in the primary school (K–2). *The Mathematics Enthusiast, 10*(1), 35–60.

Lesh, R., Hoover, M., Hole, B., Kelly, A., & Post, T. (2000). Principles for developing thought-revealing activities for students and teachers. In *Handbook of Research Design in Mathematics and Science Education* (pp. 591–646). Mahwah, NJ: Lawrence Erlbaum Associates.

MacNab, D. (2000). Raising standards in mathematics education: Values, vision, and TIMSS. *Journal of Mathematical Behavior, 42*(1), 61–80.

Magiera, M. (2013). Model-eliciting activities: A home run. *Mathematics Teaching in the Middle School, 18*(6), 349–355.

Magiera, M., & Zawojewski, J. S. (2011). Characterizations of social-based and self-based contexts associated with students' awareness, evaluation, and regulation of their thinking. *Journal for Research in Mathematics Education, 42*(5), 486–520.

Maher, C. A. (1988). The teacher as designer, implementer, and evaluator of children's mathematical learning environments. *Journal of Mathematical Behavior, 6*(3), 295–303.

Merriam, S. B. (2001). *Qualitative research and case study applications in education.* San Francisco, CA: Jossey-Bass.

Miles, M. B., & Huberman, A. M. (1994). *Qualitative data analysis: An expanded source-book* (2nd ed.). Thousand Oaks, CA: Sage Publications, Inc.

National Council of Teachers of Mathematics. (2000). *Principles and standards for school mathematics.* Reston, VA: National Council of Teachers of Mathematics.

National Governors Association Center for Best Practices and Council of Chief State School Officers. (2010). *Common core state standards for mathematics.* Retrieved from http://www.corestandards.org/assets/CCSSI_Math%20Standards.pdf

Oshima, J., Oshima, R., Murayama, I., Inagaki, S., Takenaka, M., Nakayama, H., & Yamaguchi, E. (2004). Design experiments in Japanese elementary science education with computer support for collaborative learning: Hypothesis testing and collaborative construction. *International Journal of Science Education, 26*(10), 1199–1221.

Patton, M. Q. (1990). *Qualitative evaluation and research methods* (2nd ed.). Newbury Park, CA: Sage Publications, Inc.

Penuel, W. R., Fishman, B. J., Cheng, B. H., & Sabelli, N. (2011). Organizing research and development at the intersection of learning, implementation, and design. *Educational Researcher, 40*(7), 331–337. http://doi.org/10.3102/0013189X11421826

Romberg, T. A. (1997). Using knowledge of children's mathematics thinking in classroom teaching: An experimental study. In E. Fennema & B. S. Nelson (Eds.), *Mathematics teachers in transition* (pp. 357–380). Mahwah, NJ: Lawrence Erlbaum Associates.

Savery, J. R. (2006). Overview of problem-based learning: Definitions and distinctions. *Interdisciplinary Journal of Problem-based Learning, 1*(1), 9–20.

Shattuck, J., & Anderson, T. (2013). Using a design-based research study to identify principles for training instructors to teach online. *International Review of Research in Open and Distance Learning, 14*(5), 1–26.

Shulman, L. (1986). Those who understand: Knowledge growth in teaching. *Educational Researcher, 15*(2), 4–14.

Simon, M. A., & Tzur, R. (1999). Explicating the teacher's perspective from the researchers' perspectives: Generating accounts of mathematics teachers' practice. *Journal for Research in Mathematics Education, 30*(3), 252–264. http://doi.org/10.2307/749835

Strauss, A. C., & Corbin, J. (1998). *Basics of qualitative research: Techniques and procedures for developing grounded theory* (2nd ed.). Thousand Oaks, CA: Sage Publications, Inc.

Swafford, J. O., Jones, G. A., Thornton, C. A., Stump, S. L., & Miller, D. R. (1999). The impact on instructional practice of a teacher change model. *Journal of Research and Development in Education, 32*(2), 69–82.

Zawojewski, J., Chamberlin, M., Hjalmarson, M., & Lewis, C. (2008). Designing design studies for professional development in mathematics education: Studying teachers' interpretive systems. In A. Kelly, R. Lesh, & J. Baek (Eds.), *Handbook of design research in education: Innovations in science, technology, engineering and mathematics learning and teaching* (pp. 219–245). New York, NY: Routledge.

Margret A. Hjalmarson is an associate professor of mathematics education in the Graduate School of Education at George Mason University. She received her BA in mathematics from Mount Holyoke College. She received her MS in mathematics and her PhD in mathematics education from Purdue University. She is currently director of the Mathematics Education Center at George Mason and has served as the academic program coordinator for the Mathematics Education Leadership programs. Her research interests include design research, mathematics teacher leadership, STEM faculty development, and engineering education.

Heidi Diefes-Dux is a professor in the School of Engineering Education at Purdue University. She received her BS and MS in food science from Cornell University and her PhD in food process engineering from the Department of Agricultural and Biological Engineering at Purdue University. She is a member of Purdue's Teaching Academy. Since 1999, she has been a faculty member within the First-Year Engineering Program, teaching and guiding the design of one of the required first-year engineering courses that engages students in open-ended problem solving and design. Her research focuses on the development, implementation, and assessment of modeling and design activities with authentic engineering contexts.

6

The Grand Challenge: Using a PBL Approach to Teach Cutting-Edge Science

Peggy A. Ertmer, Sarah Schlosser, Kari Clase, and Omolola Adedokun

Introduction

Recent data from national and international reports (e.g., National Center for Educational Statistics, 2008; National Science Board, 2008) suggest that U.S. high school students continue to perform poorly in science subjects and hold low aspirations for becoming science majors or entering science careers. Given this, numerous programs have been initiated across the country to enhance K–12 science learning and increase students' interest, motivation, and aspirations for careers in STEM (science, technology, engineering, and mathematics) fields (National Academies, 2007; National Research Council, 2012). However, despite this national push to increase STEM learning in K–12 schools, rural students still appear to be "underserved and underrepresented in the teaching of STEM" (Avery & Kassam, 2011, p. 2). Due to a number of factors (e.g., reduced state funding, outdated infrastructure, high teacher turnover), rural students often lack access to effective STEM education (Barley, 2009; Mollekopf, 2009).

Engaging Rural Students in STEM Content: The Potential of PBL

According to Avery and Kassam (2011), rural students are likely to embrace STEM subjects, majors, and careers if STEM instruction is made relevant to their daily lives as well as to the economic viability of their communities.

Because many of the grand challenges facing the world today (e.g., climate change, energy supply) have direct implications for rural life in terms of both job growth and career opportunities, it is important to engage students in efforts to address these challenges. For example, many of the rural communities in Indiana are involved in providing resources for sustainable energy through crop production and wind farm development. By examining specific sustainable energy concepts, students and teachers in these historically isolated districts can begin to understand how they can play an important role in the future economy of the state, as well as the nation as a whole. Connecting the cutting-edge research in bioscience to the core curricula for high school students can motivate student learning by demonstrating both the urgency and the significance of the needed solutions.

The challenge for STEM educators, however, is to connect these grand societal challenges to STEM content in ways that are relevant to students' *current* lives as well as effective in motivating and preparing them to tackle future challenges in STEM fields. One curricular model that holds strong potential is technology-enhanced problem-based learning (PBL), which promotes students' active construction of knowledge through engagement in meaningful problem solving (Hmelo-Silver, 2000). A PBL curriculum is organized around a series of ill-structured, authentic problems that encompass discipline-based content (Ertmer & Simons, 2006). Students learn to analyze these problems, using authentic tools of the discipline (e.g., primary source documents, graphing calculators, scientific probes), in order to identify what information they need, how to integrate facts and concepts from different disciplines and sources, and how to evaluate the strength of their proposed solutions. In addition, the curriculum is structured so as to foster group work, self-directed learning, critical thinking, and self-reflection (Hmelo-Silver & Barrows, 2006).

Technology plays a key role during the PBL process, serving as an important tool for both teachers and students (Park & Ertmer, 2008). For teachers, technology supports both the planning and implementation processes. Not only can teachers use technology to access specific background information about the issue/problem to be addressed, but they also can use it as an authentic means to introduce and engage students in the problem (Kim et al., 2011; Liu, 2002). For students, technology can increase their engagement in the problem (Liu, Horton, Olmanson, & Toprac, 2011; Zumbach, Kumpf, & Koch, 2004), as well as scaffold their efforts during the problem-solving process (e.g., through use of thinking aids such as calculators, concept-mapping tools, or computer-based scaffolds; Kim & Hannafin, 2011). In addition, technology can support students' organization and collaborative efforts, allowing them to interact with both local and distant peers and experts and providing the means to track their progress over time.

Evidence has shown that PBL is effective in helping students master both discipline-based content and higher-order thinking skills, including problem solving, critical thinking, and decision making (Glazewski & Ertmer, 2010; Mergendoller, Maxwell, & Bellisimo, 2006; Murray & Savin-Baden, 2000). Furthermore, there is evidence to suggest that PBL can help both preservice (Park & Ertmer, 2008) and inservice teachers (Derry, Siegel, Stampen, & the STEP Research Group, 2002) change their ideas about how to structure instruction in their current and future classrooms. The emphasis in PBL on student-centered learning requires teachers to explicitly confront the traditional paradigm typically used in classrooms today (Barrett, 2005; Park & Ertmer, 2008).

In addition to helping teachers confront their pedagogical beliefs (Ertmer, 2005), PBL offers an assortment of strategies and techniques that can be applied within a variety of teaching approaches. Facilitation strategies, including questioning, are examples of key components of PBL that have value across a variety of instructional settings (Bhattacharyya & Bhattacharya, 2009; Savery, 2006; Zhang, Lundeberg, McConnell, Koehler, & Edberhardt, 2010). Other examples include classroom management (Bhattacharyya & Bhattacharya, 2009; Thomas, 2000), collaboration (Hmelo-Silver, 2004), assessment (Macdonald 2005; Thomas, 2000), integration of interdisciplinary material (Hmelo-Silver, 2004), scaffolding and building on students' prior knowledge (Ertmer & Glazewski, in press; Simons & Ertmer, 2005; Thomas, 2000), and the integration of technology (Bhattacharyya & Bhattacharya, 2009; Thomas, 2000). Additionally, PBL offers ideas for fostering student reflection and metacognition (Hmelo-Silver, 2004), as well as helping students take responsibility for their own learning (Yadav, 2011). Thus, courses such as the one described in this study offer inservice and preservice teachers a vehicle for engaging their students with content and pedagogy in a collaborative, technology-enhanced environment designed to foster student learning (Bhattacharyya & Bhattacharya, 2009).

However, teachers' ability to implement PBL *effectively* is dependent on a number of factors. Chief among these are teachers' confidence for and ability to (1) assume a facilitative role (Ertmer & Glazeski, 2015; Ertmer & Simons, 2006; Hmelo-Silver & Barrows, 2006); (2) transition students into more active, accountable roles (Glazewski & Ertmer, 2010; Grant & Hill, 2006); and (3) design and implement alternative assessment measures that adequately capture growth in both student knowledge and problem-solving skills (Grant, 2011). In addition, teachers must be confident in their own STEM knowledge (Kolodner et al., 2003) and be willing to engage students in topics with which they, themselves, may have had little experience (Organization for Economic Cooperation and Development [OECD], 2009). According to Brush and Saye (2000), "successfully implementing student-centered learning requires skills and resources that are very different from those required by more traditional, teacher-centered classroom activities" (p. 80).

Research Purpose and Questions

This research was motivated by the need to improve rural STEM teachers' abilities to engage their students in global issues such as climate change and renewable energy. Although PBL methods offer a viable approach for introducing these issues in the context of meaningful problems that encompass students' subject area courses (e.g., biology, physics, chemistry, math, technology), learning outcomes ultimately are dependent on teachers' confidence for and ability to implement PBL effectively, as well as their understandings of the specific content being targeted by the PBL unit. As part of a two-week summer course that simultaneously addressed the content area of sustainable energy and a PBL approach to teaching, we examined changes in teachers' confidence for using PBL methods to teach this content in their future 6–12 grade science and math classes. Specific research questions included:

1. What is the impact of a two-week summer course on pre- and inservice teachers' knowledge and confidence for teaching specific STEM content?
2. What is the impact of a two-week summer course on teachers' confidence for using technology-enhanced PBL methods in their middle and high school classrooms?
   a. With which aspects do they feel most comfortable?
   b. With which aspects are they most concerned?
3. What is the relationship between teachers' STEM knowledge and confidence and their PBL knowledge and confidence?

Methods

We used a mixed-methods research design to examine teachers' knowledge of and confidence for implementing a STEM-based PBL unit in their high school or middle school classrooms following an integrated summer workshop focused

Table 6.1 *Data collection instruments.*

Instrument	Data Collected/Measurement	Participants	Research Question
Content Knowledge Test	Teachers' content knowledge related to sustainable energy (pre and post)	21	RQ1
Science Teaching Efficacy Beliefs Instrument (STEBI)	Teachers' content confidence (pre and post)	21	RQ1
PBL Survey	Teachers' PBL confidence and knowledge (pre and post)	18	RQ2
Workshop Daily Reflections	Teachers' changing knowledge and confidence related to both content and PBL	21	RQ2
Focus Group Interviews	Teachers' changing knowledge and confidence related to both content and PBL (post)	11	RQ1 & 2
PBL Unit (developed, in groups, in the workshop)	PBL knowledge (post)	21	RQ2

on teaching STEM content through a PBL approach. Data collection focused on the preservice and inservice teachers who participated in the workshop. For consistency, the terms *participants* or *teachers* are used to refer to this group. The term *student* is used to refer to the 6–12 grade students who will eventually participate in these PBL activities. The term *instructors* refers to both the content and PBL faculty who led the workshop. Table 6.1 summarizes the data sources used to examine teachers' knowledge, perceptions, and confidence related to both sustainable energy content and PBL methods.

Context: Conceptual Framework

This research was part of a larger NSF I-3 project, *Research Goes to School*, designed to provide cutting-edge science content to rural middle and high school STEM teachers. More specifically, the project aimed to enable teachers to transform their curricula by developing and implementing PBL units that addressed the grand challenge of sustainable energy in order to help their 6–12 grade students embrace the relevance of math and science in their daily lives. Drawing on work at Purdue's Center for Direct Catalytic Conversion of Biomass to Biofuels (C3Bio), the goal was to enable both teachers and students to explore the scientific and technological challenges related to increasing the efficiency by which biomass is converted to fuel (Agrawal, Singh, Ribiero, & Delgass, 2007). Not only did this topic have the potential to engage students in the interdisciplinary nature of research (Wyman, 2009), but it also was likely to be directly relevant to rural students, many of whom have lived or worked on farms that grew soybeans and corn.

Participants

Twenty-one teachers participated in EDCI 62700, Problem-Based Learning in the Science and Math Classroom, a two-week intensive course offered in the summer of 2011. Seven of the participants were inservice teachers (three male, four female) who at the time of the study were teaching in rural districts across the state. Thirteen were second-career preservice teachers (nine male, four female) who at the time of the study were completing their master's degrees, and who had been hired by various rural districts to begin teaching the following fall. In general, participants taught more than one subject (e.g., chemistry and physics) and more than one grade level (see Table 6.2).

Inservice teachers were selected via an application process; preservice teachers comprised the second cohort of the Woodrow Wilson Fellowship Program at Purdue University, which was designed to bring highly qualified STEM teachers into rural secondary schools. In addition, one male preservice teacher participated who, as an undergraduate sophomore, was just beginning his math and science teaching methods courses. Additional demographic details are included in Table 6.2.

Context: Summer Workshop

Participants met daily over nine days for approximately 6.5 hours each day. The primary goal of the course was to enable teachers to develop a PBL unit, relevant to their designated curricula, that revolved around issues related to the conversion of biomass to biofuels. To support teachers in these efforts, a number of activities were facilitated: teachers participated in a mini-PBL unit, listened to a variety of guest speakers (both content- and PBL-focused), and engaged in activities related to both content (field trips, lab experiments) and PBL (gallery walk, designing rubrics). A majority of the time during the second week was devoted to the development and refinement of teachers' PBL units. Participants worked in self-selected groups of three; as much as possible, groups were composed of teachers from the same discipline, although some cross-disciplinary

Table 6.2 ***Demographic details for research participants.***

Descriptions	Inservice (n = 7)	Preservice (n = 14)	Total (n = 21)
Gender			
Male	3	8	11
Female	4	6	10
Ethnicity			
White/Caucasian	7	13	20
Other	—	1	1
Years Spent Teaching in Current School			
2 years	1	N/A	1
5 years	1	N/A	1
8 years	1	N/A	1
11 years	2	N/A	2
No response	2	N/A	2
Subjects Taught in Past Year			
Biology	5	4	9
Earth science	3	2	5
Engineering	—	2	2
Chemistry	1	4	5
Mathematics	1	4	5
Physics	2	2	4
Technology	—	3	3
Other subjects	3	2	5
Grade Levels Taught			
Grade 9	4	13	17
Grade 10	5	10	15
Grade 11	7	11	18
Grade 12	7	13	20

teams were formed. In general, pre- and inservice teachers worked together, although two teams were not mixed.

The course was co-taught by a content expert and a PBL pedagogical expert, both faculty members. In addition, assistance was provided by a graduate student with expertise in both PBL and chemistry, two graduate students with expertise in STEM content areas (biology, chemistry), an undergraduate student majoring in biology education, and a middle school STEM teacher. As much as possible, the instructors modeled a PBL approach during the course and engaged teachers in the types of activities (e.g., use of a driving question, mini-lectures, ongoing formative assessment using detailed rubrics) that the teachers were expected to develop and implement in their own classrooms. Technology was integrated, when appropriate, throughout the workshop (e.g., digital probes, video, Blackboard course site), although little time was given to actually teaching *about* the technology. Teachers created their PBL units using Google Sites so they could be readily accessed and modified after the workshop.

Table 6.3 summarizes the key workshop activities. In general, each class session began by debriefing the previous day's activities and addressing any concerns raised in the teachers' reflections from the previous day. This was typically followed by a specific energy activity and/or field trip. During the first week of the workshop, teachers worked in small groups to explore different types of renewable energy, including solar, wind, and water. In the second week, the focus shifted to PBL, with a different component emphasized each day. Guest speakers (content and PBL experts) were included each day during lunch. These guest presentations were followed by a short debriefing session designed to help participants examine how they could apply the information or activities to their own units and classes. Each day also provided time for groups to work on their PBL units.

Data Collection and Analysis

To answer the knowledge component of research question 1, a 30-item, multiple choice pre-post content assessment was used. The content assessment was created and validated by the Environmental Literacy and Inquiry Working Group (Bodzin, 2011; Bodzin, Fu, & Peffer, 2012; Bodzin, Peffer, & Kulo, 2012). Initial review of the instrument by a panel of five earth and environmental scientists and science educators ensured content accuracy, alignment with benchmark ideas drawn from the *AAAS Atlas of Science Literacy Maps* (2007), and construct validity. After pilot testing, the revised instrument was validated in 2010 with 1,043 students in five middle schools in two cities in the northeast. Total score reliability (Cronbach alpha) was .776. For our purposes—measuring changes in teachers' knowledge of sustainable energy—we modified the original instrument by removing nine items that did not relate to topics covered in the course. Cronbach alpha for the modified instrument was .73 at the time of the pretest and .48 at the time of the posttest. The lower reliability measure

Table 6.3 ***Key workshop activities.***

Activity	Description
Content area speakers	Scientists described the biology, chemistry, economics, etc. involved in the C3Bio Project.
PBL speakers	K–12 teachers, currently using PBL approaches in their classrooms, shared their experiences and resources.
Energy activities/field trips	Teachers in the course participated in hands-on activities and field trips.
PBL Unit	Websites created by each group included the following PBL components: driving question, objectives and standards, student activities (e.g., investigations, grouping strategies, and scaffolds), materials and resources, implementation management plan (e.g., timeline, debriefing, questioning), evaluation plan, and materials.
Individual reflections	Teachers wrote individual explanations of how each of their unit components modeled PBL best practice.
Small group presentations	Small groups explored a specific renewable energy source and presented their findings to the class.
PBL presentations	Instructors made short presentations and facilitated activities on PBL components (e.g., gallery walk for developing driving questions, brainstorming characteristics that make a specific PBL component effective, evaluating sample facilitation, and questioning videos).
Unit presentations	Teachers presented their group units to the class, as well as invited guests, on the last day.
Technology resources	Instructors modeled various tools and resources throughout; teachers built their units using technology as an implementation tool.

at the time of the posttest could mean that the instrument was not stable, or it may have been due to our small sample size. Regardless, interpretations of teachers' content test performance should be made with caution.

The pretest was completed on the first day of the course, prior to engaging in any other course activities. The posttest was completed on the last day of the course, after the teachers had presented their final units to their peers. Sample questions included: Which of the following is *not* a renewable biofuel? [four answer choices provided]; Photovoltaic cells convert [choose one of four possible answers] directly into electricity. To compare pre-post differences on the content assessment, responses were scored as 1 (correct) or 0 (incorrect) and summed for a total score. A paired *t*-test was used to examine the statistical differences (if any) between pre-post means.

The confidence portion of our first research question was examined using the Science Teaching Efficacy Beliefs Instrument (STEBI) developed by Riggs and Enochs (1990). The STEBI was modeled after scales "designed to measure self-efficacy and outcome expectancy beliefs for teaching behaviors in general" (Gibson & Dembo, cited in Riggs & Enochs, 1990, p. 627). There are two versions of the instrument: STEBI-A for inservice teachers and STEBI-B for preservice teachers. Both versions consisted of 22 items, rated on a five-point Likert scale (1 = strongly disagree, 5 = strongly agree), with the inservice version referring to *actual* teacher practices and the preservice version referring to *intended* practices. In addition to the 22 similar items, the inservice version had an additional item ("Even teachers with teaching abilities in science/math cannot help some students learn science/math") that was not included on the preservice instrument. This study used only the 22 items that appeared on both versions. Items were divided into two subscales reflecting: (1) personal science teaching efficacy (n = 12 items; e.g., "I will continually find good ways to teach science") and (2) science teaching outcome expectancies (n = 10 items; e.g., "When the science grades of students improve, it is most often due to their teacher having found a more effective teaching approach"). The Personal Science Teaching Efficacy subscale reflects teachers' beliefs about their personal abilities to impact science learning, whereas the Science Teaching Outcome Expectancy subscale reflects teachers' beliefs about whether student learning can be influenced by effective teaching (Riggs & Enochs, 1990). Although originally developed for use with elementary teachers, the STEBI has since been used by numerous researchers to examine science teacher efficacy among high school teachers (Anderson, Dragsted, Evans, & Sorensen, 2004; Enochs, 1999; Khoury-Bowers & Simonis, 2004; Lumpe, Haney, & Czerniak, 2000).

Changes in teachers' confidence for using PBL in their classrooms were assessed using a 15-item pre-post survey that had been developed and piloted by the authors the previous summer. For the first 14 items, participants rated their levels of confidence for performing tasks in the PBL environment on a five-point scale, from 1, not at all confident, to 5, extremely confident. Alpha coefficients were .90 for both the pretest and posttest, suggesting a highly reliable instrument. The 15th item asked participants to rate their perceptions of their current knowledge of PBL on a five-point scale from 1, extremely low, to 5, extremely high. To examine changes from pre- to post-course, participants' responses were summed for a total score, and then compared using a paired *t*-test. Although the total score provided a general measure of teachers' overall confidence for using PBL, comparison of pre-post scores on individual items provided a more detailed understanding of teachers' confidence for implementing specific components of an effective PBL unit (e.g., developing a driving question, scaffolding students' inquiry).

Finally, two data sources were used to triangulate findings related to the subquestions for research question 2 (i.e., teachers' perceptions of comfort and concern for teaching biofuels content using a PBL approach): teachers' daily reflections and focus group interviews. At the end of each day's session, the teachers were asked to respond to two to six questions. Reflections included both general (e.g., What are your thoughts about PBL? Based on today's activities, what additional comments or suggestions do you have?) and specific (e.g., What are the goals of biofuels research and how are they accomplished? What did you learn about the economics of energy?) questions. As illustrated by these sample questions, participants were prompted to think about both PBL and STEM content, as well as to consider how the two could be integrated in their units (e.g., How could you use information from today's biofuels presentation in your PBL unit?). Reflections were analyzed using a simple pattern-seeking approach; that is, we looked for commonalities among responses to each question to illustrate participants' perceptions of the workshop activities and to provide recommendations for changes to future workshops.

Two 75-minute focus groups were conducted by the project's internal evaluator and another staff member at the end of the summer workshop, one for inservice teachers and one for preservice teachers. Participants (*n*'s = five preservice and six inservice teachers) were asked to provide their thoughts about the workshop, lessons learned, implementation plans, and perceived benefits and challenges to implementing the PBL biofuels unit. Each session was audiotaped and transcribed. Data were analyzed using open coding, to identify initial themes and patterns, followed by constant comparison methods (Creswell, 2009), to combine codes and create categories of similar themes. An additional researcher, not involved in the initial data analysis, reviewed the codes and themes and collaborated with the internal evaluator to reduce the data into the final categories.

Research question 3 was examined using Pearson correlations. Participants were classified as either a 1 (preservice teacher) or 0 (inservice teacher), and then the total (e.g., content knowledge) or average (e.g., PBL, STEBI surveys) scores were used for each of the variables under consideration.

Legitimation in Mixed-Methods Research

Given that our research methods involved both quantitative and qualitative methods, we examined issues of legitimation, using the framework proposed by Onweugbuzie and Teddlie (2003). According to these authors, researchers continuously strive to assess and document the legitimacy—for example, the "validity, credibility, trustworthiness, dependability, confirmability, and transferability"—of their methods and their findings (p. 354). Onweugbuzie and Teddlie noted that mixed-methods studies have increased legitimation over pure quantitative or qualitative studies because they integrate data/information from both approaches. This comparison of information across types of sources corresponds to Lincoln and Guba's (1985) description of triangulation, which included the comparison of data from different sources. In this study, we compared findings from our quantitative instruments with the patterns and themes that emerged from our qualitative data sources using a constant comparative approach (Creswell, 2009), with each being used to triangulate or check what the other indicated. In addition to the use of triangulation among different data sources, legitimation of the study was strengthened by triangulation among four different researchers.

Results

Changes in Teachers' STEM Knowledge and Confidence

Changes in STEM knowledge. Results from participants' pre- and post-knowledge tests showed an average gain, from pre- to post-workshop, of 1.8 points on a 30-item knowledge test related to sustainable energy, which was significant for the combined sample (pre- and inservice teachers) at the .02 level ($t = -2.65$). On the pretest, scores ranged from 10 to 27, with an average of 23.3. Posttest scores ranged from 21 to 30, with an average of 25.1. When analyzing the data separately for inservice and preservice teachers, the results showed significant pre-post increases for inservice but not preservice teachers (see Table 6.4). Interestingly, a one-way ANOVA of group differences in gain scores showed no statistically significant group differences ($F = 0.002$, $p > 0.05$), suggesting that both groups increased their content knowledge, even though the pre-post change was more pronounced among inservice teachers.

Table 6.4 ***Effects of workshop on teachers' biofuels knowledge.***

		Pre		Post		Gain	
Total score on content test	**N**	**M**	**SD**	**M**	**SD**	**1.8**	***t***
All participants combined	21	23.33	3.61	25.14	2.48	1.86	2.65*
Inservice teachers	7	24.71	1.80	26.57	2.07	1.86	3.65*
Preservice teachers	14	22.64	4.13	24.43	2.41	1.79	1.77

NOTE: Maximum possible score on content test = 30; * = significant at $p < .05$.

Data from the focus group interviews support the observed pre-post significant increases in content knowledge. Both pre- and inservice teachers indicated that the workshop gave them a better understanding of the concepts of sustainable energy, including the conversion of biomass to biofuels and distinctions among the fuels made from biomass. Participants also reported that they learned important facts about sustainability. However, it is important to note that sample sizes for these focus group interviews were small and thus may not be representative of all participants. A few sample comments, taken from the six inservice teachers who participated in the focus group interview, include the following:

> I learned a lot about the C3Bio at Purdue and chemistry department mainly and in particular how to convert biomass into biofuel.

> There were some very interesting, specific things about the science side of things that I picked up on that were enjoyable

> I didn't know that we were only getting 30% efficiency out of our ethanol, of our corn.... I didn't realize how much electricity we lost in the power lines. I knew it was inefficient, but I didn't know it was more than 50%.

Sample comments from the five preservice teachers who participated in the focus group interview included:

> I knew there was a number, but I didn't have it in mind, but he said by the time [you] load the biomass and drive it, say 80 miles, uh, 50 miles, you've now burned more energy trucking it than is in it.

> [Prior to this class], I didn't know the difference between biodiesel and biofuels.

Changes in STEM confidence. As reported by the authors (Goodpaster et al., 2012) in a previous paper, statistically significant pre-post increases were observed for the combined groups (inservice and preservice teachers) on the STEBI Science Teaching Outcome Expectancy (OE) subscale, but nonsignificant changes were observed on the Personal Science Teaching Efficacy (SE) subscale. ANOVA analyses revealed nonsignificant group differences (i.e., inservice vs. preservice) in gain scores for both subscales (OE: $F = 4.04$, $p = .06$; SE: $F = .11$, $p = .75$). For specific details about these results, please refer to the Goodpaster and colleagues (2012) report.

Changes in Teachers' PBL Knowledge and Confidence

Changes in PBL knowledge. A two-tailed paired *t*-test ($df = 17$) indicated a significant increase in participants' ratings of *perceptions of knowledge* of PBL ($t = 2.83$; $p = .006$) from pre- to post-course. Average ratings of knowledge increased from 3.06 to 3.83 on a five-point scale. Although separate paired sample *t*-tests revealed significant increases in pre-post perceptions of knowledge for preservice and not inservice teachers, a one-way ANOVA showed no statistically significant differences ($F = .35$, $p = .57$) in pre-post gains across groups (see Table 6.5).

Data from the post-course focus group interviews also suggest that the program enhanced participants' understanding of problem-based learning and how to implement PBL units in their classrooms. Inservice teachers indicated that they learned new teaching strategies; for example, they spoke about

Table 6.5 *Changes in teachers' knowledge and overall confidence for implementing problem-based learning.*

		Pre		Post		Gain	
	N	M	SD	M	SD	1.8	*t*
Average knowledge score							
Combined sample	18	3.06	1.11	3.83	0.71	0.78	2.83*
Inservice teachers	7	3.29	0.95	3.86	0.90	0.57	1.08
Preservice teachers	11	2.91	1.22	3.82	0.60	0.91	2.89*
Average confidence score							
Combined sample	18	2.98	0.908	4.00	0.43	1.02	7.61***
Inservice teachers	7	2.92	0.59	4.23	0.41	1.30	5.25**
Preservice teachers	11	3.02	0.64	3.85	0.39	0.83	6.29***

NOTE: * $p < .05$; ** $p < .01$; *** $p < .001$.

their excitement in using "exit tickets" to motivate their students to work and to check for comprehension at the end of class. Sample comments from the inservice teachers include:

> I've had an introduction to inquiry-based learning before, but have just had pieces and parts, and it's never been in any kind of order. This was in an order and it encompassed everything that we needed to know in order to carry out a problem-based unit. And everything to plan it and everything to finish it up, just to wrap it up and leave it [in] a neat little package. So that was very helpful.

> I think for me, the fact that we were actually immersed in problem-based learning. It wasn't something we were shown. It's just like what we are going to expect our children to do, our students to do. It was modeled for us and now that our product is just about finished, it's kind of exciting.

Preservice participants also mentioned that the program enhanced their teaching skills and provided them with practical opportunities to develop lesson units—a skill that is necessary for successful teaching careers. Sample comments from the preservice teachers include:

> I felt like [it] was good for me to practice more. I haven't done a lot of unit planning. I didn't do as much as probably they did in their student teaching. So just to have that opportunity to do it and not only do it by myself but to do it with a group of people helped me out.

> We learned, [and] we did a lot of inquiry-based stuff.

> We're all very interested in this type of program, [and] I think, especially [for] some of us with industry experience, this feels more like what we're used to. It's not necessarily what we had in school, but it is more like what we find in the workplace, and this has given us some of the skills and tools to develop this [unit].

Finally, PBL units created by the teachers suggested the ability to apply knowledge gained from the workshop to the development of their own PBL units. While some units were more complete than others, all included the primary components related to the driving question, student activities, implementation strategies, and an evaluation plan. Although we were not able to evaluate teachers' implementation of their units, the final products created by the teachers indicate sufficient knowledge of PBL to allow effective implementation.

Changes in PBL confidence. Scores on the 14 items of the PBL confidence survey were added and averaged to account for those with missing values on one or more of the items. A two-tailed paired *t*-test ($df = 17$) indicated a significant increase in participants' ratings of overall *confidence* for implementing PBL in their classrooms ($t = 7.61$, $p < .000$) from pre- to post-workshop. Average ratings of confidence increased from a mean of 2.98 ($SD = .36$) to 3.99 ($SD = .18$) for the combined sample (see Table 6.5).

Separate analyses of pre-post changes in total scores for pre- and inservice teachers also showed statistically significant gains in confidence for both groups. A one-way ANOVA examining possible group differences in average gains in confidence showed no statistically significant differences ($F = 3.34$, $p > 0.05$). This suggests that the impact of the program on PBL confidence was similar for both pre- and inservice teachers.

To explore pre-post differences further, a paired samples *t*-test was conducted to examine differences in pre-post responses to confidence ratings on individual items, as shown in Table 6.6. The results revealed statistically significant differences for all 14 items for the combined group. Post-participation confidence ratings were significantly higher than preparticipation ratings.

Confidence and Concern for Implementing Specific PBL Components

As illustrated by PBL confidence scores listed in Table 6.6, participants rated their post-confidence at the highest levels ($M = 4.00$ or greater on a five-point scale) for items related to using the internet to find PBL materials ($M = 4.61$) as well as to access state and national standards ($M = 4.89$). This indicates that the technology-embedded approach utilized in the workshop helped participants feel more confident using technology to prepare their lessons. Teachers also rated their confidence at relatively high levels for using questions to prompt higher-order thinking ($M = 4.06$) and facilitating student questioning in an ill-structured environment ($M = 4.00$). As noted by one preservice teacher in her Day 3 reflection: "Group discussion is critically important in order to link content with the 'messing about' activity. How questions are asked is also important. Let students answer rather than answering as the teachers." Another preservice teacher noted the importance of debriefing: "Debriefing

Table 6.6 ***Pre-post changes in teachers' confidence for implementing individual components of PBL.***

		Pre		Post		
Item	N	M	SD	M	SD	t
Developing problems for student-based inquiry	18	2.89	0.90	3.78	0.65	5.78***
Developing driving questions	18	2.72	0.90	3.86	0.72	6.68***
Mapping inquiry activities to unit objectives	18	2.94	0.94	3.89	0.59	4.27**
Using Internet to find PBL materials	18	3.44	1.25	4.61	0.61	4.51***
Using Internet to find state/ national standards	18	4.39	0.78	4.89	0.32	2.70*
Developing scaffolds to support students' content learning	17	2.53	0.87	3.88	0.70	5.28***
Developing scaffolds to support students' inquiry	18	2.44	0.92	3.81	0.71	5.34***
Developing scaffolds to support students' metacognition	18	2.39	0.85	3.78	0.73	5.15***
Effectively facilitating PBL discussion	18	2.72	1.07	3.78	0.65	4.04**
Using questions to prompt higher-order thinking	18	3.39	0.85	4.06	0.64	3.69**
Facilitating student questioning in ill-structured environment	18	2.61	0.92	4.00	0.77	8.44***
Providing ongoing formative feedback to students	18	3.28	0.83	3.83	0.77	2.23*
Creating rubrics to assess learning	17	3.18	0.95	3.88	0.93	3.17**
Developing/implementing alternative assessment measures	17	2.76	1.15	3.85	0.82	4.11**

NOTE: *t = T statistic; PBL = problem-based learning; * = significant at $p < .05$; ** = significant at $p < .01$; *** = significant at $p < .001$.

after a project is very important so students get a chance to reflect about what they did."

At the time of the posttest, participants showed the lowest levels of confidence (M = 3.78) on three items related to (1) developing problems for student-based inquiry, (2) developing scaffolds to support student metacognition, and (3) effectively facilitating PBL discussions. This may simply be a function of the relatively low levels of confidence participants had for these specific PBL components at the time of the pretest (*M* = 2.89, 2.39, and 2.72, respectively). Although the participants made significant gains by the end of the course, there was still room for growth.

Table 6.7 presents results of a series of ANOVA tests conducted to examine group differences in the confidence change scores (i.e., posttest minus pretest scores) for implementing individual PBL components.

Overall, inservice teachers showed greater gains in confidence for implementing the various components of PBL than preservice teachers (see Table 6.7). These differences were significant between groups on three items: (1) developing problems for student-based inquiry ($F = 4.83, p < .05$), (2) developing scaffolds to support student inquiry ($F = 4.91, p < .05$), and (3) developing scaffolds to support student metacognition ($F = 11.28, p < .01$). On all three items, the inservice teachers made greater gains than the preservice teachers. As noted by one preservice teacher in his Day 4 reflection: “It’s challenging developing activities that properly scaffold and allow students to construct their own knowledge while keeping the scope reasonable.” Another preservice teacher described being worried that “PBL won’t fly without preparing the students to do inquiry, basic lab methods, and safe practice.” A third preservice teacher expressed concern that “students need to get the content out [of the activity] and not just have fun.” It is clear from these teachers’ reflections that they were not yet completely comfortable developing a unit that would effectively support students’ learning within a PBL framework.

On three different items, preservice teachers showed a higher, but insignificant, gain than the inservice teachers. These items included (1) creating rubrics to assess learning, (2) developing and implementing alternative assessment measures, and (3) effectively facilitating PBL discussions. One inservice teacher noted the following in her Day 5 reflection: “It’s challenging creating a question that is ambiguous enough for students to form their own investigative question but focuses enough to ensure mastery of the targeted content/curriculum.”

Relationships Among Variables

In addition to teachers’ perceptions of PBL knowledge, PBL confidence, and content knowledge, we also collected pre-post data on teachers’ science teaching self-efficacy beliefs, using the STEBI instrument described earlier (Riggs & Enochs, 1990); our findings regarding pre-post changes in SE have been reported elsewhere (Goodpaster et al., 2012). For the current study, we

Table 6.7 ***Group differences in gain scores on confidence for implementing PBL components.***

	Combined		Preservice		Inservice		
Item	**M**	**SD**	**M**	**SD**	**M**	**SD**	***F***
Developing problems for student-based inquiry	0.89	0.68	0.64	0.50	1.29	0.76	4.83^{*}
Developing driving questions	1.14	0.72	0.96	0.78	1.43	0.53	1.94
Mapping inquiry activities to unit objectives	0.94	0.94	0.64	0.92	1.43	0.79	3.50
Using Internet to find PBL materials	1.17	1.10	0.91	1.22	1.57	0.79	1.61
Using Internet to find state/national standards	0.50	0.79	0.46	0.82	0.57	0.79	0.90
Developing scaffolds to support students' content learning	1.35	1.06	1.00	1.00	2.00	0.89	4.16^{+}
Developing scaffolds to support students' inquiry	1.36	1.08	0.96	1.06	2.00	0.82	4.91^{*}
Developing scaffolds to support students' metacognition	1.39	1.14	0.82	0.75	2.29	1.11	11.28^{**}
Effectively facilitating PBL discussion	1.05	1.10	1.09	1.30	1.00	0.82	0.03
Using questions to prompt higher-order thinking	0.67	0.77	0.63	0.67	0.71	0.95	0.04
Facilitating student questioning in ill-structured environment	1.39	0.70	1.18	0.60	1.71	0.76	2.75
Providing ongoing formative feedback to students	0.56	1.06	0.46	0.72	0.71	1.50	0.25
Creating rubrics to assess learning	0.71	0.92	0.82	0.60	0.50	1.38	0.45
Developing/implementing alternative assessment measures	1.09	1.09	1.14	1.14	1.00	1.10	0.06

Note: M = mean; SD = standard deviation; $^{*} = p < .05$; $^{**} = p < .01$; $^{+} = p = 0.059$; *F* = ANOVA F statistic.

conducted correlation analyses to examine relationships among participants' specific science content knowledge, their SE, perceptions of PBL knowledge, overall PBL confidence (i.e., average on all 14 PBL confidence items), and teacher classification (i.e., pre- vs. inservice teachers).

Students' classification as a preservice or inservice teacher was not significantly correlated with any of the other measures. Although one might predict that inservice teachers would have greater content knowledge and/or greater confidence for using PBL or for teaching science, that was not the case in this study. There were no significant relationships between a participant's "classification" and any of the other variables examined in this study.

At the time of the pretest, significant correlations were found between participants' ratings of their PBL confidence and their ratings of their PBL knowledge ($r = .60$; $p < .01$, see Table 6.8). In general, those who rated themselves as having greater levels of PBL knowledge also rated themselves as having higher levels of confidence for implementing PBL in their classrooms. This is not surprising, as ratings of confidence are often determined by how knowledgeable you judge yourself to be in a given domain (Schunk, 2000). Also, at the time of the pretest, a significant correlation ($r = .76$, $p < .01$) was found between PBL confidence and the STEBI Personal SE subscale (i.e., teacher's judgments of their abilities to affect student science learning). Those who felt more confident implementing PBL also rated their abilities to impact students' science learning at higher levels. This possibly suggests that, at the time of the pretest, participants judged that PBL teaching skills and science teaching skills were similar in nature, feeling relatively confident in their ability to be effective in both domains.

At the time of the posttest, there were no significant correlations among any of the variables examined (see Table 6.9). Only one variable, content knowledge,

Table 6.8 *Correlation among variables: pretest.*

Variable	Classification	PBL Confidence	PBL Knowledge	Content Knowledge	Outcome Expectancy	Personal Efficacy
Classification	1.00					
PBL Confidence	−0.08	1.00				
PBL Knowledge	0.17	0.60**	1.00			
Content Knowledge	0.28	−0.01	0.14	1.00		
Outcome Expectancy	−0.39	0.18	0.01	−0.17	1.00	
Personal Efficacy	−0.13	0.76**	0.32	0.05	0.07	1.00

Note: Classification = pre- versus inservice; * = significant at $p < .05$; ** = significant at $p < .01$.

had a strong, but nonsignificant, relationship to a participant's "classification" ($r = .42, p = .059$). In general, inservice teachers were more likely to have greater content knowledge than preservice teachers at the time of the posttest.

To get a better picture of how the participants changed over the duration of the course, we conducted an additional correlation using gain scores (see Table 6.10). There was a significant correlation between gains in teachers' ratings of PBL confidence and gains on the two subscales on the STEBI ($r = .52, p < .05$ on the Outcomes Expectancy subscale; $r = .68, p < .01$ on Personal Efficacy subscale). Participants with higher confidence for using PBL methods also tended to have higher confidence for affecting science learning and for believing that effective teaching can positively influence student science learning.

Discussion

Changes in Teachers' Content Knowledge and Confidence

Results indicated a significant gain in energy content knowledge for the combined sample of pre- and inservice teachers at the end of the workshop. Furthermore, pre-post changes were more pronounced for the inservice teachers. Some of the reasons for this result may relate to the increased teaching experience and expertise of our inservice teachers. Others have observed relationships between content knowledge and both teaching experience

Table 6.9 *Correlation among variables: posttest.*

Variable	Classification	PBL Confidence	PBL Knowledge	Content Knowledge	Outcome Expectancy	Personal Efficacy
Classification	1.00					
PBL Confidence	0.26	1.00				
PBL Knowledge	−0.05	0.22	1.00			
Content Knowledge	0.42^{+}	0.04	−0.16	1.00		
Outcome Expectancy	−0.11	0.29	0.10	0.03	1.00	
Personal Efficacy	0.10	0.24	0.14	0.26	0.16	1.00

Note: Classification = pre- versus inservice; * = significant at $p < .05$; ** = significant at $p < .01$; $^{+}$ = $p = 0.059$.

Table 6.10 *Correlation among variables: gain scores.*

Variable	Classification	PBL Confidence	PBL Knowledge	Content Knowledge	Outcome Expectancy	Personal Efficacy
Classification	1.00					
PBL Confidence	0.42	1.00				
PBL Knowledge	−0.15	0.39	1.00			
Content Knowledge	0.01	0.04	−0.11	1.00		
Outcome Expectancy	0.44	0.52*	−0.01	−0.10	−1.00	
Personal Efficacy	0.08	0.68**	0.31	0.19	0.34	1.00

NOTE: Classification = pre- versus inservice; * = significant at $p < .05$; ** = significant at $p < .01$.

and expertise, specifically within the context of biology (Gess-Newsome & Lederman, 1995; Khalick, 2006). In addition, the inservice teachers were less diverse than the preservice teachers in terms of the subjects taught the previous year (see Table 6.2), perhaps providing them with a more developed framework, or a deeper content knowledge representation, on which to build. However, as stated earlier, the results from this test must be interpreted with caution, as the sample size was small and the reliability score suggested that the instrument could be unstable. Based on the use of this instrument and demonstrated reliability from other studies (Bodzin, 2011; Bodzin, Fu, et al., 2012; Bodzin, Peffer, et al., 2012), the reliability scores obtained were more likely reflective of the small sample size.

In addition, as reported by Goodpaster and colleagues (2012), significant gains were observed in STEM confidence, as measured by the OE subscale (but not the Self-Efficacy subscale) of the STEBI (Riggs & Enochs, 1990). As stated by Bandura (1997), and discussed by Cantrell, Young, and Moore (2003), personal self-efficacy is the "belief in one's capabilities to organize and execute the courses of action required to produce given attainments, whereas outcome expectancy is a judgment of the likely consequence such performances will produce" (p. 177). Our results suggest that the teachers believed their units would produce strong learning outcomes for their students but were less convinced of their abilities to effectively teach the PBL units. It is quite possible that the two-week workshop was insufficient to produce a significant change in self-efficacy because participants did not have the opportunity to implement their units with students. Perhaps, if the STEBI were administered after classroom implementation, we would observe an impact on the self-efficacy subscale. This would support the observations of Cantrell and colleagues (2003), who found larger effect sizes in SE when participants had spent time actually "teaching science to children in an elementary classroom" (p. 188). Others have reported that variables such as gender, number of science courses taken, and positive school science experiences can impact SE (Bleicher, 2004). Since the pre- and inservice teachers were diverse, these variables may also have impacted the results we obtained.

Changes in Teachers' PBL Knowledge and Confidence

At the end of the two-week workshop, participants rated their knowledge of PBL at a significantly higher level than at the beginning of the workshop. Engaging participants in the PBL process and requiring them to apply their knowledge to the development of their own units appeared to be effective in increasing their perceived understandings of "how to do PBL." This is not surprising, as best practices in teacher professional development emphasize the importance of engaging teachers in both active and collaborative design work (Garet, Porter, Desimone, Birman, & Yoon, 2001; Koehler & Mishra, 2005). Specifically, results from a recent meta-analysis demonstrated that PBL is effective when participants engage in design problems (d = 0.74; Walker & Leary, 2009). In this study, participants engaged in the design problem of developing an authentic PBL unit for their own students. Using a similar approach, Walker and colleagues (2011) reported significant gains in teachers' PBL knowledge after participating in a professional development workshop in which they designed and later implemented PBL units.

Overall confidence for implementing PBL also increased significantly from pre- to post-workshop. However, participants' responses to individual items uncovered nuances in ratings of confidence. For example, at the time of the posttest, participants' ratings ranged from 3.78 to 4.89 on a five-point scale, suggesting that they felt more confident implementing some aspects of PBL than others. Although a lot of time was spent during the workshop helping participants learn how to facilitate student inquiry, including the development and use of specific scaffolds, it is likely that in the two-week timeframe teachers did not gain sufficient understanding to enable them to feel as confident implementing these aspects. Previously, Ertmer and Simons (2006) reported the difficulties teachers face transitioning into these types of facilitative roles. In addition, in this study, teachers did not get the opportunity to *practice* facilitating student inquiry, thereby giving them less concrete information on which to base their confidence ratings. As noted by Bandura (1997), one of the best ways to increase confidence is by engaging participants in actual mastery of the task. Unfortunately, this was not possible in the summer workshop setting.

In addition, there were noted differences between the pre- and inservice teachers on individual confidence ratings. On all but three items, the inservice teachers showed greater gains at the time of the post-survey. It is plausible that the inservice teachers' prior classroom experiences and existing pedagogical content knowledge (Shulman, 1987) enabled them to glean more from the workshop than the preservice teachers. According to Crawford (1999), "pre-service teachers typically struggle with many pedagogical issues" (p. 176). However, it is noteworthy that the workshop was able to help both groups of teachers grow in confidence regarding pedagogical skills that could be transferred to a variety of settings.

Relationships Among Variables

At the time of the posttest, a significant correlation was noted between gains in overall PBL confidence and gains on the two subscales of the STEBI (see Table 6.8), suggesting that as teachers gain confidence in one area (e.g., implementing PBL in the classroom), they also feel more confident that their students' learning will benefit from effective science teaching (OE), and that they have the *personal* ability to positively impact their students' science learning (personal efficacy). Although judgments of efficacy are commonly believed to be context-specific (Henson, 2002), Bandura (1997) argued that efficacy judgments *may* transfer between domains, especially if those domains share common characteristics. In this study, participants learned about PBL while also learning new STEM content. One of the main goals of the workshop was to simultaneously increase teachers' knowledge of both STEM and PBL so that they, in turn, could use the same methods to teach STEM content to their students. In this way, efficacy for effective STEM teaching and for using PBL may have become intertwined. That is, specifically demonstrating/modeling how to teach science and math content via PBL methods may have led to simultaneous increases in teachers' confidence for both using PBL and for teaching STEM. Confidence is known to increase by observing effective models (Schunk, 2000). Furthermore, according to Henson (2002), teachers with high efficacy/confidence tend to "experiment with methods of instruction, seek improved teaching methods, and experiment with instructional materials" (p. 128). Similar results have been reported for preservice teachers (Tribble, cited in Henson, 2002). As such, increases in teaching efficacy may correspond to increases in efficacy for using new instructional methods, including PBL.

Limitations and Suggestions for Future Research

Given the relatively small number of participants in this study, results are not readily generalizable. In order to verify these results, a larger sample is needed. In addition, our participants were all teachers assigned to teach, or currently teaching, in rural schools. It is unclear whether or how this specific teaching context impacted our findings. Comparisons with teachers assigned to urban or suburban schools would shed additional light on this question. Finally, we were unable to capture observation data to verify the extent to which teachers actually implemented their PBL units in their STEM classrooms. Gathering follow-up observation data would enhance our understanding of how the knowledge and confidence gained during the two-week workshop translated into classroom practice. Future studies are also needed to gather *student* data to verify how K–12 rural students engaged in these PBL units, as well as the impact of these units on their STEM learning and their motivation for learning future STEM content and/or pursuing STEM careers.

Implications and Conclusions

The results of this study have implications for the professional development of rural STEM teachers. Engaging pre- and inservice teachers in a professional development experience that integrates STEM content and PBL methods has the potential to simultaneously increase their knowledge of both STEM content and PBL. In addition, this approach can increase teachers' confidence for being effective science teachers. According to the Carnegie Commission on Mathematics and Science Education (CCMSE, 2009), "no school factor is more important to learning than the quality of their teachers" (p. 34). If we are to improve STEM learning for all our students, we must "increase the supply of teachers who have strong working knowledge of mathematics and science *and* the pedagogical techniques necessary to teach math and science effectively" (p. 35). Based on the results of this study, a two-week PBL/STEM-integrated workshop offers a promising method for achieving both increased content knowledge and increased understanding of effective pedagogical techniques among STEM teachers.

Traditional approaches to teaching science typically have involved learning facts about science (CCMSE, 2009), as opposed to engaging in science. However, the National Research Council (1996) has long stressed the importance of engaging learners in "inquiry into authentic questions generated from students' experiences" (pp. 32–33). In this study, participants learned new STEM content by engaging in the kind of experiences they were expected to provide for their students. This, then, increases the likelihood that they will employ similar techniques in their own classrooms (Penuel, Fishman, Yamaguchi, & Gallagher, 2007). As noted earlier, making STEM instruction relevant to rural students' lives increases the likelihood that they will pursue STEM majors and careers (Avery & Kassam, 2011). Helping teachers experience these kinds of engaging activities, themselves, is a critical first step in effecting the kind of changes recommended for the K–12 classroom. According to CCMSE (2009), students and parents give high marks to teachers who use engaging instructional practices, such as PBL. Furthermore, students who rate their science teachers highly are more likely to see math and science in their futures.

Although pre- and inservice teachers both gained STEM and PBL knowledge through the two-week workshop, there were differences among groups, suggesting that professional developers should consider their individual *and* shared needs. According to Crawford (1999), inquiry-based instruction challenges even "the most expert of teachers" (p. 175). As noted by Dexter, Anderson, and Becker (1999): "For teachers to implement any new instructional strategy, they must acquire new knowledge about it and then weave this together with the demands of the curriculum, classroom management, and existing instructional skills" (p. 223). Given that preservice teachers are novices in all aspects of classroom instruction, they are more likely to require additional mentoring and support as they implement innovative approaches in their STEM classrooms. This is not to suggest that inservice teachers will not struggle, only that they are likely to face different challenges, perhaps related to changing from traditional or comfortable approaches to those with which they are less familiar and/or confident. It is important that professional developers be prepared to support teachers' various needs in ways that are most relevant to them.

Given the severe shortage of highly qualified STEM teachers in classrooms today, as well as noted weaknesses in terms of both content and pedagogy for many career teachers in STEM fields (CCMSE, 2009), it is important to empower our future STEM teachers to make STEM learning exciting, accessible, and challenging for all students. As stated by Carnegie/Institute for Advanced Study (2011), "Tools are needed that deepen teachers' STEM knowledge and help them deliver personalized, rigorous STEM learning to all students" (p. 12). An integrated PBL/STEM approach may offer one of the best tools available at this time.

Acknowledgments

This chapter is an updated version of an article previously published in the *Interdisciplinary Journal of Problem-based Learning.* Original citation: Ertmer, P. A., Schlosser, S., Clase, K., & Adedokun, O. (2014). The grand challenge: Helping teachers learn/teach cutting-edge science via a PBL approach. *Interdisciplinary Journal of Problem-based Learning, 8*(1), 4–20.

This work was supported, in part, by the NSF Innovations through Institutional Integration Project (DUE-0963621). The contents of this chapter are the authors and do not necessarily represent the views or policies of the National Science Foundation. The authors wish to acknowledge support provided by the staff of the Discovery Learning Center, Purdue University, particularly Ms. Lisa Kirkham, project coordinator.

References

Agrawal, R., Singh, N. R., Riberio, F. H., & Delgass, W. N. (2007). Sustainable fuel for the transportation sector. *Proceedings from the National Academy of Sciences of the United States of America, 104*(12), 4828–4833.

Anderson, A., Dragsted, S., Evans, R., & Sorensen, H. (2004). The relationship between changes in teachers' self-efficacy beliefs and the science teaching environment of Danish first-year elementary teachers. *Journal of Science Teacher Education, 15*(1), 25–38.

Avery, L. M., & Kassam, K. (2011). Phronesis: Children's local rural knowledge of science and engineering. *Journal of Research in Rural Education, 26*(2), 1–18.

Bandura, A. (1997). *Self-efficacy: The exercise of control.* New York, NY: Freeman.

Barley, Z. (2009). Preparing teachers for rural appointments: Lessons from the mid-continent. *The Rural Educator, 30*(3), 10–15.

Barrett, T. (2005). Understanding problem-based learning. In T. Barrett, I. MacLabhrainn, & H. Fallon (Eds.), *Handbook of enquiry and problem based learning*. Galway: CELT.

Barrows, H. (1986). A taxonomy of problem-based learning methods. *Medical Education, 20*(6), 481–486.

Basu, S. J., & Barton, A. C. (2007). Developing a sustained interest in science. *Journal of Research in Science Teaching, 44*(3), 446–489.

Bhattacharyya, S., & Bhattacharya, K. (2009). Technology-integrated project-based approach in science education: A qualitative study of in-service teachers' learning experiences. *Electronic Journal of Science Education, 13*(3), 1–26.

Bleicher, R. (2004). Revisiting the STEBI-B: Measuring self-efficacy in preservice elementary teachers. *School Science and Mathematics, 104*(8), 383–391.

Bodzin, A. M. (2011, April). *What do eighth grade students know about energy resources?* Paper presented at the annual meeting of the National Association for Research in Science Teaching (NARST), Orlando, FL.

Bodzin, A., Fu, Q., & Peffer, T. (2012, January). *Investigating curriculum enactment with a GT-supported science curriculum on students' geospatial thinking and reasoning.* Paper presented at the annual meeting of the Association for Science Teacher Education (ASTE), Clearwater Beach, FL.

Bodzin, A., Peffer, T., & Kulo, V. (2012, January). *The impact of a geospatial technologies-integrated curriculum to promote energy literacy.* Paper presented at the annual meeting of the Association for Science Teacher Education (ASTE). Clearwater Beach, FL.

Brush, T., & Saye, J. (2000). Design, implementation, and evaluation of student-centered learning: A case study. *Educational Technology Research and Development, 48*(3), 79–100.

Cantrell, P., Young, S., & Moore, A. (2003). Factors affecting science teaching efficacy of pre-service elementary teachers. *Journal of Science Teacher Education, 14*(3), 177–192.

Carnegie Commission on Mathematics and Science Education. (2009). *Transforming mathematics and science education for citizenship and the global economy.* Carnegie Corporation of New York/Institute for Advanced Study. Retrieved from https://www.carnegie.org/media/filer_public/80/c8/80c8a7bc-c7ab-4f49-847d-1e2966f4dd97/ccny_report_2009_opportunityequation.pdf

Carnegie Corporation of New York and the Institute for Advanced Study. (2011). *Growing opportunity: A two-year update on the Opportunity Equation: Transforming mathematics and science education for citizenship and the global economy.* Retrieved from https://www.carnegie.org/media/filer_public/aa/a9/aaa9549c-34d4-49e3-9531-39b0c4980be4/ccny_report_2011_growing.pdf

Crawford, B. A. (1999). Is it realistic to expect a preservice teacher to create an inquiry-based classroom? *Journal of Science Teacher Education, 10*(3), 175–194.

Creswell, J. W. (2009). *Research design: Qualitative, quantitative, and mixed methods approaches* (3rd ed.). Thousand Oaks, CA: Sage Publications.

Derry, S. J., Siegel, M., Stampen, J., & the STEP Research Group. (2002). *The STEP system for collaborative case-based teacher education: Design, evaluation and future directions.* Proceedings of Computer Support for Collaborative Learning (CSCL) (pp. 209–216). Mahwah, NJ: Erlbaum.

Enochs, L. G., Posnanski, T., & Hagedorn, E. (1999). *Science teaching self-efficacy beliefs: Measurement, recent research, and directions for future research.* Paper presented at the National Association of Research in Science Education, Boston, MA.

Environmental Literacy and Inquiry Working Group. (2009). *The energy resources content assessment.* Retrieved from http://ei.lehigh.edu/eli/research/erca.pdf

Ertmer, P. A. (2005). Teacher pedagogical beliefs: The final frontier in our quest for technology integration? *Educational Technology Research and Development, 53*(4), 25–39.

Ertmer, P. A., & Glazewski, K. D. (2015). Essentials for PBL implementation: Fostering collaboration, transforming roles, and scaffolding learning. In A. Walker, H. Leary, C. Hmelo-Silver, & P. A. Ertmer (Eds.), *The essentials of problem-based learning: Exploring and extending the legacy of Howard S. Barrows* (pp. 89–106). West Lafayette, IN: Purdue University Press.

Ertmer, P. A., & Glazewski, K. D. (in press). Scaffolding in PBL environments: Structuring and problematizing relevant task features. In N. Dabbagh, M. Moallem, & W. Hung (Eds.), *Wiley handbook of problem-based learning.* Malden, MA: Wiley.

Garet, M., Porter, A., Desimone, L., Birman, B., & Yoon, K. (2001). What makes professional development effective? Results from a national sample of teachers. *American Educational Research Journal, 38*(4), 915–945.

Gess-Newsome, J., & Lederman, N. G. (1995). Biology teachers' perceptions of subject matter structure and its relationship to classroom practice. *Journal of Research in Science Teaching, 32*(3), 301–325.

Glazewski, K. D., & Ertmer, P. A. (2010). Fostering socio-scientific reasoning in problem-based learning: Examining teacher practice. *International Journal of Learning, 16*(12), 269–282.

Goodpaster, K., Adedokun, O., Kirkham, L., Ertmer, P., Clase, K., & Weaver, G. (2012,

March). *The impact of a professional development workshop on rural STEM teachers' self-efficacy and biofuels knowledge.* Paper presented for presentation at the annual meeting of National Science Teacher Association, Indianapolis.

Grant, M. M. (2011). Learning, beliefs, and products: Students' perspectives with project-based learning. *Interdisciplinary Journal of Problem-based Learning, 5*(2), 37–69. http://docs.lib.purdue.edu/ijpbl/vol5/iss2/6/

Grant, M. M., & Hill, J. (2006). Weighing the risks with the rewards: Implementing student-centered pedagogy within high-stakes testing. In R. Lambert & C. McCarthy (Eds.), *Understanding teacher stress in an age of accountability* (pp. 19–42). Greenwich, CT: Information Age.

Henson, R. K. (2002). From adolescent angst to adulthood: Substantive implications and measurement dilemmas in the development of teacher efficacy research. *Educational Psychologist, 37*(3), 137–150.

Hmelo-Silver, C. E. (2000). Knowledge recycling: Crisscrossing the landscape of educational psychology in a problem-based course for preservice teachers. *Journal on Excellence in College Teaching, 11*(2&3), 41–56.

Hmelo-Silver, C. E. (2004). Problem-based learning: What and how do students learn? *Educational Psychology Review, 16*(3), 235–266.

Hmelo-Silver, C. E., & Barrows, H. S. (2006). Goals and strategies of a problem-based learning facilitator. *Interdisciplinary Journal of Problem-based Learning, 1*(1), 22–40. http://docs.lib.purdue.edu/ijpbl/vol1/iss1/4/

Khalick, F. (2006). Preservice and experienced biology teachers' global and specific subject matter structures: Implications for conceptions of pedagogical content knowledge. *Eurasia Journal of Mathematics, Science and Technology Education, 2*(1) 1–29. Retrieved from http://www.ejmste.com/012006/ab1.htm

Khourey-Bowers, C., & Simonis, D. (2004). Longitudinal study of middle grades chemistry professional development: Enhancement of personal science teaching self-efficacy and outcome expectancy. *Journal of Science Teacher Education, 15*(3), 175–195.

Kim, M., & Hannafin, M. J. (2011). Scaffolding 6th graders' problem solving in technology-enhanced science classrooms: A qualitative case study. *Instructional Science, 39*(3), 255–282.

Kim, M. C., Ertmer, P. A., Fang, J., Kim, W., Tomory, A., & Freemyer, S. (2011, April). *Challenges of facilitating technology-enhanced inquiry among high school students: A multiple case study.* Paper presented at the annual convention of the American Educational Research Association (AERA), New Orleans, LA.

Koehler, M., & Mishra, P. (2005). Teachers learning technology by design. *Journal of Computing in Teacher Education, 21*(3), 94–102.

Kolodner, J. L., Camp, P. J. Crismond, D., Fasse, J. G., Holbrook, J., Puntambekar, S., & Ryan, M. (2003). Problem-based learning meets case-based reasoning in the middle school science classroom: Putting learning by design into practice. *Journal of the Learning Sciences, 12*(4), 495–547.

Liu, M. (2002). *Alien Rescue*: A problem-based hypermedia learning environment for middle school science. *Journal of Educational Technology Systems, 30*(3), 255–270.

Liu, M., Horton, L., Olmanson, J., and Toprac, P. (2011). A study of learning and motivation in a new media enriched environment for middle school science. *Educational Technology Research and Development, 59*(2), 249–265.

Lumpe, A., Haney, J., & Czerniak, C. (2000). Assessing teachers' beliefs about their science teaching context. *Journal of Research in Science Teaching, 37*(3), 275–292.

Macdonald, R. (2005). Assessment strategies for enquiry and problem-based learning. In T. Barrett, I. MacLabhrainn, & H. Fallon (Eds.), *Handbook of enquiry and problem-based learning: Irish case studies and international perspectives* (pp. 85–93). Galway: CELT.

Mergendoller, J. R., Maxwell, N., & Bellisimo, Y. (2006). The effectiveness of problem-based instruction: A comparative study of instructional methods and student characteristics. *Interdisciplinary Journal of Problem-based Learning, 1*(2), 49–69.

Mollekopf, D. (2009). Creating highly qualified teachers: Maximizing university resources to provide professional development in rural areas. *The Rural Educator, 30*(3), 28–32.

Murray, I., & Savin-Baden, M. (2000). Staff development in problem-based learning. *Teaching in Higher Education, 5*(1), 107–120.

National Academies. (2007). *Rising above the gathering storm: Energizing and employing America for a brighter economic future.* Washington, DC: Author.

National Center for Education Statistics. (2008). *Highlights from TIMSS 2007: Mathematics and science achievement of US fourth- and eighth-grade students in an international context.* Washington, DC: U.S. Department of Education. Retrieved from https://nces.ed.gov/pubs2009/2009001.pdf

National Research Council. (1996). *National science education standards.* Washington, DC: National Academies Press.

National Research Council. (2012). *A framework for K–12 science education: Practices, crosscutting concepts, and core ideas.* Washington, DC: National Academies Press.

National Science Board. (2008). *Science and engineering indicators 2008.* Retrieved from https://wayback.archive-it.org/5902/20160210152939/http://www.nsf.gov/statistics/seind08/

Onwuegbuzie, A. J., & Teddlie, C. (2003). A framework for analyzing data in mixed methods research. In A. Tashakkori & C. Teddlie (Eds.), *Handbook of mixed methods in social and behavioral research* (pp. 351–383). Thousand Oaks, CA: Sage Publications.

Organization for Economic Cooperation and Development (OECD). (2009). *Top of the class: High performers in science in PISA 2006.* Retrieved from https://eric.ed.gov/?id=ED523051

Park, S. H., & Ertmer, P. A. (2007). Impact of problem-based learning (PBL) on teachers' beliefs regarding technology use. *Journal of Research on Technology in Education, 40*(2), 247–267.

Penuel, W. R., Fishman, B. J., Yamaguchi, R., & Gallagher, L. P. (2007). What makes professional development effective? Strategies to foster curriculum implementation. *American Educational Research Journal, 44*(4), 921–958.

Riggs, I. M., & Enochs, L. G. (1990). Toward the development of an elementary teacher's science teaching efficacy belief instrument. *Science Education, 74*(6), 625–637.

Savery, J. R. (2006). Overview of problem-based learning: Definitions and distinctions. *Interdisciplinary Journal of Problem-based Learning, 1*(1), 9–20.

Schunk, D. H. (2000). *Learning theories: An educational perspective* (3rd ed.). Upper Saddle River, NJ: Merrill/Prentice Hall.

Shulman, L. S. (1986). Those who understand: Knowledge growth in teaching. *Educational Researcher, 15*(2), 4–14.

Simons, K. D., & Ertmer, P. A. (2005). Scaffolding disciplined inquiry in problem-based learning environments. *International Journal of Learning, 12*(6), 297–306.

Thomas, J. W. (2000). *A review of research on project-based learning.* San Rafael, CA: Autodesk Foundation.

Walker, A., & Leary, H. (2009). A problem based learning meta analysis: Differences across problem types, implementation types, disciplines, and assessment levels. *Interdisciplinary Journal of Problem-based Learning, 3*(1), 12–43.

Walker, A., Recker, M., Robertshaw, M. B., Osen, J., Leary, H., Ye, L., & Sellers, L. (2011). Integrating technology and problem-based learning: A mixed methods study of two teacher professional development designs. *Interdisciplinary Journal of Problem-based Learning, 5*(2), 70–94.

Wirkala, C., & Kuhn, D. (2011). Problem-based learning in K–12 education: Is it effective and how does it achieve its effects? *American Educational Research Journal, 48*(5), 1157–1186.

Wyman, P. D. (2009). The interdisciplinary study of biofuels. *Science Teacher, 76*(2), 29–34.

Yadav, A., Subedi, D., Lundeberg, M. A., & Bunting, C. F. (2011). Problem-based learning: Influence on students' learning in an electrical engineering course. *Journal of Engineering Education, 100*(2), 253–280.

Zhang, M., Lundeberg, M., McConnell, T. J., Koehler, M. J., & Edberhardt, J. (2010). Using questioning to facilitate discussion of science teaching problems in teacher professional development. *Interdisciplinary Journal of Problem-based Learning, 4*(1), 57–82.

Zumbach, J., Kumpf, D., & Koch, S. (2004). Using multimedia to enhance problem-based learning in the elementary school. *Information Technology in Childhood Education Annual, 2004*(1), 25–37.

Peggy A. Ertmer is professor emerita in the learning design and technology program area at Purdue University. Her research interests relate to technology integration, teacher beliefs, and helping students become expert instructional designers, specifically through the use of case- and problem-based learning methods. She is the founding editor of IJPBL and teaches courses to preservice and inservice STEM teachers, using a PBL approach.

Sarah Schlosser received her PhD in chemistry education from Purdue University and currently serves as an assistant professor of chemistry in the Department of Natural Science and Mathematics at Lee University in Cleveland, Tennessee. Her teaching and research interests include the use of instructional tools (e.g., demonstrations, animations, videos, and simulations) and strategies (e.g., problem-based and case-based learning) for teaching science.

Kari Clase is an associate professor in the College of Technology with a partial appointment in the Department of Agricultural and Biological Engineering at Purdue University. An expert in educational methods and approaches for biotechnology, Clase has extensive experience in bringing grand challenge research problems into the classroom to engage students in the process of research and help them learn in an authentic interdisciplinary context. Her currently funded projects include collaborators from multiple disciplines and an impact that spans K–12 to graduate education.

Omolola Adedokun is a senior extension evaluation specialist in the University of Kentucky's School of Human and Environmental Science, where she leads evaluation activities for statewide nutrition education programs. She previously served as an assessment specialist for Purdue University's Discovery Learning Research Center, where she conducted research and evaluation studies to examine the effectiveness and overall impact of STEM education programs.

7

Using Technology-Enhanced Learning Environments to Support Problem-Based Historical Inquiry in Secondary School Classrooms

John Saye and Thomas Brush

Despite a century of advocacy, problem-based inquiry is seldom practiced in social studies classrooms (Saye & SSIRC, 2013, 2015). For almost twenty years, we have investigated how we might promote and support inquiry practice in a greater number of classrooms.

In this chapter, we focus on findings from the Decision Point project, a series of design-based studies investigating how learning environments might be designed to scaffold students in meeting the challenges of problem-based historical inquiry (PBHI). We differentiate between hard scaffolding, support that may be built into the learning environment based on typical learner difficulties, and soft scaffolding, spontaneous support that a teacher provides to students as they are engaged in knowledge construction (Saye & Brush, 2002). Although this chapter gives particular attention to hard scaffolding, our findings also highlight the centrality of soft scaffolding in moving student inquiry forward. In the epilogue to this chapter, we situate the Decision Point work within our more recent research in problem-based inquiry.

Introduction

For more than two decades, researchers in science and mathematics have explored the potential of inquiry activities in which students use technology-enhanced learning environments to explore authentic, ill-structured problems (CTGV, 1992, 1993; Hmelo-Silver, 2004; Jonassen, 1997, 1999; Kolodner et al., 2003). Despite persistent arguments for problem-based inquiry in social education, few social studies or history teachers have implemented such activities (Dundis & Fehn, 1999; Shaver, 1996). Technology-enhanced social studies inquiry has been even more rare, and little research has examined the design, implementation, or effects of such a practice (Berson, Lee, & Stuckart, 2001; Saye & Brush, 2006; Zukas, 2000).

For nine years, we investigated how we might assist teachers and learners who engage in inquiry about ill-structured historical problems. This chapter describes our instructional model, reviews challenges to developing the expertise required for disciplined inquiry about historical dilemmas, and summarizes what our work suggests about the potential of interactive technologies for mitigating those challenges.

We argue that the primary role for precollegiate history study should be to promote civic competence: the ability to make informed, reasoned decisions for the public good as citizens of a diverse, democratic society in an interdependent world (NCSS, 1994). Historical study can provide perspective and habits of mind that help citizens make sound decisions about contemporary problems (Barton & Levstik, 2004; Khong, 1992; Lichtman & French, 1978; VanSledright, 2002). Our model for history study springs from a long tradition of advocacy for developing citizenship through engagement with social problems (Dewey, 1933; Engle & Ochoa, 1988; Hunt & Metcalf, 1955), and most specifically from the work of Oliver, Shaver, and Newmann (1966, 1970), who organized social studies around inquiry into persistent societal issues.

Our model is also grounded in the more general concept of authentic intellectual work that has emerged from research on improving the quality of student learning (Newmann & Associates, 1996). Authentic intellectual work requires students to: (1) use prior knowledge and rules of evidence to engage in disciplined inquiry about meaningful problems, (2) communicate their conclusions in complex ways, and (3) produce work that has value beyond school. Consistent evidence across content areas supports the effectiveness of authentic intellectual work for developing complex understanding, problem solving, and decision making (Hickey, Moore, & Pellegrino, 2001; Saye & Brush, 1999; Schneider, Krajcik, Marx, & Soloway, 2002). Research also suggests that students whose classes emphasize authentic intellectual work perform as well or better on tests of content knowledge as do students who experience more traditional instruction (e.g., Levin, Newmann, & Oliver, 1969; Newmann, Bryk, & Nagaoka, 2001; Smith & Neimi, 2001).

We apply the standards of authentic intellectual work specifically to the challenge of using history to prepare competent democratic citizens. We refer to our model for history study as PBHI. Some models of historical inquiry focus primarily on interpreting historical artifacts and constructing historical narratives. Although these acts are integral parts of the PBHI process, our end purpose is to reason about fundamental societal questions as they arise in particular historical events (Massaro, 1993; Oliver & Shaver, 1996; Saye & Brush, 2004a). For instance, we might ask "Was the Washington administration justified in the actions it took to exert national authority over states and individual citizens?" Students investigate Washington's presidency in order to form a defensible conclusion. This question represents a larger, enduring social issue: "What standards must be met to give leadership legitimate authority?" To develop a defensible answer to the question, students apply their prior knowledge, develop deep knowledge of the early Federalist era, consider alternative perspectives and solutions, and justify their conclusions with evidence. A culminating unit task requires them to communicate their ideas in complex ways to explain and persuade others to their point of view. Although learners must respect the historical context in which a specific event occurred, reasoning about the larger issue as it is instantiated in Washington's presidency can deepen student understanding about later historical instances of the issue, such as the Civil War and contemporary instances such as the Iraqi constitution process.

The PBHI Line of Inquiry

Examinations of social studies classrooms engaged in inquiry reveal the complexity and difficulty of this practice (e.g., Rossi & Pace, 1998). Theorists operating in other content areas have suggested that the qualities inherent in rich, authentic multimedia learning environments can help promote student engagement and encourage students to explore content more deeply and develop more complex views of issues (CTGV, 1992; Dwyer, 1994; Pedersen & Liu, 2003). Instructional designers have also argued that resources and support structures can be integrated into multimedia learning environments to help support more disciplined inquiry into ill-structured problems (Hannafin, Land, & Oliver, 1999; Jacobsen, Maouiri, Mishra, & Kolar, 1996; Land & Zembal-Saul, 2003; Masterman & Rogers, 2002; Reiser, 2004). Lee and Clarke (2003) examined student exploration of a historical event using rich digital archives and concluded that students are likely to flounder in such environments without a great deal of structuring support. However, recent research looking specifically at using highly structured Internet-based WebQuests to support student inquiry in history projects has reported disappointing results for student performance (Lipscomb, 2002; Milson, 2002).

We have focused our work on understanding the underlying mechanisms that facilitate PBHI and how technology and other support structures might be configured to ease the demands of this practice for students and teachers. Our studies represent a series of generative design experiments that inform problem-based curriculum development. Design experiments are "crucibles for the generation and testing of theory" that might result in the development of more robust designs over time (Cobb, Confrey, diSessa, Lehrer, & Schauble, 2003, p. 9). Unlike the controlled environment of a laboratory experiment, design experiments study a design in practice in the "multiply confounded" world of specific real-world educational settings (Brown, 1992; Collins, Joseph, & Bielaczyc, 2004). Innovative educational environments and activities are simultaneously designed, implemented, and studied. The goals of such research are both pragmatic, with the idea of progressively refining practice, and theoretical, with the view that these specific cases represent "paradigm cases of a broader class of phenomena" (Cobb et al., 2003, p. 10) to which the emerging design principles should apply.

Our work has been with fine-grained data, drawn from small samples. Although our designs prohibit broad generalizations, the evolving nature of these studies has allowed us to look closely at the challenges of implementing PBHI, to test and refine key features of our design framework, and to gain some sense of the possibilities and limitations of technology for helping mitigate obstacles to effective inquiry. After a long period of investigation, much remains that we do not know. However, we maintain with others who conduct design-based research that it is critical to do the lengthy work required for deep understanding and refinement of essential aspects of innovation before subjecting it to larger studies aimed at summative generalizations (Cobb et al., 2003; Lewis, Perry, & Murata, 2006).

We have drawn from work done in authentic intellectual achievement (e.g., Newmann & Associates, 1996), cognitive science (e.g., Bransford, Brown, & Cocking, 2000; Brown, Collins, & Duguid, 1989), instructional design (e.g., Land & Zemball-Saul, 2003), and the characteristics of inquiry-based social studies classrooms (e.g., Newmann, 1991; Rossi & Pace, 1998) to develop a set of assumptions about the criteria for establishing enabling learning environments (Figure 7.1). We then considered the potential attributes, or affordances (Kennewell, 2001; Ryder & Wilson, 1996), of interactive technologies that might

Characteristics of Thoughtful, Inquiry-Based Social Studies Classrooms

- Emphasis on in-depth study of a limited number of topics
- Knowledge is situated in authentic, holistic learning contexts
- Lesson design provides students with time to think about substantive issues
- Unit problems and tasks challenge students to connect information and construct new knowledge
- Teacher models thoughtful approaches to reasoning
- Teacher demands rigorous inquiry and provides timely support for such thinking

Figure 7.1 Characteristics of thoughtful, inquiry-based social studies classrooms.

enhance such environments. We applied selected affordances to construct technology-supported open learning environments in which complex concepts can be realistically represented, manipulated, and explored (Land, 2000).

Challenges to Development of Expertise for Disciplined PBHI

Teachers and curriculum developers face at least three interrelated challenges in assisting learners to gain the expertise necessary for genuine inquiry into historical issues. Learners must (1) become deeply engaged with the historical content, (2) build a sound model of the problem under consideration, and (3) be able to reason critically about an ethical issue from another time. Although it is tempting to view the process as a linear progression from engagement to model-building to reasoning, the relationship among these challenges is better conceptualized as complex interplay in which each element provides necessary ingredients for the development of disciplined inquiry into past problems.

Engagement With Historical Content

Developing the expertise required for disciplined inquiry into the past requires sustained, focused effort to develop a rich understanding of the historical period under study. Researchers have noted the difficulties teachers encounter in motivating students to undertake in-depth study (Onosko, 1991; Rossi, 1995). Studies of engagement suggest that learners must perceive intrinsic worth and purpose in the task if they are to make the effort required to develop deep knowledge of a subject (Newmann, Wehlange, & Lamborn, 1992). Authentic tasks that pose problems similar to the work done by people in the world beyond school may promote deeper levels of student engagement (Brown, Collins, & Duguid, 1989; Newmann & Associates, 1996; VanSickle & Hoge, 1991). However, students can develop enthusiasm for a topic and still produce superficial problem solutions. Engagement is necessary for rigorous inquiry, but it does not guarantee rigor.

Model-Building

Rigor requires that the products of inquiry address disciplinary standards for knowledge construction. Ill-structured, multilogical social problems such as those presented in the PBHI model are particularly difficult for novices (Perkins, Allen, & Hafner, 1983). To develop a defensible solution to a historical controversy, one must construct a sound model of the situation under study: the problem landscape. Novices lack the domain-specific knowledge that experts in the field use for model-building (Rossi, 1995; Voss, Greene, Post, & Penner, 1983; Wineburg, 1991a). In order to build sound models of historical problems, learners must hold certain epistemological assumptions about knowledge and history, develop the knowledge required to situate the posed dilemma within its historical context, and understand the complexities of the issue for the people living at the time.

Epistemological Assumptions

Most novices hold absolutist assumptions about knowledge (Kuhn, 1999). Reality is directly knowable, and knowledge is certain and received from authoritative sources. Novices regard historical texts as authoritative expositions of past reality and are confused by conflicting accounts (VanSledright, 2002; Wineburg, 1991b). Because historians view historical narratives as speech acts, they look beyond the written text for subtexts that allow them to "summon the world" surrounding the historical document and evaluate the arguments and evidence put forward by the author of the narrative (Holt, 1990). For novices, such an approach to texts is an "unnatural act" (Wineburg, 1999).

Before novices can engage in historical thinking, they must perceive knowledge as uncertain and constructed by the knower. Only then can they view historical texts as claims and develop the nuances of historical thinking necessary to weigh those claims.

Developing Adequate Knowledge for Historical Contextualization

As novices begin to weigh evidence for claims, they cannot lose sight of the "pastness" of a historical event. To build a sound model of the problem, they must situate the dilemma in its historical context. Accomplishing this task requires several types of domain-specific knowledge. First, novices must acquire foundational or declarative knowledge about the historical place and time. However, they cannot effectively contextualize without also developing conceptual knowledge that allows them to perceive connections beyond the surface features of the problem to more abstract conceptual structures that provide complexity and nuance to the model under construction (Chi, Glaser, & Farr, 1988). For instance, more advanced or expert thinkers considering the issues surrounding Washington's presidency might reference such relevant concepts as consent, rule of law, and implied powers. They might make connections to the French Revolution and colonial trade patterns as phenomena that help explain the motivations of various historical actors. Beyond foundational and conceptual knowledge, novices must acquire metacognitive knowledge that allows them to monitor and manage their thinking and apply prior knowledge (VanSickle & Hoge, 1991), and develop strategic knowledge that provides guidance in how to proceed in their investigation, what questions to ask of data, and what rules to apply as they source, corroborate, and contextualize evidence (VanSledright, 2002).

Perspective Recognition

As learners begin to assemble the requisite knowledge for situating an issue in its historical context, they must actively seek to understand how people of that period viewed the problem (Yeager & Foster, 2001). Although this understanding is often called historical empathy, Barton and Levstik (2004) argued that historical empathy can be more precisely conceptualized as two cultural tools: perspective recognition and caring. Empathy as caring involves concern for people in the past and is a key part of ethical reasoning about past problems.

However, disciplined use of empathy as caring is impossible without attention to the other dimension of empathy, perspective recognition. Perspective recognition requires learners to fight against presentism and imagine how people in a much different time and place perceived their world and its issues. It also requires learners to overcome the temptation to construct oversimplified models of past perspectives. They must assume that issues in the past were as complex as those of the present day and seek to understand the multiple, conflicting viewpoints about a problem that were held by historical actors (Barton & Levstik, 2004).

Learners may acquire complex understandings of the perspectives of past actors and still be "unready" to reason about past social controversy. Having abandoned absolutist epistemological assumptions, they may hold the multiplist view that since knowledge is subjective, assertions are merely opinions, and everyone has a right to an opinion. From this view, it is impossible to make judgments that value one assertion over another. Learners cannot use historical thinking to build complex, nuanced historical models and engage in PBHI if they do not hold an evaluative epistemological assumption that assertions may be compared and judged by the quality of evidence and reasoning used to support them (Kuhn, 1999). Essential to true historical thinking, evaluative assumptions are also a prerequisite for learners to be able to engage in critical reasoning about persistent ethical issues in the past or the present.

Critical Reasoning

Critical dialectical reasoning requires learners to overcome natural egocentric and ethnocentric tendencies and genuinely consider views that differ from their own before making a final judgment (Parker et al., 1989). Difficult under any circumstances, seriously entertaining multiple views of people in the past poses even greater challenges. Empathy as caring comes into play because it can provide the motivating sense of worth that stimulates the reasoning process (Newmann et al., 1992). Learners must feel enough concern for those past actors who were confronted with difficult decisions to want to understand the arguments that the various parties of the day would use to try to convince others of their position (Barton & Levstik, 2004). They must care about the consequences of societal decisions for the people of that time and place if they are to make the effort to reason through the dilemma.

Dialectical reasoning further requires that learners not rush to judgment. Learners might master and champion one authentic historical view and make a sophisticated persuasive argument for that position. However, dialectical reasoning demands that they go beyond simple advocacy to an honest consideration of competing arguments before arriving at a final position.

This complex web of challenges makes the achievement of the expertise required for PBHI complicated and difficult. Acknowledging these obstacles, our research has experimented with how we might create enabling learning environments that help learners and teachers surmount these difficulties so that they may engage in rigorous investigations of historical problems. We have given particular attention to the role that interactive technologies might play in such environments.

The Potential of Technology to Support Enabling Learning Environments

Our work has been based around design experiments with a single open learning environment (OLE): *Decision Point (DP): Civil Rights*. The *DP: Civil Rights* OLE contains more than 1,000 multimedia artifacts related to the 1950s–1960s civil rights movement. We developed a chronological and conceptual architecture for the *DP: Civil Rights* OLE that grouped 23 pivotal civil rights events conceptually around three common change strategies (legal challenges, nonviolent protest, and Black Power) and grouped source documents within each pivotal event by document type (e.g., newspaper articles, personal accounts, artifacts). Each event menu contains not only the artifacts associated with it but a timeline and an introductory essay An integrated electronic notebook provides learners with support tools to assist in gathering, organizing, analyzing, and evaluating data, and with the ability to access evidence to construct sentations (Figure 7.2).

Over the course of four design iterations, we worked with classroom teachers to develop and modify the *DP: Civil Rights* OLE and a problem-based inquiry unit that used the resources of that environment to explore the issue: "What strategies were civil rights activists justified in using to achieve social justice?" The first three *DP* iterations examined the processes and outcomes of the *DP: Civil Rights* inquiry unit in the classroom of a traditional, expository-oriented teacher. The fourth *DP* study examined similar issues in the classrooms of two teachers who already practiced some form of inquiry-based instruction. In each of the studies, we collected data from a wide variety of sources: individual dialectical student essays and persuasive and dialectical group presentations, completed student scaffolds, records of the paths of student investigations

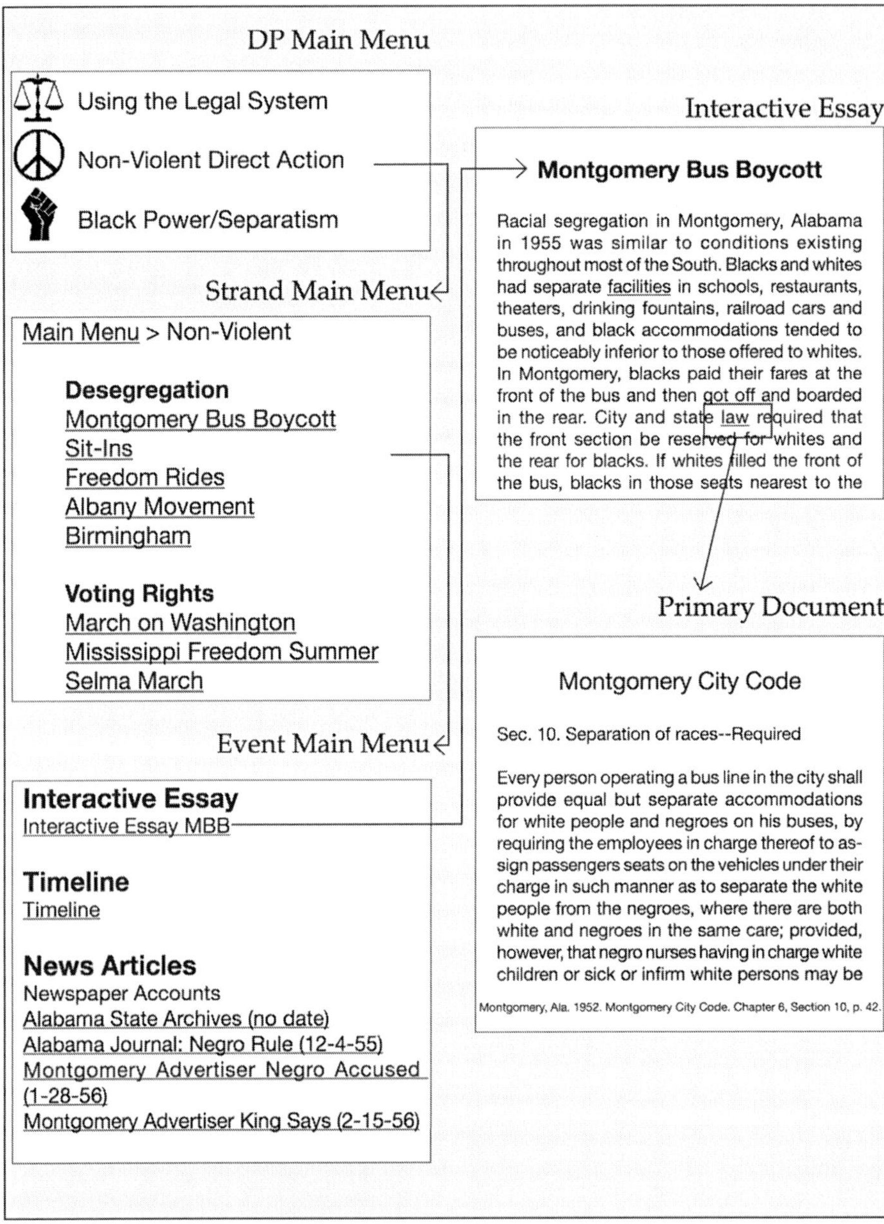

Figure 7.2 Conceptual structure of *DP* database.

through the OLE, class discussions, classroom observations, student surveys, and student and teacher interviews. Refer to Table 7.1 for a summary of the research methodologies employed in each of the four studies.

The learners who participated in the *DP* studies were diverse in gender, ethnicity, and socioeconomic status. Each classroom featured a range of learner abilities as measured by past performance and test scores (one *DP4* class was remedial and had a greater percentage of students who had struggled in the past). Although students in the more inquiry-oriented classes (*DP4*) had more prior experience with higher-order thinking challenges than those in the *DP1–DP3* classes, the *DP4* teachers stated that their students had not done assignments that were as complex or demanding as the *DP* unit. Other studies have noted that even in classes that commonly ask students to go beyond lower-order thinking tasks, learners struggle to conduct authentic inquiry (Krajcik et al., 1998). Indeed, researchers who have looked extensively at the cognitive skills required for inquiry have found that adults often do not have adequate inquiry skills (Kuhn & Dean, 2004). Anticipating the same learner deficits in the *DP* classrooms, we sought methods to help learners and teachers overcome these obstacles to reasoning.

Table 7.2 outlines the overall progression of our line of inquiry. In each iteration of the *DP* studies, we examined challenges for both students and teachers. The focus for each study emerged from the findings of our previous experiments and our speculations about how design modifications might improve results for particular problematic elements. Although we have investigated support for inquiry for both students and teachers, this report focuses on student work since our efforts in that area are most closely related to issues of technological support. We address teacher data when it is relevant to design decisions and to larger issues for which we are now developing technology-supported solutions.

Rather than describing each study individually, our discussion addresses our work holistically by examining the design hypotheses that have animated our investigations, reviewing the interventions that we have attempted and what our findings suggest about wise practice, and identifying areas for future research to illuminate those questions for which we have too little data.

In our work, we have speculated about ways that the affordances of technology might be used to address the multiple challenges to problem-based inquiry. Two broad design hypotheses have shaped our investigations of student learning in a history-based OLE:

Table 7.1 *Summary of decision point studies: methodology.*

	Decision Point 1	Decision Points 2 & 3	Decision Point 4
Participants and Setting	• 45 students in two 11th grade U.S. history classes • Traditional teacher • Same teacher for both classes • High school in small southeastern city home to a land-grant university	• 39 students in two 11th grade U.S. history classes • Traditional teacher • Same teacher for both classes • High school in small southeastern city home to a land-grant university	• 26 students in one 11th grade U.S. history class (School A) • 19 students in one 11th–12th grade remedial U.S. history class (School B) • Inquiry-oriented teachers • Different teachers for two classes • School A: High school in small southeastern city home to a land-grant university • School B: High school in a small southeastern industrial city
Data Sources	• Classroom observations • Teacher debriefings • Student and teacher interviews • Student artifacts (completed scaffolds, planning documents) • Resources accessed in DP database • Objective test • Essay test • Student group presentations • Attitudinal survey	• Classroom observations • Teacher debriefings • Student and teacher interviews • Resources accessed in DP database • Student group presentations • Student artifacts (completed scaffolds, planning documents	• Classroom observations • Teacher debriefings • Student and teacher interviews • Student group presentations
Design and Data Analysis	• Exploratory study with control group • Quantitative: Descriptive statistics, nonparametric inferential statistics • Qualitative: Analytic induction	• Design experiments • Quantitative: Descriptive statistics • Qualitative: Analytic induction	• Design experiments • Qualitative: Content analysis, analytic induction

Table 7.2 *Summary of research focus for each* Decision Point *study.*

	Decision Point 1	Decision Points 2 & 3	Decision Point 4
Summary	• Exploratory study • Traditional teacher • Control group	• Design experiments • Traditional teacher • No control groups	• Design experiments • 2 inquiry-oriented teachers • No control groups
Student Focus	• Engagement • Empathy • Model-building • Critical ethical reasoning (Saye & Brush, 1999)	• Epistemology • Model-building • Critical ethical reasoning • Support for teacher's work with students (Brush & Saye, 2000; Saye & Brush, 2002)	• Engagement • Empathy • Epistemology (Brush & Saye, 2005)
Teacher Focus	• Teacher conception of PBHI • Scaffolding teacher obstacles to PBHI • Limits to teacher scaffolding (Saye & Brush, 2004)		• Teachers' conceptions of PBHI • Teacher PBHI strategies • Factors to account for teacher differences (Saye & Brush, 2006)

1. Technological affordances allow the construction of more realistic, vivid representations of reality that encourage learner engagement and empathy.
2. Technological affordances may be used to stimulate and support the development of expertise.

Design Hypothesis: More Realistic, Vivid Representations of Reality Encourage Learner Engagement and Empathy

When we ask students to examine a world distant in time and culture from their own, they must grapple with a nuanced, ill-structured, and foreign social reality (Perkins, Allen, & Hafner, 1983; VanSledreight, 2002). The affordances of hypermedia and the Internet allow us to create more realistic representations of complex social phenomena. In the *Decision Point: Civil Rights* OLE, we situated a wide variety of multimedia artifacts within a framing historical context that allows students to explore the multiple views held by historical actors of the period (Figure 7.2). We hypothesized that by joining photographs, audio- and video-recorded personal accounts, and period television news footage with textual news accounts, personal accounts, and artifacts (in a conceptually organized, easily navigable framework), we could provide a richer sense of the time and place that would encourage both engagement and empathy.

Design Hypothesis: Technological Affordances Stimulate and Support the Development of Expertise

OLEs allow us to support learners who encounter a challenging scenario with which they have little experience. Novices in any learning domain often attend to surface features while ignoring important underlying conceptual structures necessary for comprehending the nuances of a problem. Superficial understanding often leads novices to unreflective, shallow solutions (Chi, Glasser, & Farr, 1988). With appropriate scaffolding, novices may perform at a level that more closely approximates that of an expert, for example, a historian working with a set of source documents (Parker et al., 1989; Vygotsky, 1978). In our curriculum design, we conceptualize two forms of scaffolding: soft and hard (Saye & Brush, 2002). Teachers provide soft scaffolding when they engage learners in supportive dialogue based on their diagnoses of immediate learner difficulties. Hard scaffolding, on the other hand, can be planned in advance by anticipating common learner problems. Interactive technologies allow us to embed foundational, conceptual, metacognitive, and strategic hard scaffolds into the learning environment and examine questions about their effects on the development of learner expertise (Hannafin, Land, & Oliver, 1999).

Our research proceeds from socioconstructivist assumptions that conceive of students and teachers as active agents who construct their own knowledge (Vygotsky, 1978). We do not assume that hard scaffolding in a technology-enhanced environment can substitute for effective teachers in creating an enabling context for inquiry learning. However, given the heavy demands that inquiry places on teachers (Rossi, 1995; Rossi & Pace, 1998; Saye, 1998), we wished to discover if OLEs might be joined with offline hard scaffolds and soft scaffolding to maximize the possibilities for improving historical model-building and critical ethical reasoning.

Four more specific hypotheses regarding expertise have guided our efforts in these areas. We hypothesized that technological affordances could

1. facilitate challenges to epistemological assumptions;
2. support the development of foundational, conceptual, strategic, and metacognitive knowledge;

3. support perspective recognition and empathetic caring; and
4. support the development of critical ethical reasoning.

Efforts to assist learners in solving complex, ill-structured problems will necessarily address multiple challenges simultaneously. As a result, it is often difficult to specify the effect of any single intervention. We might have chosen to change only one element in each new iteration, but practical and ethical considerations of time, opportunity, and need compelled us to make revisions that account for as many observed difficulties as possible. We may speculate on the relative effect of any single intervention feature, but the interplay of the various features of enabling learning environments are far too complex to make definitive claims in that regard.

Recognizing that model-building and critical reasoning were inextricably linked, we nonetheless conceptualized our challenge as first helping students begin to assemble a realistic problem model, and then assisting them in developing defensible problem solutions. In the *DP* study unit, students had three major tasks: (1) a collaborative investigative task that required groups to gather, analyze, and synthesize data about civil rights events; (2) a collaborative presentation that used acquired understandings to argue for a solution to the unit problem; and (3) an individual essay that used acquired understandings to reason dialectically about a problem closely related to the unit problem.

As we observed learners' progress and difficulties in successive design experiments, we continued to refocus our inquiry and enhance the learning environment in response to our evolving theories about ways to improve student performance. Table 7.3 illustrates the evolution of unit tasks with the most significant adaptations highlighted. These changes reflect an emphasis on the collaborative presentation task and reductions in problem scope. In the following sections, we describe design interventions related to specific hypotheses.

Using Historical Thinking for Model-Building

Challenges to epistemological assumptions. To weigh evidence and construct a defensible model of the past, learners must assume that the narratives they will encounter are claims from biased witnesses rather than authentic reproductions of a past reality. We hypothesized that a combination of scaffolds might challenge the absolutist epistemology typical of novice thinking. We purposefully included alternative narratives in each *DP* event but saw little evidence in *DP1* that students attended to these competing accounts. In *DP2*, we added

Table 7.3 *Evolution of* DP *unit task design.*

Task	*DP1*	*DP2*	*DP3*	*DP4*
Model-Building	• Each expert group investigates five events representing one of three featured change strategies • Data gathering/ analysis scaffolds	• Investigation task unchanged from DP1 • Revised data gathering/ analysis scaffolds	• Investigation task unchanged from DP1 • Revised data gathering/ analysis scaffolds • **Models for scaffolds provided**	• Each expert group investigates **two events that convey experiences of a particular interest group (client)** • Revised data gathering/ analysis scaffolds • Revised model scaffolds
Group Presentation	Dialectical Presentation • New decision-making teams with members from each expert group • Teams develop two alternative courses of action for addressing unit problem • Teams argue for chosen position; account for opposing arguments • Simple decision tree scaffold provided	Dialectical Presentation • Team assignment unchanged from DP1 • Team tasks unchanged from DP1 • **Argumentation storyboard and storyboard model provided**	**Persuasive Presentation** • **Expert group synthesizes findings on effectiveness of assigned strategy** • Group presents best case arguments for/ against the strategy • Group recommends continuing, abandoning, or modifying the strategy • Revised argumentation storyboard and model	Persuasive Presentation • Expert group synthesizes findings to **address a subquestion related to the unit question** • Group presents best case arguments for/ against **client position** • Group responds to opponents' arguments • Revised argumentation storyboard and model
Individual Essay	• Scaffolded essay requiring dialectical argument	• Not analyzed	• Not analyzed	• Not analyzed

Note **Bolded text** highlights key design changes from previous iterations.

hyperlinks in introductory event essays to direct students' attention explicitly to these conflicting perspectives. As student groups constructed presentations of their solutions to the unit problem, we provided an argumentation storyboard scaffold that guided learners toward an examination of conflicting arguments, as well as a model presentation that reflected that process.

Development of foundational, conceptual, strategic, and metacognitive knowledge. The chronological and conceptual architecture of the *DP: Civil Rights* OLE (Figure 7.2) directly addressed the deficits in foundational and conceptual knowledge that prevent learners from situating evidence in its historical context and weighing claims using disciplinary standards. We anticipated that the organizational structure of the OLE would assist students by providing a supporting framework that situated the mass of civil rights artifacts in their historical contexts and directed learners' attention to more subtle dimensions of the problem.

However, to acquire the foundational and conceptual understandings needed for model-building, learners must also know how to organize their investigations, evaluate data, and synthesize their results. Strategic knowledge directs learners in how they should proceed and what questions they should ask of data. Metacognitive knowledge helps them know when to ask those questions, when to apply prior knowledge, and how to assess and adjust the effectiveness of their strategies. We hypothesized that providing data gathering and data analysis scaffolds would assist learners in organizing their investigations and asking questions of evidence in a more expert manner. A hyperlink utility allowed students to link database documents directly to their scaffolds. We also provided a metacognitive "journal" scaffold that investigative groups were to complete at the end of each day to reflect on the progress of their investigations.

Despite the supporting structure of the *DP* OLE, students in *DP1* often seemed overwhelmed by the volume of available data and were unsure how to move forward in their investigations or to which data they should most closely attend. Students used scaffolds superficially and sometimes not at all (Brush & Saye, 2001; Saye & Brush, 1999, 2002). Those problems notwithstanding, *DP1* student essays demonstrated a greater ability to situate factual knowledge in meaningful contexts than those of peers who studied the unit without the OLE. *DP1* essay scores were also superior to the control group in the use of evidence to make persuasive and dialectical arguments (albeit aggregate reasoning scores for the class were not at the level required for competent citizenship). However, culminating group presentations were extremely shallow and demonstrated little nuanced understanding of events or use of historical evidence to substantiate claims (Saye & Brush, 1999). Believing that the ability to reason together to arrive at workable problem solutions was a critical need in a democratic society, we chose to concentrate our efforts in succeeding iterations on adjustments to the learning environment that might improve collaborative presentations.

Findings from the first two iterations led us to hypothesize that the original problem landscape was too large for effective student model-building and critical reasoning. We made progressive efforts to limit the problem scope by modifying and shrinking the investigative task and by focusing the culminating group presentation on a smaller data set and a more limited problem (Table 7.2). In *DP1* and *DP2*, we had used a jigsaw strategy in which students were assigned to expert investigatory teams that gathered data related to one of the three principal change strategies. The students then joined experts who had investigated other change strategies to form new decision-making groups. The new groups synthesized their findings and developed dialectical presentations. Since we were disappointed in the quality of these syntheses and problem solutions, in *DP3* we kept students in expert groups throughout the project and asked them to synthesize data and construct presentations that assessed the merits of a single change strategy. Although groups were expected to acknowledge and respond to the arguments of opponents, their presentations were to be primarily empathetic and persuasive rather than dialectical. In *DP4*, we limited the focus of investigation and argumentation even further by having expert groups investigate a smaller number of events within a given change strategy and make persuasive presentations that focused on a problem that represented only one aspect of the larger unit problem. For instance, rather than synthesizing data from the experience of a range of 1960s groups to answer the question "What strategies were civil rights activists justified in using to achieve social justice?," groups representing the federal government and the Mississippi Freedom Democratic Party addressed a more limited question: "What is the proper response of federal authorities to the events of the civil rights movement?"

We also searched for ways that hypermedia and improved scaffolding might be used to target specific learner needs for knowledge development. We hypothesized that embedded hypermedia links could help learners make connections from source documents to related foundational knowledge and abstract conceptual principles. From *DP2* forward, we embedded hyperlinks within introductory event essays as sense-making tools that placed discrete documents within the sort of framing conceptual schema that a historian might possess. We further speculated that perhaps students underused scaffolding because they did not appreciate the complexity of the task or understand how a scaffold might be helpful (Land, 2000). In succeeding iterations, we made scaffolding more explicit. In *DP2*, we added exemplary models of completed argumentation storyboard scaffolds (Figure 7.3) and did the same for data gathering and analysis scaffolds in *DP3*. We asked teachers to give explicit attention to those models. Unlike the more global metacognitive support provided earlier by the student journal scaffold, we hoped that modeling work with documents in one event would give students insight into how they should employ specific metacognitive processes to interpret text and subtext, and corroborate the accounts that they encountered in their own investigations.

Perspective recognition and empathetic caring. Strategic and metacognitive knowledge are integral to the process of perspective recognition. As learners attempt to make sense of new data and fit it into their emerging problem model, they must make a conscious effort to understand how the data and the larger event were viewed from diverse perspectives of that time. Only when they have made this effort can learners responsibly employ empathetic caring to reason through a historical dilemma.

We hypothesized that a number of design elements already discussed would support the development of complex perspective recognition and a sense of empathetic care: realistic representations of the past, alternative narratives, directing hyperlinks to alternative perspectives, and explicit modeling and scaffolding of persuasive and dialectical reasoning in considering problem solutions.

Critical Ethical Reasoning

Once learners construct a sound model of a historical situation, a final challenge remains for critical reasoning: using constructed understandings to genuinely consider alternative arguments before taking and defending a position. Culminating unit tasks examined students' abilities to reason collaboratively and individually. We hypothesized that we could improve dialectical reasoning—the genuine juxtaposition and interrogation of conflicting arguments prior to making a decision—through explicit modeling and step-by-step strategic scaffolding of the dialectical process. We provided such scaffolding in both individual dialectical essay assignments and in the argumentation storyboards that student groups completed in preparation for presentations of their positions on the unit question. An interactive presentation tool provided the same support format as the storyboard template and facilitated locating and incorporating

Presentation Storyboard: Screen 3

Support for Claims

[May use more than one screen]

Text Showing on the Screen:

A Danger to Community Order

- Boycott increases tension and intolerance among the races
- Incidents of gunshots taken at four buses
- Bombings at homes of several boycott leaders
- Revival of Ku Klux Klan activity

List of Supporting Media

MFS-ART D: Klan Ledger

Script for This Screen:

1. The boycott endangers the peace of the community
   - Tension and intolerance have increased among the races
     - Incidents of gunshots taken at four buses
     - Bombings at homes of several boycott leaders including Dr. King
     - Revival of Ku Klux Klan activity
       - Driving through black neighborhoods in robes shouting/ blowing horns
       - Mass rally in Montgomery

Figure 7.3 Sample page from model argumentation storyboard.

multimedia evidence from the DP database. As discussed previously, based on our observations of students' struggles to develop nuanced problem solutions or to demonstrate deep dialectical reasoning, we reduced the scope of the problem and the presentation task and investigated whether we might elicit persuasive, empathetic reasoning and an incipient level of dialectical reasoning that presented a fair account of opposing views.

Findings

The development of the expertise necessary for PBHI is such a complex, interrelated process that it is difficult to isolate the effects of technological or other hard scaffolding interventions from the support efforts made by teachers. However, our first three unit implementations (*DP1–3*) occurred in a traditional classroom where the teacher provided minimal levels of soft scaffolding. We hoped that growing familiarity with PBHI and our continued encouragement and support would lead our study teacher to provide greater levels of soft scaffolding over time, but she remained reluctant to do so (Saye & Brush, 2004b). Although not an intentional part of our design, her continued reluctance allowed us to examine the effects of hard scaffolding when little soft scaffolding was present. Convinced after three iterations that it would be difficult for students to develop meaningful expertise without substantial soft scaffolding, we shifted our experiments to other classrooms where that vital element was present (*DP4*). The evolution of other design elements complicates comparisons based on the level of soft scaffolding; however, some observed differences raise useful speculations for future design work. Additionally, the consistency of some findings across all cases regardless of the soft scaffolding condition or, in some cases, the existence of comparative data across groups with the same teacher allows us to make other assertions in which we have reasonable confidence.

Table 7.4 summarizes the interventions we made in response to our hypotheses and the key assertions that we draw from our work. Although we gathered a variety of data, student performances on culminating unit products provide the most comprehensive indicators of how our design interventions may have affected learners' abilities to employ sound models to develop evidence-based problem solutions. Interim products such as completed scaffolds, field notes, and videotape documenting classroom sessions offer insight into why students may have improved or continued to struggle. Taken as a whole, our findings suggest considerable promise for using technological affordances to engage learners, encourage empathy, and challenge epistemological assumptions. However, findings for improving deep knowledge development and critical reasoning are more mixed. We begin with those findings in which we feel most confident, and then move to areas for which the data is suggestive but more limited.

Consistent evidence across all studies indicates that experiences with the *DP* unit increased student engagement and empathy (Brush & Saye, 2005; Saye & Brush, 1999, 2002). Authenticity of tasks and deliberate support for active learning appear to be key factors, but, as hypothesized, the realism of the OLE also seems to have played a critical role.

Engagement

In all *DP* studies, the vast majority of students remained on task for lengthy periods of time each day, often talking animatedly about their work. In classes where teachers created opportunities for genuine discussion (*DP4*), students often took ownership of classroom dialogue, persisted in discussions after the teacher was ready to move on, and actively raised questions about peers' interpretations of artifacts and events. Teachers in all studies remarked that the levels of student involvement were unusually high. For instance, one teacher described the differences he observed in two students:

> One ... student was not very motivated in the past, didn't have a lot of skills, didn't exhibit a great interest for school at all, but really took this project and ran with it. He just loved it. He showed that genuine interest and was doing his work without having to have any prompting by me, which was unusual. And [in] the Black Panther group, [another] student, he would sleep, show up late, ... chronic absenteeism, but he was there every day. Their presentation was one that I wasn't expecting to be outstanding, and it really was. (*DP4*)

Typical of many comments we encountered, a student linked the realism of the *DP* OLE to his heightened interest: "You really felt like you were there ... in that time when you could really see in actuality, like, what happened instead of just hearing it from someone else" (*DP2*). Another student explained, "It was more realistic because you could actually see, like, the people talking about it ... and see the newspaper reports where somebody actually wrote it down, rather than just have a textbook saying this happened and that happened" (*DP1*).

Table 7.4 *Summary of design interventions and results.*

Hypothesis	Decision Point 1	Decision Points 2 & 3
More realistic representations of reality encourage engagement and empathy	• Realistic, multimedia representations (*DP1*)	• OLEs can promote: • Greater learner engagement • Greater empathetic caring
Affordances facilitate challenges to epistemological assumptions	• Alternative narratives in source documents (*DP1*) • Essay hyperlinks to alternative perspectives (*DP2*) • Presentation argumentation scaffolds (*DP2–DP4*) • Presentation models (*DP2–DP4*)	• Affordances can stimulate consideration of tentative, interpretive nature of history; recognition of alternative narratives
Historical contextualization: Affordances support development of foundational and conceptual knowledge	• Conceptual OLE architecture (*DP1*) • Hyperlinks in introductory essays (*DP2*)	• Expansive OLE problem landscapes inhibit model-building • Conceptual design assists contextualization of factual knowledge • Hypermedia affordances improve ability to contextualize source documents • OLE affordances not sufficient to develop nuanced problem models
Historical contextualization: Affordances support development of strategic and metacognitive knowledge	• Hyperlinked data gathering and analysis scaffolds (*DP1–DP4*) • Exemplary models for scaffolds (*DP3*) • Dialectical essay scaffold (*DP1*)	• Guiding scaffolds may be ineffective without sufficient modeling • Hard scaffolds with models can improve data gathering; support for high-level conceptual tasks is more problematic

Continued

Table 7.4 *Continued.*

Hypothesis	Decision Point 1	Decision Points 2 & 3
Historical contextualization: Affordances support development of strategic and metacognitive knowledge (*continued*)	• Presentation argumentation scaffolds (*DP2–DP4*) • Presentation models (*DP2–DP4*)	• Hard scaffolds with models can assist strategic decisions; support for metacognition is more problematic
Affordances support perspective recognition and empathetic caring	• Realistic, multimedia representations (*DP1*) • Alternative narratives in source documents (*DP1*) • Essay hyperlinks to alternative perspectives (*DP2*) • Dialectical essay scaffold (*DP1*) • Presentation argumentation scaffolds (*DP2–DP4*) • Presentation models (*DP2–DP4*)	• Affordances can support improved understanding of a past perspective • Affordances can stimulate greater empathetic caring
Affordances support the development of critical ethical reasoning	• Same as for perspective recognition • Interactive presentation tool (*DP1*)	• OLEs and hard scaffolding can support improved persuasive and dialectical reasoning but may be limited in ability to promote deep consideration of alternative views

Empathy

Evidence also consistently suggested that the realism of the OLE and the directed support for discovering and understanding past perspectives facilitated the imaginative act of perspective recognition and stimulated a sense of empathetic care for historical individuals and their dilemmas.

For instance, as students explored the varied resources of the *DP* OLE, one student explained:

> I could imagine it better.... We had more of a picture of what people were like ... like, there was a video of [George] Wallace; just the accent ... the attitude, everything combined gives you an idea of what they were like back then, and you wouldn't really know all about that just reading a book.... We knew about it before, but when you hear it and when you, like, see it, it just kind of takes you there.... You don't [usually] really get to put yourself into history, you know; it's just kind of like facts, and you're just instilling them. (*DP1*)

A classmate commented that his experiences with the *DP* materials were "more like on a personal level.... You got into how somebody felt about this, or, you know, what they did and how strongly they felt about it. Because sometimes books don't actually convey that to you."

Evidence from later *DP* implementations illustrates the critical linkage between empathy and the advancement of critical reasoning. Findings suggest that modeling an empathetic historical argument and providing explicit scaffolding for the elements to be considered in constructing a persuasive argument promoted improved argumentation from a particular historical perspective (Brush & Saye, 2005; Saye & Brush, 2002). Although understandings of the perspectives of past actors were never as nuanced or complex as we would have hoped, the best group presentations from the perspective of an assigned historical client authentically reflected the views of that client (*DP4*).

In the *DP4* study, the translation from perspective recognition to empathetic care was suggested by the fact that some groups maintained their assigned perspectives throughout post-presentation discussions even though they were free to voice their own opinions. The most striking evidence in this regard was the strenuous advocacy of the black separatists' position by middle-class white students who persisted in arguing passionately for a perspective that might be expected to be very different from their own experience and views (Brush & Saye, 2005).

Epistemology

Findings suggest that learner engagement with alternative perspectives also stimulated movement toward more complex epistemological assumptions about knowledge and history. We found consistent evidence that that intentional juxtaposition of competing accounts in a realistic multimedia environment may prompt students to consider the tentative, interpretive nature of historical claims. For instance, one student commented:

> Just to see different people's viewpoints on one subject, I mean, you have probably twelve different viewpoints, you know, these links, on one subject, so you could get, you know, a segregationist's point of view, you know, from different people, which is interesting, which is always good when you're doing a project, like we did, where we have to persuade the audience in one case or another. It's really helpful to have different viewpoints to look at and to choose from so you can get kind of an overview of the opposing sides and what they thought ... I thought that made it a lot easier to make your own opinion, from looking at others opinions. (*DP4*)

A student in an earlier *DP* study expressed similar insights:

> You saw what the press saw and what everyone else in the world saw about it at the time, you know, and see what you think about it. Even though you can't always, you know, tell if it's true ... you just kind of got to see that story from all different sides ... cause usually we just go by the side that's in the book. (*DP2*)

Ironically, the realism of rich multimedia may also complicate efforts to encourage more evaluative epistemological views. In some cases, authentic multimedia such as photographs and period news footage seemed to lead students to believe that they understood "what exactly was going on"—suggestive of an absolutist epistemology. In other cases, students seemed to have become more sensitive to varying perspectives regarding events but reached the multiplist epistemological conclusion that all claims must be given equal warrant.

However, even if students develop an awareness of the existence of alternative interpretations and a belief that standards exist for weighing the merits of those claims, they still may not be ready to weigh competing views prior to coming to a judgment. Before they can fairly weigh accounts, learners must build a sound problem model that allows them to grasp and interpret those views within the complex fabric of their time and place. Despite evidence that learners had increased levels of empathy and some had developed more complex epistemologies, important deficits in student-constructed problem models continued to inhibit rigorous critical reasoning.

Knowledge Construction and Critical Reasoning

Student performances suggest mixed results for improving learner abilities to gather and contextualize data and reason critically about historical problems. Results over time supported our early hypothesis that expansive problem landscapes inhibit students' abilities to construct acceptable models of an ill-structured problem. They also reinforced our entering assumption that OLE affordances without accompanying soft scaffolding are not sufficient for developing successful model-building or critical reasoning. As we progressively limited the problem scope (*DP3* and *DP4*), student performances on culminating presentations became more authentic and less school-like, and demonstrated more cohesive narratives. As we moved from a condition in which students received minimal soft scaffolding (*DP1–3*) to substantial teacher support (*DP4*), presentations improved to reflect more genuine understandings of the perspectives of historical actors (see Table 7.2).

Data analysis suggests that the affordances of the OLE assisted in improved data gathering and in guiding students to construct more integrated argumentation narratives. Even with minimal soft scaffolding, *DP1* students were able to access and contextualize factual knowledge in written essays at a deeper level than peers who studied the unit without the OLE (Saye & Brush, 1999). In *DP2*, student groups with minimal soft scaffolding but with access to hyperlinked introductory *DP* event essays performed better on culminating presentations than groups who had encountered those essays without hyperlinks. Interviews suggested that the addition of contextual hyperlinks in the *DP* database assisted students in making relational connections between source documents and the events surrounding them. This improved performance notwithstanding, constructed narratives failed to demonstrate nuanced understandings of the problem landscape (Saye & Brush, 2002).

Evidence also suggests that the guidance provided by strategic and metacognitive hard scaffolds may improve some aspects of model-building but have less effect in other areas. Moreover, our findings suggest that hard scaffolding is unlikely to succeed in any instance unless students are provided with exemplary models of completed work that help them understand how that support might be employed to improve historical thinking. Students reported that models helped them understand the investigative task, and their work reflected improved depth in data gathering. Modeling also seemed to improve student understanding and application of strategies for approaching the investigation and for constructing cohesive arguments that referenced some historical evidence (Brush & Saye, 2005; Saye & Brush, 2002). However, even with modeling, hard scaffolds did not appear to assist greatly with higher-level conceptual tasks such as synthesizing evidence and finding patterns in data. Hard scaffolds also appeared much less successful in helping students perform either global metacognitive tasks such as monitoring their progress or more specific metacognitive tasks such as corroborating accounts and noting discrepancies in evidence (Brush & Saye, 2001; Saye & Brush, 2002, 2006). The student journal scaffold, designed to help students monitor their progress, was ineffective. Most students either ignored the journal or entered very superficial, unreflective information such as "Our group is working well together" (Brush & Saye, 2001). Our attempts to demonstrate more specific metacognitive thinking with models of completed scaffolds did not seem to transfer when students attempted to do the same work with their own document sets.

With the most severe restriction of the problem landscape and the addition of substantial soft scaffolding (*DP4*), most groups demonstrated better abilities to represent the views of an assigned historical perspective than had been typical of previous iterations. In our discussion of empathy, we referred to a best-case presentation by a group representing black separatists. This performance illustrates unmet challenges in helping students build robust models. Although the group's persuasive argument for their client indicated that they had developed considerable understanding of the experiences and motivations of that historical group, they had difficulty recognizing and accounting for the motivations of competing perspectives that they had encountered in their investigations but not studied as intensively. They also struggled to make connections beyond the surface features of the separatist case to influential events such as Mississippi Freedom Summer and more abstract concepts such as internal colonization and alternative power structures that underlay the separatist arguments. These gaps in their model of the 1960s civil rights landscape limited their ability to consider the intricacies of their own group's position, give a fair hearing to competing arguments, and develop a nuanced problem solution.

In summary, our work suggests that when reasoning challenges are limited in scope, OLEs can be paired with other scaffolding to help students improve in persuasive argumentation from a past perspective. Although later iterations of the *DP* presentation task did not call for true dialectical argumentation, earlier studies suggest some promise in encouraging students to consider competing views (Saye & Brush, 1999, 2002). However, if students have not developed models that provide reasonably deep understandings of those views and the events and ideas that shaped them, their reasoning will remain superficial. Supporting robust model-building remains the critical unresolved issue for our project. Can we help students develop adequate models so that they can grasp competing views at a reasonable level of complexity? Until students have this depth of understanding, it is not possible to gauge the degree to which they are able to genuinely suspend judgment and give serious consideration to multiple views before arriving at their own decision. Students may have the disposition to reason dialectically but have too little knowledge with which to reason rigorously.

Soft scaffolding is critical to any attempts to meet this challenge. We are not surprised that hard scaffolding has proven more successful at supporting strategic thinking than conceptual and metacognitive thinking. Although curriculum designers can examine expert thinking and develop general strategic models for approaching a problem, the ill-structured nature of social problems invites multilogical reasoning paths and raises varied conceptual challenges for diverse individuals that cannot be predicted in advance. Skilled teachers must diagnose and address those difficulties as they arise.

Our work has caused us to question the generally accepted practice of gradually "fading" or withdrawing the support offered to learners. Advocates of cognitive apprenticeship assume that over time scaffolding and questioning will develop sufficient expertise so that learners can operate independently of support and that such independence is critical to genuine learning (Brown et al., 1989; Pea, 2004). However, our observations of teachers engaged in soft scaffolding suggest the complexity of that support and raise questions of whether most adolescents will ever reach a level of expertise that allows them to independently address ill-structured social problems. In one instance, a teacher spent four minutes in an intense interchange with a single student to help her consider the subtext behind the production of a single, brief source document. He hoped that this investment would allow the student to do such sourcing independently with other artifacts, but the degree of questioning required to produce a satisfactory analysis in this instance caused us to wonder when the student would be ready for such independent metacognition. Even with such intensive scaffolding, *DP4* presentations were often inadequate. Both study teachers invested considerable time after each group presentation in leading the class to perceive conceptual and cause-effect connections. That expert questioning seemed indispensable in prodding students to think more deeply about the meaning of events and to link work done by each group with work done by others so that students might develop a broader sense of how individual events fit within the larger historical context of the civil rights movement (Saye & Brush, 2006).

At least one other group of researchers has recently posited that we should rethink the notion of fading scaffolds over time—particularly hard scaffolds that are embedded within a learning environment. Sherin, Reiser, and Edelson (2004) argued that hard scaffolds are designed to provide learners with support for tasks that have already been determined to be difficult for learners to accomplish independently and that we should not always anticipate that this support will be withdrawn. Our observations of student needs revealed in soft scaffolding exchanges lead us to conclude that the fading of some soft scaffolding may be equally unlikely.

Conclusion

Our work corroborates findings by other investigators that students may be able to gather data from source documents but have difficulty synthesizing that data to create well-reasoned narratives or arguments (Barton & Levstik, 2004; Lee & Ashby, 2000; VanSledreight, 2002). Barton and Levstik (2004) hypothesized that projects such as ours—situating evidence gathering within authentic tasks that seek to answer meaningful questions—would improve student performance in narrative construction. We believe that our limited successes in this endeavor may be due in part to the problem of bounded rationality (Shulman & Carey, 1984; Simon, 1982). Even with meaningful encounters and multiple layers of support, students may have difficulty in holding complex, competing perspectives and numerous conceptual connections in their heads so that they are available for constructing the sort of complex models needed for rigorous problem solving.

This belief does not imply surrender. Rather, it argues for looking more deeply at those areas that do make a difference to discover how far we can push the boundaries of competent problem solving and reasoning for adolescents. The results of our design experiments lead us to two overarching recommendations for future design work.

Emphasizing the developmental nature of complex thinking, Kuhn (2005) concluded that engaging learners in small, fairly simple investigations whose primary purpose is to uncover the inquiry process can best promote inquiry competence. Rather than direct instruction in the rules of inquiry, students are guided in the practice of it so that they can discover its power and worth. Similarly, our investigations have led us to believe that more tightly bounded problems are necessary to produce optimal improvement in student performances. We created the expansive *DP: Civil Rights* OLE in the hope that students could follow their curiosity to construct knowledge about their own questions as they arose as part of their investigations. However, we must balance this potential against the disorientation and superficiality that such an embarrassment of riches seemed to engender. We are currently developing much smaller problem landscapes with much more tightly defined sets of source documents. Smaller document sets will allow us to attend more closely to student conceptual and metacognitive needs by embedding supporting information and questions directly into the documents, a level of support that was impractical in the more open-ended *DP* event investigations.

For instance, as Figure 7.4 illustrates, students exploring first encounters between Christopher Columbus and the Taino Indians might be assisted in interpreting Columbus's journal through metacognitive cues that prompt them to compare accounts over time and ask questions about the subtext that may help explain changing behaviors among the Taino. We anticipate that this support would be needed on a long-term basis. Although most inquiry advocates would likely endorse this degree of support as students are introduced to the idea of interpreting source documents, many would worry that the continued availability of this level of scaffolding would not allow students to gain ownership of the process. This may be so, but we have doubts that most adolescents in most classrooms will be ready—or will be provided adequate time—to do this work at a level that will allow them to build robust problem models. Class time is limited, and we should be clear about priorities. Making meaning from source documents is important. However, our central mission remains to encourage critical reasoning about essential societal questions. By reducing the learners' cognitive load for constructing problem models, students may not only have more complete information for reasoning but more time and energy to devote to reasoning tasks.

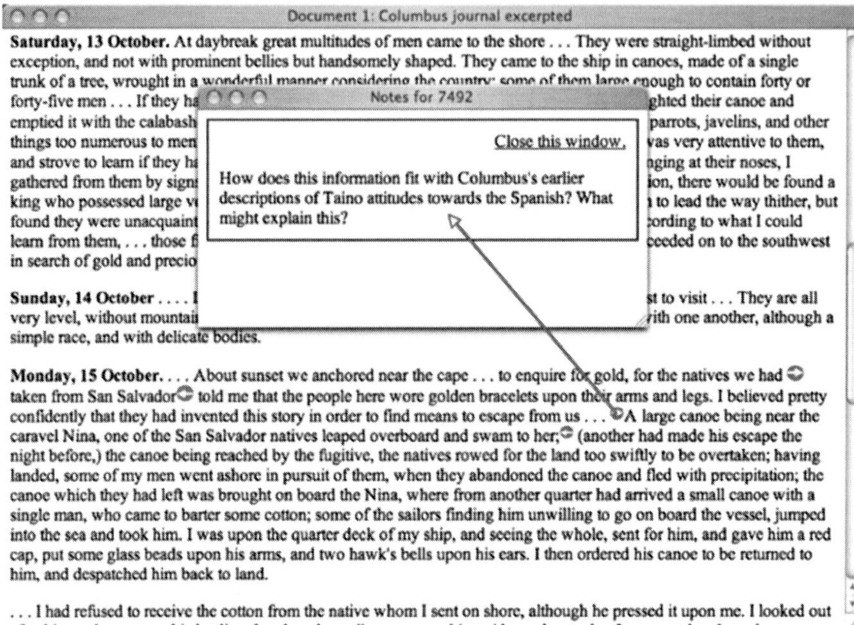

Figure 7.4 Embedded metacognitive scaffold.

Our second major recommendation argues for narrowing the research scope. Given the indispensability of soft scaffolding, designers should focus their energies on work in classrooms where teachers are disposed and skilled at providing this essential support. Only by optimizing this element are we likely to discover the potential and limits of hard scaffolding supports for improving student performance. A number of researchers have suggested that teacher personalities affect their willingness and ability to tolerate the open-endedness and uncertainty associated with practices such as inquiry (Johnston, 1990; Saye, 1998; Shaver, 1996). Our current work emphasizes exploring soft scaffolding–wise practices and developing materials and experiences that enhance the scaffolding skills of those teachers who already have the dispositions to engage their students in these ambiguous, cognitively challenging encounters (Saye & Brush, 2009; Saye, Kohlmeier, Brush, Mitchell, & Farmer, 2009). As we expand our partnership network with such teachers, we are designing a series of studies, each of which will focus on individual elements of hard scaffolding to understand what combination of hard and soft scaffolding supports may have the greatest effect. As we seek to optimize the problem size and the scaffolding conditions for effective PBHI, we can also revisit the issue of fading to determine whether consistent, optimal soft and hard scaffolding in these more defined problem environments allows some of that support to be faded over time. We hope that the insights and models that flow from this work assist in expanding the corps of inservice and preservice teachers who are willing and able to practice PBHI.

Compared to the disciplines of science and mathematics, social studies has been slow to consider how technology can be leveraged to provide powerful holistic learning experiences for students and teachers. In mathematics, for example, researchers have had the opportunity to explore the benefits of multimedia learning environments for more than 15 years with products such as the *Jasper Woodbury* series (e.g., CTGV, 1992; Hickey, Moore, & Pelligrino, 2001). Through multiple trials, researchers have found that these resources promoted increased engagement with mathematics subject matter and significantly increased student success in problem-solving and interpretation tasks. In science, extensive research on multimedia learning environments such as *Alien Rescue* (Pedersen & Liu, 2003), *Learning By Design* (Kolodner et al., 2003), and *Model-It* (Krajcik, Soloway, Blumenfeld, & Marx, 1998) has reported benefits such as increased engagement, awareness of alternative perspectives regarding science problems, and the ability to scaffold challenging tasks to assist both students and teachers with inquiry-based science activities.

Our investigations emphasize how much we do not yet know about technology's potential as a tool for encouraging rigorous historical investigation and problem solving. The mixed results we have obtained stimulate our thinking and challenge us to conceptualize more powerful ways that we might harness the potential of technological tools to promote the development of expertise in problem-based teaching and learning. Design experiments are particularly beneficial in this regard, because their results can immediately inform practice while also generating broader theories and principles that may be applied to our field and others.

Clearly, technology is no panacea for the challenges students and teachers face when engaging in disciplined inquiry into social problems. Technology may ease certain burdens associated with inquiry, but success hinges on skilled, energetic teachers and motivated learners. The challenge remains for social educators to expand our understanding of how technology-enhanced learning environments might be best designed and used to increase the likelihood of powerful history and social studies learning that results in civic competence.

Epilogue

As we observed the struggles of *Decision Point* teachers in meeting the soft scaffolding challenges of inquiry, we gradually shifted our research focus from students to teachers, recognizing that until teachers could navigate these instructional challenges, efforts to support students were likely to be unproductive (Saye & Brush, 2006). In our work since the *Decision Point* studies, we have focused on how we might support teachers in conceptualizing and mastering PBHI practice. We have concentrated on using scaffolded lesson study to build sustained collaborative communities of PBHI practice. This work has shown some promise in encouraging a deeper grasp of PBHI practices (Howell & Saye, 2015; Saye et al., 2009, 2013). However, even intensive, three-year projects have achieved only modest success for the full range of teacher participants (Kohlmeier et al., 2015; Saye et al., 2013). Consistent with our earlier work and that of others (Johnston, 1990; Saye, 1998; Shaver, 2006), teacher responses continue to suggest the importance of dispositions and epistemological beliefs on teachers' openness to entertaining inquiry practices in their classrooms.

Our continuing work also corroborates other research suggesting the limits of scaffolding in supporting inquiry into ill-structured social problems. The greatest successes in social studies have been with small, tightly bounded problem landscapes (De La Paz et al., 2014; Kohlmeier, 2005), and even then students have struggled with some disciplinary inquiry practices (Reisman, 2012). The successes reported in such studies offer little comfort if problem-based social inquiry is to prepare students for the demands of democratic citizenship. Tightly bounded settings do not authentically reflect the complexity of the real world, and scaffolding has been less successful in helping students or teachers navigate larger problem landscapes that more closely approximate social reality (Barton, 1997; Parker et al., 2013; Saye, 2017). Researchers who believe that civic competence is central to the mission of the social studies must continue to explore how we might make social inquiry more manageable for both students and learners while also supporting inquiry learning progressions that ready students for effective civic decision making as adult citizens.

Acknowledgments

The body of this chapter was previously published as Saye, J. W., & Brush, T. A. (2007). "Using technology-enhanced learning environments to support problem-based historical inquiry in secondary school classrooms." *Theory & Research in Social Education, 35*(2), 196–230. Copyright 2007 by the College and University Faculty Assembly of National Council for the Social Studies; adapted with permission.

References

Barton, K. C. (1997). "I just kinda know": Elementary students' ideas about historical evidence. *Theory & Research in Social Education, 25*(4), 407–430. http://dx.doi.org/10.1080/00933104.1997.10505821

Barton, K. C., & Levstik, L. S. (2004). *Teaching history for the common good.* Mahwah, NJ: Erlbaum.

Berson, M., Lee, J., & Stuckart, D. (2001). Promise and the practice of computer technologies in the social studies: A critical analysis. In W. E. Stanley (Ed.), *Critical issues in social studies research for the 21st century.* Greenwich, CT: Information Age Publishing.

Bransford, J. D., Brown, A. L., & Cocking, R. R. (2000). *How people learn: Brain, mind, experience, and school.* Washington, DC: National Academy Press.

Brown, A. L. (1992). Design experiments: Theoretical and methodological challenges in creating complex interventions in classroom settings. *Journal of Learning Sciences, 2*(2), 141–178.

Brown, J. S., Collins, A., & Duguid, P. (1989). Situated cognition and the culture of learning. *Educational Researcher, 18*(1), 32–42.

Brush, T. A., & Saye, J. W. (2000). Implementation and evaluation of a student-centered learning unit: A case study. *Educational Technology Research and Development, 48*(3), 79–100.

Brush, T. A., & Saye, J. W. (2001). The use of embedded scaffolds with a hypermedia-supported student-centered learning activity. *Journal of Educational Multimedia and Hypermedia, 10*(4), 333–356.

Brush, T. A., & Saye, J. W. (2005, April). *The effects of multimedia-supported problem-based inquiry on student engagement, empathy, and assumptions about history.* Paper presented at the Annual Meeting of the American Educational Research Association, San Diego, CA.

Chi, M. T. H., Glaser, R., & Farr, M. J. (1988). *The nature of expertise.* Mahwah, NJ: Lawrence Erlbaum.

Cobb, P., Confrey, J., diSessa, A., Lehrer, R., & Schauble, L. (2003). Design experiments in educational research. *Educational Researcher, 32*(1), 9–13.

Cognition and Technology Group at Vanderbilt. (1992). The Jasper experiment: An exploration of issues in learning and instructional design. *Educational Technology Research and Development, 40*(1), 65–80.

Cognition and Technology Group at Vanderbilt. (1993). Anchored instruction and situated cognition revisited. *Educational Technology Research and Development, 33*(3), 52–70.

Collins, A., Joseph, D., & Bielaczyc, K. (2004). Design research: Theoretical and methodological issues. *Journal of the Learning Sciences, 13*(1), 15–42.

De La Paz, S., Felton, M., Monte-Sano, C., Croninger, R., Jackson, C., Deogracias, J. S., & Hoffman, B. P. (2014). Developing historical reading and writing with adolescent readers: Effects on student learning. *Theory & Research in Social Education, 42*(2), 228–274. http://dx.doi.org/10.1080/00933104.2014.908754

Dewey, J. (1938). *Experience and education*. New York, NY: Macmillan.

Dundis, S. P., & Fehn, B. R. (1999). Historical thinking skills and conceptualized archives: Exploring the American Journey CD-ROMs. *The Social Studies, 90*(6), 273–277.

Dwyer, D. (1994). Apple classrooms of tomorrow: What we've learned. *Educational Leadership, 51*(7), 4–10.

Engle, S., & Ochoa, A. (1988). *Educating citizens for democracy: Decision-making in social studies*. New York, NY: Teachers College Press.

Hannafin, M., Land, S., & Oliver, K. (1999). Open learning environments: Foundations, methods, and models. In C. Reigeluth (Ed.), *Instructional design theories and models* (Vol. II, pp. 115–140). Mahwah, NJ: Erlbaum.

Hickey, D. T., Moore, A. L., & Pellegrino, J. W. (2001). The motivational and academic consequences of elementary mathematics environments: Do constructivist innovations and reforms make a difference? *American Educational Research Journal, 38*(3), 611–652.

Hmelo-Silver, C. (2004). Problem-based learning: What and how do students learn? *Educational Psychology Review, 16*(3), 235–266.

Holt, T. (1990). *Thinking historically: Narrative, imagination, and understanding*. New York, NY: College Entrance Examination Board.

Howell, J. B., & Saye, J. W. (2016). Using lesson study to develop a shared professional teaching knowledge culture among 4th grade social studies teachers. *Journal of Social Studies Research, 40*(1), 25–37. http://dx.doi.org/10.1016/j.jssr.2015.03.001

Hunt, M. P., & Metcalf, L. E. (1968). *Teaching high school social studies: Problems in reflective thinking and understanding* (2nd ed.). New York, NY: Harper & Row.

Jacobsen, M. J., Maouiri, C., Mishra, P., & Kolar, C. (1996). Learning with hypertext learning environments: Theory, design and research. *Journal of Educational Multimedia and Hypermedia, 5*(3/4), 239–281.

Johnston, M. (1990). Teachers' backgrounds and beliefs: Influences in learning to teach in the social studies. *Theory and Research in Social Education, 18*(3), 207–233.

Jonassen, D. (1999). Designing constructivist learning environments. In C. M. Reigeluth (Ed.), *Instructional design theories and models* (Vol. 2, pp. 89–121). Mahwah, NJ: Erlbaum.

Jonassen, D. (1997). Instructional design models for well-structured and ill-structured problem-solving learning outcomes. *Educational Technology Research and Development, 45*(1), 65–94.

Kennewell, S. (2001). Using affordances and constraints to evaluate the use of information and communications technology in teaching and learning. *Journal of Information Technology for Teacher Education, 10*(1&2), 101–116.

Kohlmeier, J. (2005). The impact of having ninth graders "do history." *The History Teacher, 38*(4), 499–524.

Kohlmeier, J., Saye, J., McCormick, T., Howell, J., Jones, C., Shannon, D., & Brush, T. (April, 2015). *Promoting problem-based historical inquiry through scaffolded lesson study.* Presented at the annual meeting of the American Educational Research Association, Chicago, IL.

Khong, Y. F. (1992). *Analogies at war.* Princeton, NJ: Princeton University Press.

Kolodner, J., Camp, P., Crismond, D., Fasse, B., Gray, J., Holbrook, J., … Ryan, M. (2003). Problem-based learning meets case-based reasoning in the middle-school science classroom: Putting Learning by Design into practice. *Journal of the Learning Sciences, 12*(4), 495–547.

Krajcik, J., Soloway, E., Blumenfeld, P., & Marx, R. (1998). Scaffolded technology tools to promote teaching and learning in science. In C. Dede (Ed.), *ASCD 1998 Yearbook: Learning with Technology.* Alexandria, VA: ASCD.

Kuhn, D. (1999). A developmental model of critical thinking. *Educational Researcher, 28*(2), 16–26, 46.

Kuhn, D. (2005). *Education for thinking.* Cambridge, MA: Harvard University Press.

Kuhn, D., & Dean, D. (2004). Connecting scientific reasoning and causal inference. *Journal of Cognition and Development, 5*(2), 261–288.

Land, S. M. (2000). Cognitive requirements for learning with open-ended learning environments. *Educational Technology Research and Development, 48*(3), 61–78.

Land, S., & Zembal-Saul, C. (2003). Scaffolding reflection and articulation of scientific explanations in a data-rich, project-based learning environment: An investigation of Progress Portfolio. *Educational Technology Research and Development, 51*(4), 65–84.

Lee, J. K., & Clark, W. G. (2003). High school social studies students' use of online historical documents related to the Cuban Missile Crisis. *Journal of Interactive Online Learning, 2*(1). Retrieved from http://www.ncolr.org/issues/jiol/v2/n1/high-school-social-studies-students-uses-of-online-historical-documents-related-to-the-cuban-missile-crisis

Lee, P., & Ashby, R. (2000). Progression in historical understanding among students ages 7–14. In P. N. Stearns, P. Sexias, & S. Wineburg (Eds.), *Knowing, teaching, and learning history: National and international perspectives* (pp. 199–222). New York, NY: New York University Press.

Levin, M., Newmann, F., & Oliver, D. (1969). *A law and social science curriculum based on the analysis of public issues* (Final Report Project No. HS 058. Grant No. OE 310142). Washington, DC: Department of Health, Education, and Welfare.

Lewis, C., Perry, R., & Murata, A. (2006). How should research contribute to instructional improvement? The case of lesson study. *Educational Researcher, 35*(3), 3–14.

Lichtman, A., & French, V. (1978). *Historians and the living past: The theory and practice of historical study.* Arlington Heights, IL: AHM Publication Corporation.

Lipscomb, G. (2002). Eighth graders' impressions of the Civil War: Using technology in the history classroom. *Education Communication and Information, 2*(1), 51–67.

Massaro, T. M. (1993). *Constitutional literacy: A core curriculum for a multicultural nation.* Durham, NC: Duke University Press.

Masterman, E., & Rogers, Y. (2002). A framework for designing interactive multimedia to scaffold young children's understanding of historical chronology. *Instructional Science, 30*(3), 221–241.

Milson, A. J. (2002). The Internet and inquiry learning: Integrating medium and method in a sixth grade social studies classroom. *Theory and Research in Social Education, 30*(3), 330–353.

National Council for the Social Studies. (1994). *Expectations of excellence: Curriculum standards for the social studies.* Washington, DC: National Council for the Social Studies.

Newmann, F. M. (1991). Higher order thinking in the teaching of social studies: Connections between theory and practice. In J. Voss, D. Perkins, & J. Segal (Eds.), *Informal reasoning and education* (pp. 381–400). Mahwah, NJ: Erlbaum.

Newmann, F., & Associates. (1996). *Authentic achievement: Restructuring schools for intellectual quality.* San Francisco, CA: Jossey-Bass.

Newmann, F., Bryk, A. S., & Nagaoka, J. K. (2001). *Authentic intellectual work and standardized tests: Conflict or coexistence?* Chicago, IL: Consortium on Chicago School Research.

Newmann, F. M., & Oliver, D. (1970). *Clarifying public controversy: An approach to social studies*. Boston, MA: Little, Brown.

Newmann, F. M., Wehlage, G. G., & Lamborn, S. D. (1992). The significance and sources of student engagement. In F. Newmann (Ed.), *Student engagement and achievement in American secondary schools* (pp. 11–39). New York, NY: Teachers College Press.

Oliver, D. W., & Shaver, J. P. (1966). *Teaching public issues in the high school*. Boston, MA: Houghton Mifflin.

Onosko, J. (1991). Barriers to the promotion of higher order thinking in social studies. *Theory and Research in Social Education, 19*(4), 341–366.

Parker, W. C., Lo, J., Yeo, A. J., Valencia, S. W., Nguyen, D., Abbott, R. D., … Vye, N. J. (2013). Beyond breadth-speed-test: Toward deeper knowing and engagement in an advanced placement course. *American Educational Research Journal, 50*(6), 1424–1459. http://dx.doi.org/10.3102/0002831213504237

Parker, W. C., Mueller, M., & Wendling, L. (1989). Critical reasoning on civic issues. *Theory and Research in Social Education, 19*(4), 7–32.

Pea, R. (2004). The social and technological dimensions of scaffolding and related theoretical concepts for learning, education, and human activity. *Journal of the Learning Sciences, 13*(3), 423–451.

Pedersen, S., & Liu, M. (2003). Teachers' beliefs about issues in the implementation of a student-centered learning environment. *Educational Technology Research and Development, 51*(2), 57–76.

Perkins, D., Allen, R., & Hafner, J. (1983). Difficulties in everyday reasoning. In W. Maxwell (Ed.), *Thinking: The expanding frontier* (pp. 177–189). Philadelphia, PA: Franklin Institute Press.

Reiser, B. (2004). Scaffolding complex learning: The mechanisms of structuring and problematizing student work. *Journal of the Learning Sciences, 13*(3), 273–304.

Reisman, A. (2012). Reading like a historian: A document-based history curriculum intervention in urban high schools. *Cognition and Instruction, 30*(1), 86–112. http://dx.doi.org/10.1080/07370008.2011.634081

Rossi, J. A. (1995). In-depth study in an issues-centered social studies classroom. *Theory and Research in Social Education, 23*(2), 87–120.

Rossi, J. A., & Pace, C. M. (1998). Issues-centered instruction with low achieving high school students: The dilemmas of two teachers. *Theory and Research in Social Education, 26*(3), 380–409.

Ryder, M., & Wilson, B. (1996, February). *Affordances and constraints of the Internet for learning and instruction*. Paper presented at the Annual Meeting of the Association for Education and Communications Technology, Indianapolis, IN.

Saye, J. W. (1998). Technology in the classroom: The role of dispositions in teacher gatekeeping. *Journal of Curriculum & Supervision, 13*(3), 210–234.

Saye, J. W. (2017). Disciplined inquiry in social studies classrooms. In M. M. Manfra & C. M. Bolick (Eds.), *The handbook of social studies research* (pp. 336–359). Boston, MA: Wiley-Blackwell. Manuscript in preparation.

Saye, J. W., & Brush, T. A. (1999). Student engagement with social issues in a multimedia-supported learning environment. *Theory and Research in Social Education, 27*(4), 472–504.

Saye, J. W., & Brush, T. A. (2002). Scaffolding critical reasoning about history and social issues in multimedia-supported learning environments. *Educational Technology Research and Development, 50*(3), 77–96.

Saye, J. W., & Brush, T. A. (2004a). Promoting civic competence through problem-based history learning environments. In G. E. Hamot & J. J. Patrick (Eds.), *Civic learning in teacher education* (Vol. 3, pp. 123–145). Bloomington, IN: ERIC Clearinghouse for Social Studies/Social Science Education.

Saye, J. W., & Brush, T. A. (2004b). Scaffolding problem-centered teaching in traditional social studies classrooms. *Theory and Research in Social Education, 32*(3), 349–378.

Saye, J. W., & Brush, T. A. (2006). Comparing teachers' strategies for supporting student inquiry in a problem-based multimedia-enhanced history unit. *Theory and Research in Social Education, 34*(2), 183–212.

Saye, J. W., & Brush, T. A. (2009). Using the affordances of technology to develop teacher expertise in historical inquiry. In J. K. Lee & A. Friedman (Eds.), *Research in technology and the teaching of history and social studies* (pp. 19–38). Charlotte, NC: Information Age Publishing.

Saye, J. W., Kohlmeier, J., Brush, T., Mitchell, L., & Farmer, C. (2009). Using mentoring to develop professional teaching knowledge for problem-based historical inquiry. *Theory & Research in Social Education, 37*(1), 6–41.

Saye, J., Kohlmeier, J., McCormick, T., Howell, J., Jones, C., Shannon, D., & Brush, T. (2013, November). *Scaffolded lesson study: Promoting professional teaching knowledge for problem-based historical inquiry.* Presented at the annual meeting of the College and University Faculty Assembly of the National Council for the Social Studies, St. Louis, MO.

Saye, J., & Social Studies Inquiry Research, C. (2013). Authentic pedagogy: Its presence in social studies classrooms and relationship to student performance on state-mandated tests. *Theory & Research in Social Education, 41*(1), 89–132. http://dx.doi.org/10.1080/00933104.2013.756785

Saye, J., Stoddard, J., Gerwin, D., Libresco, A., Maddox L., & SSIRC. (2015, November). *Authentic pedagogy: Examining intellectual challenge in social studies classrooms.*

Symposium presented at the annual meeting of the College and University Faculty Assembly of the National Council for the Social Studies, New Orleans, LA.

Schneider, R. M., Krajcik, J., Marx, R. W., & Soloway, E. (2002). Performance of students in project-based science classrooms on a national measure of science achievement. *Journal of Research in Science Teaching, 39*(5), 410–422.

Shaver, J. P. (1996). The prospects for issues-centered education. In R. W. Evans & D. W. Saxe (Eds.), *Handbook on teaching social issues* (pp. 380–386). Washington, DC: National Council for the Social Studies.

Sherin, B., Reiser, B., & Edelson, D. (2004). Scaffolding analysis: Extending the scaffolding metaphor to learning artifacts. *Journal of the Learning Sciences, 13*(3), 387–421.

Shulman, L. S., & Carey, N. B. (1984). Psychology and the limitations of individual rationality: Implications for the study of reasoning and civility. *Review of Educational Research, 54*(4), 501–524.

Simon, H. (1982). *Models of bounded rationality.* Cambridge, MA: MIT Press.

Smith, J., & Niemi, R. G. (2001). Learning history in school: The impact of course work and instructional practices on achievement. *Theory and Research in Social Education, 29*(1), 18–42.

VanSickle, R. L., & Hoge, J. D. (1991). Higher cognitive thinking skills in social studies: Concepts and critiques. *Theory and Research in Social Education, 19*(2), 152–172.

VanSledright, B. (2002). *In search of America's past: Learning to read history in elementary school.* New York, NY: Teachers College Press.

Voss, J. F., Greene, T. R., Post, T. A., & Penner, B. C. (1983). Problem solving skill in the social sciences. In G. H. Bower (Ed.), *The psychology of learning and motivation: Advances in research and theory* (pp. 165–213). New York, NY: Academic.

Vygotsky, L. S. (1978). *Mind in society: The development of higher psychological processes.* Cambridge, MA: Harvard University Press.

Wineburg, S. S. (1991a). Historical problem solving: A study of cognitive processes used in the evaluation of documentary and pictorial evidence. *Journal of Educational Psychology, 83*(1), 73–87.

Wineburg, S. S. (1991b). On the reading of historical texts: Notes on the breach between the school and academy. *American Educational Research Journal, 28*(3), 495–519.

Wineburg, S. S. (1999). Historical thinking and other unnatural acts. *The Kappan, 80*(7), 488.

Yeager, E. A., & Foster, S. J. (2001). The role of empathy in the development of historical understanding. In J. O. L. Davis, E. A. Yeager, & S. J. Foster (Eds.), *Historical empathy and perspective taking in the social studies.* Lanham, MD: Rowman & Littlefield.

Zukas, A. (2000). Active learning, world history, and the internet: Creating knowledge in the classroom. *International Journal of Social Education, 15*(1), 62–79.

John Saye is the Mildred Cheshire Fraley Distinguished Professor of Secondary Social Science Education in the Department of Curriculum and Teaching at Auburn University and is director of the Persistent Issues in History Network (pihnet.org). He teaches courses in social studies education. Prior to coming to Auburn in 1994, Saye taught high school social studies for 12 years. His research interests include authentic pedagogy, problem-based inquiry, teacher thinking, and collaborative communities of practice.

Thomas Brush is the Barbara B. Jacobs Chair in Education and Technology as well as the chair of the Department of Instructional Systems Technology within the School of Education at Indiana University, Bloomington. His research interests focus on developing methods and strategies to promote inquiry-oriented learning, particularly with more open-ended instruction. This involves studying methods for integrating tools to promote collaborative problem-based learning strategies into the learning environment itself and developing alternative techniques to deliver instruction to students.

8

Engaging Teachers' Pedagogical Content Knowledge: Adopting a Nine-Step PBL Model

Karen C. Goodnough and Woei Hung

Since the study described in this chapter was first published (Goodnough & Hung, 2008), the authors have continued to use the outcomes to add to the knowledge base of PBL and teacher learning. For example, Goodnough and Hung (2009) conducted a follow-up study examining K–6 teachers' development of pedagogical content knowledge in science teaching. The results confirmed the conclusion from the previous study, that the nine-step PBL design process helped elementary school teachers systematically translate their educational philosophy, such as active learning, self-directed learning, contextual learning, higher-order thinking, and individual and social knowledge construction, into practical classroom activities. The nine-step PBL design process has helped teacher educators design PBL problems that contextualize students' understanding of classroom management principles (Hung & Holen, 2011) and enhance their motivation and engagement during the learning process (Ak, Hung, & Holen, 2012). Furthermore, Goodnough (2010) used several of the ideas and principles from this original study in designing and implementing a PBL with teacher candidates that focused on differentiating instruction. Learning through PBL helped the teacher candidates develop an understanding of the potential benefits and challenges associated with using differentiated instruction as a lens for designing and implementing science curricula for junior and senior high students. Goodnough and Hung currently use PBL as an instructional approach in their own teaching, and Hung has continued to examine the tensions associated with designing PBL and its impact on student learning (Hung, Mehl, & Holen, 2013).

Introduction

Over the past few decades, problem-based learning (PBL) has gradually gained popularity in K–12 settings (Goodnough, 2006; Lambros, 2004; McGrath & Sands, 2004; Torp & Sage, 1998) across various levels and subject areas, such as science (Koszalka, Grabowski, & Kim, 2002), biology (Sungur & Tekkaya, 2006), and high school economics (Maxwell, Mergendoller, & Bellisimo, 2005). The adoption of PBL in K–6 settings has the potential to support the goals of scientific literacy (American Association for the Advancement of Science, 1998; Atlantic Provinces Education Foundation, 1998; Council of Ministers of Education, 1997; National Research Council, 1996), which generally include developing conceptual and theoretical knowledge, developing an understanding of the nature and methods of science, and engaging in and developing expertise in scientific inquiry and problem solving (Hodson, 1998).

As more and more K–12 schools and educators adopt PBL, they will need to engage in new learning, such as gaining an understanding of the nature of PBL and how it should be implemented, designing PBL problems, and using new strategies and techniques for facilitating PBL sessions (e.g., how to guide students during problem solving and collaborative learning). In the context of science, research has shown that elementary and secondary teachers feel ill-equipped and ill-prepared to assume these tasks. This lack of preparation often translates into difficulty with teaching science, and as a result, teachers often adopt low-risk, conservative approaches to science instruction (Appleton & Kindt, 2002; Mulholland & Wallace, 2001; Tabachnick & Zeichner, 1999). For example, in a national survey of mathematics and science teachers (Fulp, 2002), 75% of 655 elementary teachers reported that they need considerable professional development to improve their science content knowledge. In addition to this perceived need, teachers reported being comfortable with using general pedagogical approaches in science but less comfortable with "developing students' conceptual understanding of science, making connections between science and other disciplines, and leading students using investigative strategies" (p. 19).

In terms of adopting PBL in the context of primary and elementary science education, designing effective problems is a critical, yet challenging, task (Angeli, 2002). Teachers need to consider a range of factors, such as ensuring problems relate to the real world and engage and motivate students, creating problems that encourage students to develop higher-level thinking and group collaboration skills, designing problems that are open ended and build on students' prior knowledge, and ensuring problems target desired learning outcomes (Duch, 2001).

Over the last two decades, some researchers have provided guidelines for developing problems. For example, Barrows (1986) provided a taxonomy of PBL problems; Dolmans and Snellen-Balendong (1997) proposed seven principles for designing effective cases for PBL; Majoor, Schmidt, Snellen-Balendong, Moust, and Stalenhoef-Halling (1990) discussed construction of PBL problems; and Duch (2001) and Schmidt (1983) identified the characteristics of good PBL problems. These guidelines focus on the aspects of problems that need to be represented during design: problems need to be authentic, ill-structured, and contextualized; stimulate reasoning; enhance problem-solving skills; promote self-directed learning; and enable students to engage their prior knowledge. These guidelines can help educators who adopt PBL develop an understanding of the necessary aspects or criteria for designing effective problems. However, these criteria are often not sufficient, for two reasons. First, many guidelines are usually discussed in a bullet-list fashion, and thus, the interconnections among various aspects of a problem are often not systematically discussed. Second, selecting and developing a PBL problem that meets these criteria, while effectively targeting intended learning outcomes, requires the adoption of a systematic design process. Developing a full understanding of what to consider when designing PBL problems will increase the likelihood that effective PBL problems are created, and consequently, optimal student learning is achieved. Undertaking such a design task without adopting a systematic process can be overwhelming and unproductive.

This chapter reports on the experiences of a teacher inquiry group consisting of five teachers (K–5) and a university researcher as they developed PBL learning modules. Hung's nine-step PBL problem design process, based on his 3C3R model (Hung, 2006, 2009), was adopted during PBL development. The study was guided by the following research questions: (1) How will various facets of teachers' pedagogical content knowledge be engaged as they design PBL modules? (2) How will teachers engage with the nine-step design process? and (3) What are teachers' perceptions of the strengths and limitations of the nine-step PBL design model? Subsequently, the authors will discuss teachers' pedagogical content knowledge (PCK) in the context of science education, the 3C3R problem design model, and the nine-step PBL design process.

Pedagogical Content Knowledge and Science Teaching

Effective teaching involves having solid subject knowledge of a discipline, as well as an in-depth understanding of how to facilitate student learning within that discipline. Shulman (1986, 1987) developed the concept of PCK to show the importance of the integration of subject matter knowledge and pedagogy in teaching. According to Shulman (1986), PCK illustrates how the subject matter of a particular discipline is transformed for communication with learners. He refers to PCK as "the most powerful analogies, illustrations, examples, explanations, and demonstrations—in a word the ways of representing and formulating the subject matter that make it comprehensible for others" (p. 9). According to Shulman, PCK illustrates how the subject matter of a particular discipline is transformed for communication with learners. It includes recognition of what makes specific topics difficult to learn, as well as the conceptions students bring to the learning of those concepts.

In this study, a PCK conceptual framework proposed by Magnusson, Krajcik, and Borko (1999) was used to examine how teachers engaged and enhanced their PCK as they designed PBL experiences. The framework consists of five distinct, yet interrelated, components for teaching science:

1. Orientations to teaching science. These are ways of viewing how science should be taught and how these views guide instructional decision making. Many teachers' choices of instructional approaches reflect several distinct orientations (content emphasis, guided inquiry, process, problem-based). The reasons for adopting particular approaches are indicative of a teacher's orientation.
2. Knowledge of science curriculum. This includes beliefs about and understanding of curriculum goals and outcomes in particular courses and across grade levels. Additionally, this category involves an awareness of the curriculum resources available at various grade levels to support instruction.
3. Knowledge of students' understanding of science. This includes teachers' beliefs about and insights into what prerequisite knowledge, abilities, and skills students need to learn particular topics, as well as an understanding of how students vary in their approaches to learning particular topics. A second area targeted in this category is teachers' knowledge of science concepts and ideas that are difficult for students to learn.
4. Knowledge of assessment. This includes teachers' beliefs about and

understanding of which aspects of students' learning are important to assess within a learning episode or unit, as well as the methods of assessment that are appropriate for determining the learning that has occurred.

5. Knowledge of instructional strategies. This includes teachers' beliefs about and understanding of which instructional strategies may be used to teach in science, as well as specific strategies (topics and representations) that would be useful to adopt when teaching particular science topics.

Because PBL is a complex strategy, it requires science teachers to extend and utilize many facets of their PCK in a highly integrated manner. For example, teachers need to consider their beliefs about teaching science (orientations) and how the philosophical underpinnings of PBL align with these beliefs. Many PBL experiences are interdisciplinary, thus teachers not only have to be able to interpret and apply curriculum outcomes to classroom practice but also need to integrate curriculum outcomes from several disciplines. PBL units and curricula are developed with the intent of improving student learning. Thus, when teachers design PBL problems, they need be cognizant of the prior knowledge and abilities students bring to the PBL context. If students have had very little experience with posing questions, conducting research, and functioning in collaborative learning environments, then teachers will need to provide appropriate scaffolding and guide students in using a range of new skills. Because PBL requires the use of a multilayered approach, teachers will need to incorporate a number of other teaching strategies or tactics (e.g., lectures and laboratory investigations). Furthermore, assessment approaches within PBL contexts are diverse, reflecting authentic, performance-based tools such as group products, self-rating scales, and so forth. This study provides insight into how facets of teachers' PCK are engaged as they design PBL experiences using a nine-step design model (Hung, 2006).

A Conceptual Framework for Designing PBL Problems

When adopting PBL experiences, considerable attention needs to be given to several areas (e.g., learning outcomes to be targeted, complexity of the problem, student readiness to engage with PBL) during the PBL design process. To facilitate problem design that is systematic and attends to these areas, Hung proposed a design model and a corresponding nine-step process to apply the model.

The 3C3R PBL Problem Design Model

The 3C3R PBL problem design model (Hung, 2006) consists of two classes of components: core components and processing components. Core components, which include content, context, and connection, support content and concept learning in a discipline, while processing components, which include researching, reasoning, and reflecting, support the development of cognitive processes such as problem-solving skills. These components are aspects of a problem that need to be considered at each step in the design of a problem.

The core components are primarily concerned with the issues of appropriateness and sufficiency of content knowledge, contextualization, and integration. The content component aims to reconcile the issues of breadth versus depth of content acquisition by addressing the essence of sound content design of a PBL problem. The context component addresses the degree of contextualization of the problem that would, in turn, influence researching and reasoning processes. The connection component addresses the importance of helping students integrate knowledge learned throughout the curriculum. Conversely, processing components are used to facilitate mindful and meaningful engagement in PBL by supporting learners' cognitive processes of problem-solving skills and self-directed learning. For a complete discussion of the 3C3R model, please refer to Hung (2006).

The Nine-Step PBL Problem Design Process

Based on the conceptual framework of the 3C3R model, Hung (2009) further developed the nine-step design process to provide teachers and practitioners with a step-by-step process for systematically considering the critical components of a PBL problem. The process consists of the following steps:

1. Set goals and objectives
2. Conduct content/task analysis
3. Analyze context specification
4. Select/generate PBL problem
5. Conduct PBL problem affordance analysis
6. Conduct correspondence analysis
7. Conduct calibration processes
8. Construct reflection component
9. Examine intersupporting relationships of 3C3R components

Next, each step in the problem design process is described using an example from a grade 6 mathematics curriculum. Please note that the example has been substantially reduced and simplified and is therefore incomplete due to the length limitations of this chapter.

Step 1: Set goals and objectives. Specifying the scope of the domain knowledge is the first necessary step in all instructional design methods (Gagné, Wager, Golas, & Keller, 2005; Jonassen, Tessmer, & Hannum, 1999), including PBL course/curriculum development (Drummond-Young & Mohide, 2001; Uyeda, Madden, Brigham, Luft, & Washburne, 2002). Learning goals and objectives help teachers or designers outline the breadth and depth of content and, consequently, provide a structure for aligning the scope of the problem with curriculum standards or outcomes (Trafton & Midgett, 2001). When specifying learning goals and objectives, the designer should carefully consider three aspects—domain knowledge, problem-solving skills, and self-directed learning skills. The following example illustrates this:

Example

- *Instructional goal*: In authentic life contexts, sixth grade students will apply knowledge of fractions, decimals, and percentages in solving genuine mathematical problems.
- *Domain knowledge objectives*: Within a classroom setting, and given a real-life simulated problem, sixth grade students will identify, represent, analyze, and solve mathematical structures using fractions, decimals, and percentages in order to construct a hypothetical solution to a simulated problem.
- *Problem-solving skills objectives*: Based on the students' age and corresponding cognitive readiness, students will (1) identify and define the problem, and (2) identify all necessary information to solve the problem.
- *Self-directed learning skills objectives*: Given that younger learners lack self-directed learning skills and experience with PBL, students will (1) initiate group organization and allocate member responsibilities, and (2) generate learning issues.

Step 2: Conduct content/task analysis. As Jonassen, Tessmer, and Hannum (1999) suggested, task/content analysis is critical regardless of what instructional method is employed. To conduct a content analysis for PBL curriculum, Sugrue's (1995) categorization of problem-solving competence, which includes concepts, principles, and procedures, can help to identify critical content knowledge and skills that constitute the domain. Concepts are the core ideas within a domain. Principles are defined by Sugrue (1995) as "the rules that involve relationships among the concepts" (p. 29). Appendix A provides an example of key concepts, principles, and procedures that might be targeted in a grade 6 math unit.

Step 3: Analyze context specification. Situating learning processes in an authentic context is one of the key features of PBL (Barrows, 1994; Duch, 2001; Hmelo, 1998; Hmelo & Ferrari, 1997; Koschmann, Myers, Feltovich, & Barrows, 1994; Torp & Sage, 1998). Projected context is apparent when designing PBL problems for professional training or higher education curricula, for example, medical education or vocational education. The designer also needs to identify the factors that affect the professionals' practice in the field. K–12 curricula or university general education curricula, conversely, focus on providing general foundations of knowledge. Therefore, the applications of the content knowledge can be rather general.

Step 4: Select/generate PBL problem. In the next step, the designer should explore and establish a pool of real-life problems within the specified context, and then select one problem that best matches and supports the results of the analysis in the first three steps. The selected PBL problem needs to be appealing to learners to keep them motivated (Hung, 2006).

For example, the grade 6 mathematics PBL, a list of potential needs to be generated: (1) plan a budget to treat your mother to a Mother's Day outing, (2) plan a budget for "back to school" shopping, and (3) devise a budget plan to start a school store to raise money for school activities. After considering the following factors related to the potential problems—simplicity (age-appropriateness), relevance (familiarity), and appeal (motivation)—problem one is adopted because it targets all of these factors. Problem two is a promising second, but since this project will be given to students in early May, the time frame was more conducive to the Mother's Day problem. The following problem was generated:

> Mother's Day is about four weeks away. You and your sibling want to treat your mom to a special day. Your grandparents are going to chip in $50 to get you started. You each get $25 a month total for doing your chores, and this income is available if you choose to buy your lunches. A hot lunch is $.85 per day. The sales tax where you live is 7%, and the average gratuity for a waiter

or waitress in your area is about one-fifth of your total bill. Your grandparents would like to see your budget for this day.

Step 5: Conduct PBL problem affordance analysis. The next step is to construct a comprehensive description of the problem space (Newell & Simon, 1972) for analyzing its problem affordance. This depiction is the preparation for the correspondence analysis in Step 6.

Example

Full description:

1. Understanding the problem
   a. Problem state: The children want to plan a special "Mother's Day outing."
   b. Goal state: Plan a budget for this outing for three people, listing all possible expenses and considering the total funds available and criteria set by the grandparents.
2. Problem-solving processes
   a. Determine how much money will be available to use for this event.
   b. Research unknown variables.

Domain knowledge needed for solving the problem:

Concepts Used

- Concepts of income and expense
- Concepts of decimals

Principles Used

- Rule for finding a percentage of a number (turn the percentage into a decimal and multiply it by the original amount).

Procedures Used

- Adding, subtracting, multiplying, and dividing decimals, and fractions
- Finding a percentage of a number

Factual Information Used

- Sales tax rate is 7%
- Average gratuity is 20%

Problem-Solving Skills Analysis

- Identify the known variables given in the problem
- Identify the unknown variables needed to solve the problem

Step 6: Conduct correspondence analysis. Correspondence analysis is an essential mechanism for ensuring the reliability and effectiveness of the PBL problem in the nine-step design process. This analysis detects whether the problem corresponds to the intended content coverage and the skill level of learners by examining whether the (1) problem properly affords or supports the learning goal(s), (2) key knowledge involved in solving the problem matches the intended content knowledge, (3) contextual information in the problem is sufficient to situate the learning in an authentic context, and/or (4) connection component of the problem is properly designed. An overafording (the scope of the problem is excessively larger than the scope of the intended content) or underaffording (the scope of the problem is excessively smaller than the scope of the intended content) PBL problem will need to be calibrated in the next step. Refer to Appendix B for an example of how this analysis is conducted.

Step 7: Conduct calibration processes. Based on the correspondence analyses from step 6, the problem can be calibrated or modified as needed and transformed into the problem presentation. Content, context, researching, and reasoning are the four components involved in the calibration process to craft a problem that is well aligned with the intended content and learners' characteristics. The full description of the problem case is also transformed into a "problem" to be solved during this stage.

> ***Example***
> The items that need to be revised to align with the learning objectives are as follows:
>
> - Represent the objective of having the students see equivalents. The facts were now reworded by using different language representing fractions (i.e., the gratuity used to say 20%; it was changed to one-fifth).
> - Include the grandparent stipulation that the money needed to be "equally divided."
> - Add that transportation is free (another known variable).
> - Include the information that students needed to represent their budget both in fraction and percentage form so they could visually see relationships between them.
> - Make the total money equal to $100, so that viewing percentage/fraction/decimal relationships is easier (based on 100, for that part of the problem at least).

Step 8: Construct reflection component. Student reflection is one of the major features of PBL (Barrows & Myers, 1993). Incorporating a reflection component for students as part of the problem-solving task can help cultivate learners' self-directed learning skills and habits. The design of the reflecting component should focus on (1) acquisition of all the necessary knowledge, (2) adequate depth of study, (3) effective and efficient research methods, (4) logical and effective reasoning processes, (5) conceptual integration of knowledge, and (6) effective problem-solving strategies. The following provides an example of incorporating a reflective component:

> ***Example***
> You will be grouped in pairs for this activity. Each of you needs to contribute to the project. When you and your partner meet during each class to put your ideas and research together, you should discuss the ideas that you feel strongly about and back up your ideas with proof. Bring information (menus, flyers, calculations) to show that your ideas will work in the context of the problem. When you are considering different combinations of lunch, activities, and the gift, try using "if, then" statements to support your hypothesis generation.

Step 9: Examine intersupporting relationships of 3C3R components. The last step of the 3C3R design process is an evaluation step. This step evaluates the problem by checking how the various components of the problem work together and are connected. The content, context, connection, researching, reasoning, and reflecting components in PBL problems are not independent of one another; rather, they are complementary and mutually support one another. Therefore, when designing PBL problems, this supportiveness among the six components is critical to maximizing the effect of each component within the PBL problem as a whole. At this stage, the designer should revise the problem statement based on the result of this evaluation as needed. Refer to Appendix C for the final version of the problem statement.

Methodology/Methods

Five primary/elementary teachers and a university researcher/facilitator (the first author of this chapter) adopted collaborative inquiry (Bray, Lee, Smith, & Yorks, 2000), a participatory, action-based inquiry approach, as a means to develop PBL learning experiences. In this approach to research and adult learning, participants are co-learners and co-constructors of knowledge, with

Table 8.1 ***Sevaluation results of intersupportiveness of 3C3R components.***

	Content	Context	Connection
Researching	The information that directs students' research information in solving this problem sufficiently supports the content knowledge specified in the learning goal and objectives	The contextual information sufficiently supports students to research intended content knowledge	N/A since this is a stand-alone PBL problem. However, we may need to make sure the information in the problem is sufficient to activate the students' prior knowledge for taking on these researching and reasoning processes in solving this problem
Reasoning	The information that directs students' reasoning through the problem space sufficiently supports the students' content knowledge acquisition specified in the learning goals and objectives	The contextual information sufficiently supports students to engage in the reasoning process specified in the objectives	
Reflecting	The information in the reflection component of the problem sufficiently guides the students to engage in evaluating their own acquisition/processing of content knowledge	N/A since the projected context for this learning module is general	

relationships reflecting equity among participants; the inquiry is self-directed rather than other-directed, and participants share in the exploration and development of different forms of knowledge through sustained interaction (Reason, 1989, p. 4). The group engaged in planning, reflection, dialogue, action (implementing ideas in classrooms), and learning, and capitalized on their varied knowledge and understandings to inform decision making. The study occurred over an eight-month period, from November 2005 to June 2006. The outcomes reported in this chapter focus on the design phase of the PBL process.

The group met for five individual planning days (5–6 hours) to explore the nature of PBL and to design PBL experiences using Hung's (2006, 2009) nine-step problem design process. The first author and group facilitator provided the teachers with the Hung articles and a checklist, developed from the articles, to be used as a guide as teachers progressed through the steps. Before starting the design process, participants completed a variety of readings and engaged in a range of discussions about the nature of PBL. These discussions continued throughout the design process as group members developed new insights into the nature of PBL.

In this study, the PBL approach adopted reflected the following characteristics: the learning was driven by open-ended, ill-structured, authentic problems (Evenson & Hmelo, 2000; Gallagher, 1997; Wilkerson & Gijselaers, 1996), students worked in groups (Barrows, 1996; Hmelo, 1998), learning was student-directed and facilitated by the teacher (Barrows, 1986), an emphasis was placed on the development of content knowledge (van Gessel, Nendaz, Vermeulen, Junod, & Vu, 2003), and the development of communication, problem-solving, and decision-making skills (Johnson & Tinning, 2001) was promoted.

To view the design process from multiple perspectives and gain insight into how teachers adopted the nine-step model, a variety of qualitative methods and sources were used, including:

1. Participant observation. For an eight-month period (November 2005–June 2006), the group met for more than 30 hours, on a variety of occasions, to plan the PBL experiences. Over a four-month period (September–December 2006), implementation of modules and ongoing and post-implementation debriefing/discussion occurred. All meetings were face-to-face or held synchronously using a web-based communication/collaboration tool called Elluminate Live. All meetings were audiotaped and later transcribed. In total, 50 hours of audiotapes were transcribed.
2. Electronic journal entries. Teachers made reflective entries using an online course management system, provided to university faculty to support research and teaching, during the development and implementation of their PBL experiences. These entries fostered individual reflection about the ongoing process and allowed the facilitator to provide advice and feedback, and to act as a sounding board.
3. Documents and materials generated by the group. These documents ranged from charts created by the collaborative inquiry group during planning sessions to lesson plans developed for the PBL units.
4. Pre- and post-study interviews. Each interview was 30–60 minutes, allowing insight into the various aspects of teachers' changing beliefs and thoughts. All interviews were audiotaped and later transcribed.

Data analysis was ongoing throughout the study. This entailed reading and rereading the data from all data sources. During this process, the authors engaged in writing analytic memos and recording notes about developing insights and thoughts. Initial basic coding involved assigning labels to units of text from transcripts and journal text. The PCK categories and the steps in the design process guided data analysis, while strengths and limitations were identified across the data set. Crabtree and Miller (1992) referred to this as a template strategy; sets of codes are applied to the data but may change as data analysis proceeds. A qualitative software program, *MAXqda2*, was used to organize and code data and to generate categories and themes. Ultimately, the author brought meaning to the analyzed data through interpretation, the process of making sense of the findings, offering explanations, and generating conclusions (Marshall & Rossman, 2006).

Context of the Study

This study was the result of an ongoing partnership between the Faculty of Education, Memorial University of Newfoundland, and a local school district. Teachers were recruited in the spring by sending invitations to school principals. Teacher collaborators who volunteered to participate in the project were given a small honorarium to purchase science materials for their schools, while several teacher release days were funded through a Social Sciences and Humanities Research Council grant.[1] These days were used for planning the PBL modules, sharing ideas, and reflecting on the design process. One of the teachers taught in an urban community, while the other four were from schools located in rural communities. The structure of the teachers' schools ranged from K–12 to K–5; however, the teaching assignments were at the primary/elementary levels. All teachers taught all core subjects in the curriculum, with the exception of French, music, and physical education.

Tina, an experienced teacher of 23 years, worked with a grade 2 class of 18 students (nine boys and nine girls). Four children followed a program with modified learning outcomes,[2] while the other students were average or above average in terms of academic ability. Tina had completed a graduate degree in education, a bachelor of arts (BA) and a bachelor of special education.

Anna had a BA, a bachelor of education (BEd), and a master of education (ME), and had been teaching for 23 years. She implemented her PBL unit with a group of 22 grade 4 students (8 boys and 14 girls). Five children followed programs with modified learning outcomes, and two of these children were labeled as behaviorally challenged.

Myra had worked with a grade 3 class of 12 boys and 12 girls. She described her class as being weak academically, particularly in reading (50% were below grade level). One student was following a program with modified learning outcomes, and one student had been diagnosed with dyslexia. Myra had taught for 15 years and had completed a BA, a BEd, and a MA. She had been involved in development of a new primary science program for the provincial Department of Education. It was there that she learned of the project and became interested in furthering her professional development in science education (planning meeting).

Sharon, with 18 years of experience, had completed graduate work in education, as well as a BA and BEd. She implemented her PBL module with a grade 1 class of 24 students (13 boys and 11 girls). The class was of mixed ability; four students followed a program with modified learning outcomes and one student had a hearing impairment.

Patsy had worked with a grade 4 class of 18 students, having equal numbers of boys and girls. The class had several strong students; one student followed a program with modified learning outcomes, while another student had been diagnosed with a behavioral disorder. Patsy completed a BA and BEd, and had been teaching for two years.

Anna and Patsy worked together to develop their PBL module on habitats (grade 4), while Tina developed a PBL module on life cycles. Although Myra and Sharon taught different grade levels (grade 3 and grade 1, respectively), they developed a module that focused on the needs of living things. Many of their learning and assessment activities were similar but differentiated for learners with varying abilities, interests, and motivation.

Results and Discussion

The adoption of PBL in this study was new for all teacher collaborators. Outcomes related to the design of PBL problems, the engagement of various aspects of teachers' PCK, and teachers' perceptions of the strengths and limitations of the nine-step design model are highlighted subsequently.

The Design of PBL Problems

The primary goals of adopting the nine-step 3C3R PBL design model are to facilitate the development of problems that target specified outcomes and to promote student understanding of content knowledge within a discipline, as well as the development of student problem-solving and self-directed learning skills. Furthermore, when designing a problem, consideration needs to be given to students' prior experience with learning through PBL and how the problem appropriately engages students in mindful learning of the intended content.

To provide insight into how the design process was adopted in this study and how teachers engaged with the model, the authors used an example developed by one of the teachers, Tina. Although Tina was the only one who adopted this problem for implementation, the actual design involved discussion and feedback from all group members during each step of the design process. It should be noted that all teachers followed a similar design process, as described in the subsequent example.

In step 1, Tina selected learning goals and outcomes from the science curriculum she wished to target. For example, students were expected to: (1) observe and describe changes in the appearance and activity of an organism as it goes through its life cycle, (2) identify constant and changing traits in organisms as they grow and develop, (3) propose an answer to an initial question or problem and draw simple conclusions based on observations or research, (4) identify new questions that arise from what was learned, and (5) communicate procedures and results using drawings, demonstrations, and written and oral descriptions. Outcomes from other subject areas such as language arts were also targeted (e.g., students will be expected to communicate information and ideas effectively and clearly and to respond personally and critically). Through collaborative concept mapping, Tina and the group developed maps that outlined the concepts, principles, facts, and procedures that would be targeted in their respective units (step 2). This allowed the group to examine connections among unifying ideas and concepts. Figure 8.1 provides an example of a concept map created by Tina with support and feedback from the group.

In step 3, she selected a context for the problem (where it would occur), considered the nature of the task that would be incorporated into the problem, identified resources that were available to her to support the problem, and considered the nature of professional work that would be represented in the problem. In step 4, based on the information generated in step 3, Tina selected a real world problem for the PBL: "The problem will deal with gardening and what to do when there are caterpillars in your garden."

In step 5, Tina drafted a description of the problem:

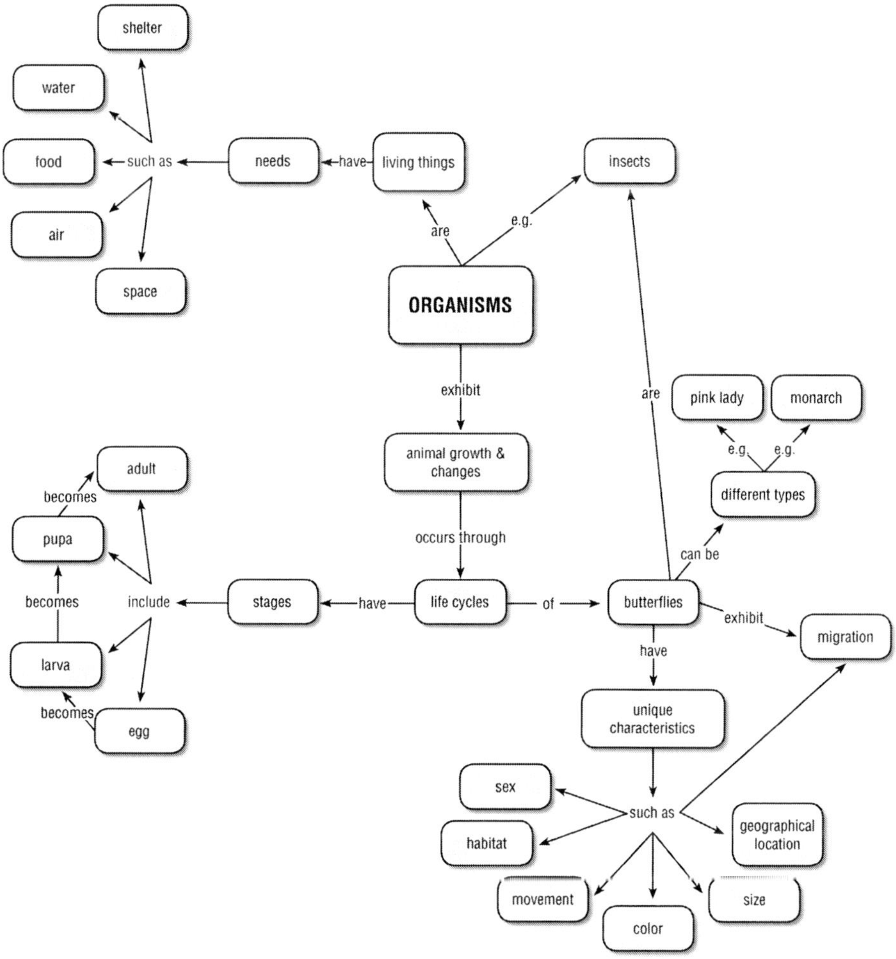

Figure 8.1 A concept map outlining the content topics targeted in Tina's PBL model.

> I have too many caterpillars in my garden. The caterpillars are starting to destroy the leaves on my flowers and/or plants. It is very difficult to have a garden on Bird Island because of the rocky, nutrient-deficient soil. With hard work, time, and money, I have managed to create a beautiful garden. How can I protect my plants from being destroyed by these insects?

This step also involved stating the goal of the problem (students will develop an understanding of life cycles and how a specific organism changes as it progresses through each stage of the life cycle), stating known variables (e.g., overabundance of caterpillars, poor soil), unknown variables (e.g., Why is the soil poor? How are the larvae destroying the plant?), and identifying the content knowledge and research and reasoning skills that would be targeted in the problem.

Next, Tina engaged in a correspondence analysis (step 6). Intended outcomes, identified early in the process, were compared to the content and reasoning skills that would be targeted in the problem as written in step 5. For example, one of the intended outcomes was for students to observe the life cycle of a butterfly. Tina examined the problem, as formulated and written in step 5, to determine if it would address the outcome. After doing this assessment, she decided that the wording of the problem would need to be changed to target this outcome. After completing the overall assessment, Tina determined if modifications to the problem were needed (step 7) as stated in step 5. Based on this analysis, the group felt the problem statement overafforded (i.e., the scope of the problem is larger than the scope of the content) the problem. Tina's comments during a planning meeting reflect this:

> The problem overaffords the intended content, and more information needs to be included in the problem statement to support the researching and reasoning components. My goal was to have students develop an understanding of life cycles and how a specific organism changes as it progresses through each stage of the life cycle. Using the butterfly as an example, I wanted them to observe firsthand how this insect goes through metamorphosis.
>
> However, I feel that the problem contains too much information (overaffordance of the intended content) because it has details about my garden and the soil in it. I don't think I need to focus on the quality of the soil or the difficulty of having a garden in this geographic area.

Subsequent revisions of the problem resulted in the following scenario:

> Every summer, Mrs. Bartlett likes to sit in a chair and enjoy her beautiful garden, where she has lots of plants and flowers with butterflies flying from one to another. However, before Mrs. Bartlett can enjoy her peaceful summers, she always has to fight with hungry caterpillars, who love to eat the leaves of her plants in the spring. She noticed that these caterpillars always appear around the same time, eating the plants, and then disappear. Then they appear again the next spring, just like the butterflies who come to visit

> the flowers in the summer, and then disappear. Mrs. Bartlett thought it would be wonderful if she could get rid of these caterpillars so that she would not have to work so hard to save the plants, and the butterflies would have more flowers to visit in the summer.
>
> You and your teammate are entomologists (bug experts) in training. Your team and other teams of entomologists are called in to help Mrs. Bartlett with her problem. These insects are devouring her plants and flowers. What can you and your team tell Mrs. Bartlett about caterpillars? What can your team do to help Mrs. Bartlett with her problem without destroying her garden? Mrs. Bartlett will choose the best solution to her problem from all the proposals.

These additions allowed a refocusing such that the content and research and reasoning skills were better integrated. Introducing butterflies into the statement directed the students' researching and reasoning toward the life cycle of caterpillars, as well as the growth and changes in appearances, the main focus of the content component (outcomes).

Further modification of step 8 allowed Tina to ensure reflection components were embedded in the problem. While Tina had identified a range of formative and summative tools that would be used in the PBL module (e.g., journal writing, paper-and-pencil tasks, student presentations, self-assessment, rubrics), the problem did not have a strong reflection component embedded in the problem statement. The final revised problem statement, which included a reflecting component, is presented in Appendix D.

Step 9, the final step, allowed the group to view the problem from a holistic perspective, examining how all the components of the problem were connected. Throughout all steps in the design process, teachers examined and engaged various facets of their PCK. The development of their PCK is described subsequently.

Engaging Teachers in the Development of PCK

During each step of the design process, teachers were engaged in considering their beliefs about and orientations to teaching science. Considerations related to their knowledge of curriculum, instruction, and assessment were prominent throughout the entire design process, as these elements were highly connected and integrated. The teacher collaborators joined the project to enhance their comfort level with the intended learning outcomes and to engage students in more "meaningful" teaching and learning in science. One teacher, Anna, had not been pleased with the types of professional development opportunities that were available through her school district and felt this project would meet many of her needs: "This project is exactly what I wanted at this time. I haven't been really pleased with the type of professional development that I've gotten, so I was getting stagnant in my teaching" (Anna, final interview).

The PBL approach aligned with teachers' *orientations and beliefs about teaching science*—that learning in science should be student-centered and foster critical and creative thinking skills. For example, when discussing the nature of PBL in an early planning meeting, teachers identified areas of student learning that could be targeted through PBL: helping students understand the role of science in the real world; developing inquiry skills, asking questions, making inferences, and drawing conclusions; evaluating sources of information; and enhancing presentation skills and written and oral communication. However, science had received little attention in the school curriculum. Thus, the teachers in the study welcomed the opportunity to renew the science curriculum, as well as recharge their knowledge of science pedagogy.

One major outcome of the design process was that teachers were engaged with developing their *knowledge of curriculum*. This was their first year working with a new curriculum framework in science, so they were not familiar with the learning outcomes. The design process allowed them to become comfortable with interpreting the learning outcomes in science. For example, in step 1 of the design process, teachers articulated the curriculum goals and outcomes (content knowledge, cognitive skills, and self-directed skills) they would be using in the PBL experience. Although these goals and outcomes were provided by the Department of Education, the teachers had to make decisions about which learning outcomes would be targeted from science and which would be targeted from other subjects, such as mathematics, social studies, and language. The following brief excerpt from a planning meeting provides an example of some of the goals and outcomes addressed in one of the PBL units:

> Scientific inquiry and collaborative problem solving were targeted; there's going to be a lot of sharing and exploring within groups. I have planned the PBL carefully, so it should be motivating for them. After targeting our science outcomes, I then looked at how it [the PBL] meets other outcomes in the other curriculum areas. Language arts are listed here and I thought they would be met through doing this PBL. In math, they will be working with numbers and number concepts, and they'll be collecting data. In social studies, they're going to be looking at their environment and how their environment changes

> over time, and they will probably be looking at how people interact within their environment, so those outcomes in social studies will be addressed, too. (Anna, planning session)

Step 2 of the design process (identifying big/unifying ideas as well as concepts, principles, procedures, skills, and factual knowledge to be targeted) helped teachers develop an in-depth understanding of their own respective content knowledge (life cycles, habitats, living things). Having competency with the subject matter knowledge is absolutely necessary if teachers are to effectively integrate content and general pedagogy to enhance their PCK. As one teacher commented, "The development of these concept maps that focus on the content for our PBLs really makes us familiar with the science content." Additionally, the teachers adopted an interdisciplinary approach by integrating outcomes from other curricular areas into the PBL design.

The design of PBL learning modules challenged teachers to consider very carefully the necessary knowledge, abilities, skills, and competencies (knowledge of students' understanding of science) students need to use or develop when engaged in a PBL experience. Early in the design process, teachers had several concerns, expressed in questions such as "How can we ensure all learners in the class will benefit from the approach? Will students be able to generate learning issues or questions about the problem? Will students like the approach? Will students who have modified learning programs be able to learn through PBL?" They also stressed the importance of finding out what students already know about a topic and the need to create PBL experiences for primary/elementary children that are fairly structured and teacher directed. This thinking about how PBL should be structured is reflected in comments made by two of the teachers: "I teach grade 2, and they are not as independent in their thinking as you would hope they would be. So, while you hope and strive for independent thinking, you need to direct the learning" and "We structure more in K–6 because of the nature of the children. They need a lot of structure and modeling. We should not take that modeling away now" (planning meeting).

While reflecting on these questions and issues, throughout step 1 (setting goals and objectives) of the design process, teachers collected and analyzed the necessary data for making informed decisions on the PBL module design. In this step, the teachers conducted a learner analysis, evaluating their targeted learners' levels of understanding in science and assessing their cognitive capabilities to engage in the problem-solving process. This facilitated the process of selecting appropriate goals and objectives for their PBL module design.

In selecting assessment and learning activities (knowledge of assessment and instructional strategies), the teachers adopted strategies and approaches that would foster learning through inquiry and collaboration; thus, student learning within collaborative groups was a critical component of the PBL process. For example, Sharon, in a planning meeting, talked about her use of cooperative learning in the context of PBL. She commented, "I use cooperative learning, but PBL will demand that I use many more cooperative learning strategies, especially if we want students to assume their fair share of work and to complete tasks collaboratively." The teachers raised concerns about how well students would function in groups, especially students following modified learning programs. These concerns are reflected in some of their comments about how to enhance group functioning:

> I think it is important to foster ownership within the groups. They can develop shared resources such as a kit or folder and allow them to generate a name for their group. This is really important for fostering rapport within the groups. (Anna)

> Yes, another thing that would help, I think, is having regular group meetings. "Ok, it's time for a meeting." They will need to talk about what they have learned, what resources they found, and the groups could talk about their questions. They need to consider if they have answered their questions and what they are going to learn next. (Sharon)

> You also need students to assume different roles ... a director to ensure everyone is paying attention, a recorder, and so forth, and these roles could alternate. (Patsy)

> And we need to constantly model what effective group work looks like, and I think we need to get them to evaluate how well their groups work. (Tina)

When planning the PBL learning experience, the teachers considered assessment and learning activities simultaneously while ensuring they were targeting the learning outcomes. As Myra said, "It is only natural that these two be considered hand-in-hand." They recognized that within a PBL environment, they would need to adopt a range of instructional and assessment strategies, stretching their thinking and classroom practices. For example, within the PBL modules, teachers orchestrated field trips; utilized guest speakers, videos, and the resources of external agencies; and used mini-lectures, graphics organizers, stories, internet resources, inquiry activities, demonstrations, student presentations, rubrics, and classroom observations.

The Nine-Step Design Model

The inquiry group identified three major strengths of the model: fostering comprehensiveness, offering a useful reflective heuristic, and catering to the learning needs of all students. However, the teachers perceived the model as being too long and time-consuming to use, lacking clarity in terms of language, and needing to include the design of learning activities as part of the process. These perceived strengths and limitations were agreed upon by the entire group after completing the design process and engaging in discussion and reflection at the end of the project.

Strengths of the model. One of the perceived strengths of the model, as identified by all teachers, is comprehensiveness. The model allowed the teachers to view the design of a PBL experience from a holistic perspective, taking into consideration how components such as the outcomes, assessment, and problem scenario within a PBL interact. Sharon commented, "It certainly forces you to think about the whole picture, how the outcomes fit with the content, context, and assessment." Patsy shared these views: "Although the process was lengthy, I felt for the first time through that the process gave me a solid understanding of how to go about planning a PBL." It is critical for teachers and instructional designers to develop a holistic view of the design of instruction. If the components of curriculum are disconnected (e.g., a mismatch between learning activities and assessment activities), it is likely that the students' literacy in a subject domain will not be well formed. A lack of cohesiveness may result in "compartmental knowledge" (Spiro, Coulson, Feltovich, & Anderson, 1988), which is one cause of students' difficulty in applying or transferring knowledge in solving real-life problems.

Teachers recognized another strength—the model provided an effective heuristic for reflection, thus "allowing one to revisit steps, make changes, and stay focused on the outcomes" (Patsy, final interview). For example, all teachers liked step 1, starting with the goals and learning outcomes to be targeted. As Sharon commented, "Outcomes drive our teaching and learning, thus the PBL needs to as well." The nine-step design process guides teachers and designers through the PBL problem design process step-by-step and, more importantly, helps them target the intended design goals and objectives. Without a structured heuristic, designers or teachers may stray from the intended learning goals/objectives in the curriculum design process.

A full depiction of the problem that enables the designer to conduct a comprehensive correspondence analysis between the scope of the problem and the intended learning goals and outcomes (see steps five and six) would, in all likelihood, improve the effectiveness of the PBL problem and module by ensuring the problem appropriately affords the intended learning goal (Hung, 2006, 2009). Furthermore, the last step of the design process (examining intersupporting relationships of 3C3R components) provides the integrity check of the PBL problem, as well as an explicit reflective tool for the teacher or the designer to refine and optimize the problem design. The importance of engaging in a thorough design process that allows for an integrity check of the problem statement and the overall PBL experience is echoed in the following comments:

> The scaffolding chart really helped wrap my head around all aspects of the problems and how students would engage with the problem. (Patsy, final interview)

> Well, the overall process certainly enhanced the design of the PBL. In the nine-step process, we had to check goals and outcomes against other parts of the problem and had to examine how everything overlapped or did not overlap. You really had to dig deep. And I think the plus of the process is that you are really focusing on those outcomes. (Sharon, group planning session)

> I would like to see the process abbreviated. However, it's really a validation process so that the problem truly is engaging and appropriate for your students and supports goals and outcomes. Without the process, you might just create your scenario and have your learning outcomes and activities and not go through this validation process. (Anna, journal entry)

Another benefit reported by three of the teachers was that the model forced them to place a greater emphasis on the learning needs of *all* students in an attempt to make PBL feasible for all learners. This is another indication, as referenced earlier, that the nine-step design process enhanced the teachers' knowledge of students' understanding of science. Considering learners' needs is a critical element of the 3C3R model and the nine-step design process. It ensures the difficulty level of the problem is appropriate for the targeted learners in terms of their cognitive capabilities, as well as their current and targeted abilities in the areas of problem solving and self-directed learning. These considerations are important because overwhelming the learners with what is beyond their capability or boring them with less-than-challenging problems would do little to foster optimal learning.

Limitations of the Model

While the teachers considered the model to be comprehensive, they suggested that the process could be streamlined and some of the steps combined. Their rationale centered on the need for creating a less time-intensive approach: "Teachers want the *Readers Digest* version of any new learning as they do not have the luxury of time that we had to work on this process," "we need something practical," and "it has to be easy and straightforward." The language used in describing the steps in the design process and the wordiness of the model were identified by the teachers as drawbacks: "Terminology is often difficult to understand." In addition to this global feedback about the design model, the teachers suggested that identification of learning activities be an explicit part of the model. As two of the teachers suggested: "The model does not indicate where to include learning activities" (Tina, planning meeting). "This is very important. When planning, we always look at our outcomes and think about learning activities to go with the outcomes together" (Myra, planning meeting).

Step 6 in the process, correspondence analysis, required the teachers to align the intended subject matter content with the subject matter content identified in step 5—affordance analysis. In addition, the teachers had to compare the learning outcomes to the research and reasoning components identified in step 5. Step 6 presented the biggest challenge for the teachers in terms of time and its lack of user-friendliness. "This was a bit confusing, and it required so much work it definitely needs to be streamlined" (Anna, interview). Overall, the teachers recommended that a modified version of the nine-step design model be developed that is "teacher-friendly" and "realistic," considering the hectic nature of teachers' daily lives. As Sharon commented, "I really see strengths in all the steps; however, I wish there was something a little more simplistic and less cumbersome" (planning meeting).

Implications/Conclusions

The adoption of the 3C3R nine-step design process in this study facilitated professional learning, assisting teachers in examining their own decision making and practice as it relates to curriculum, instruction and assessment, and student learning. Furthermore, the study provides insight into the feasibility of the process for adoption by K–12 teachers. The teachers agreed that the 3C3R model and the nine-step PBL design process provided a systematic conceptual framework, as well as an operational step-by-step means to guide the design of PBL problems. While the nine-step design process fostered the systematic PBL problem design process, the teachers also expressed practical concerns, namely lack of time and resources. This concern warrants serious consideration. A well-designed, effective PBL problem requires extensive preparation, analyses, and planning. To accomplish these tasks properly, steps 5, 6, and 7 (problem affordance analysis, correspondence analysis, and the calibration process, respectively), in particular, need to be modified so they are less time-consuming and less energy-intensive. For inservice teachers to adopt the 3C3R model and utilize the nine-step design process, the time they have for devoting to designing a PBL module would need to be taken into account.

The design of PBL learning experiences, as with many other curriculum and instructional design methods and processes, involves a series of complex tasks and needs to be approached systematically when considering the learning needs of students, as well as the practicality for the teachers. Improving the 3C3R model and the nine-step design process for K–12 educators will pose several challenges, such as finding a balance between the number of steps, analyses, and tasks necessary to make a PBL problem effective and the limited time teachers have to devote to the design process. This will continue to be one of the priorities in the continuing research of the 3C3R PBL problem design model and the nine-step design process.

Acknowledgments

This chapter is an updated version of an article previously published in the *Interdisciplinary Journal of Problem-based Learning.* Original citation: Goodnough, K., & Hung, W. (2008). Engaging teachers' pedagogical content knowledge: Adopting a nine-step problem-based learning model. *Interdisciplinary Journal of Problem-based Learning, 2*(2), 61–90.

Notes

1. The project was funded by the Social Sciences and Humanities Research Council (SSHRC), a Canadian federal granting agency that promotes and supports university-based research and training in the social sciences and humanities.
2. Students who follow modified learning programs have the learning outcomes, assessment activities, and learning experiences for courses modified from the regular curriculum, based on their unique learning needs as identified by a set of diagnostic tests and tools.

References

Ak, S., Hung, W., & Holen, J. B. (2012, April). *Problems and motivation in problem-based learning: A case study.* Paper presented at the 2012 AERA Annual Meeting, Vancouver, Canada, April 13–17.

American Association for the Advancement of Science. (1998). *Blueprints for reform.* New York, NY: Oxford University Press.

Angeli, C. (2002). Teachers' practical theories for the design and implementation of problem-based learning. *Science Education International, 13*(3), 9–15.

Appleton, K., & Kindt, I. (2002). Beginning elementary teachers' development as teachers of science. *Journal of Science Teacher Education, 13*(1), 43–61.

Atlantic Provinces Education Foundation. (1998). *Foundation for the Atlantic Canada science curriculum.* Halifax, Canada: Author.

Barrows, H. S. (1986). A taxonomy of problem-based learning methods. *Medical Education, 20*(6), 481–486.

Barrows, H. S. (1994). *Practice-based learning: Problem-based learning applied to medical education.* Springfield, IL: Southern Illinois University School of Medicine.

Barrows, H. S. (1996). Problem-based learning in medicine and beyond. In L. Wilkerson & W. H. Gijlselaers (Eds.), *Bringing problem-based learning to higher education: Theory and practice* (pp. 3–13). San Francisco, CA: Jossey-Bass.

Barrows, H. S., & Myers, A. C. (1993). *Problem-based learning in secondary schools.* Unpublished monograph. Springfield, IL: Problem-Based Learning Institute, Lanphier High School and Southern Illinois University Medical School.

Bray, J. N., Lee, J., Smith, L. L., & Yorks, L. (2000). *Collaborative inquiry in practice: Action, reflection and meaning making.* Thousand Oaks, CA: Sage Publications, Inc.

Council of Ministers of Education. (1997). *Common framework of science learning outcomes: Pan-Canadian protocol for collaboration on school curriculum.* Toronto, Canada: Author.

Crabtree, B. F., & Miller, W. L. (Eds.). (1992). *Doing qualitative research: Multiple strategies.* Newbury Park, CA: Sage Publications, Inc.

Dolmans, D. H. J. M., & Snellen-Balendong, H. (1997). Seven principles of effective case design for a problem-based curriculum. *Medical Teacher, 19*(3), 185–189.

Dolmans, D. H. J. M., Gijselaers, W. H., Schmidt, H. G., & van der Meer, S. B. (1993). Problem effectiveness in a course using problem-based learning. *Academic Medicine, 68*(3), 207–213.

Drummond-Young, M., & Mohide, E. A. (2001). Developing problems for use in problem-based learning. In E. Rideout (Ed.), *Transforming nursing education through problem-based learning* (pp. 165–191). Boston, MA: Jones & Bartlett.

Duch, B. (2001). Writing problems for deeper understanding. In B. Duch, S. E. Groh, & D. E. Allen (Eds.), *The power of problem-based learning: A practical "how to" for teaching undergraduate courses in any discipline* (pp. 47–53). Sterling, VA: Stylus Publishing.

Evenson, D. H., & Hmelo, C. E. (2000). *Problem-based learning: A research perspective on learning interactions.* Mahwah, NJ: Erlbaum.

Fulp, S. L. (2002). Status of elementary school science teaching. *2000 national survey of science and mathematics education.* Retrieved from http://www.horizon-research.com/horizonresearchwp/wp-content/uploads/2013/04/elem_science.pdf

Gagné, R. M., Wager, W. W., Golas, K. C., & Keller, J. M. (2005). *Principles of instructional design* (5th ed). Belmont, CA: Wadsworth.

Gallagher, S. A. (1997). Problem-based learning: Where did it come from, what does it do, and where is it going? *Journal for the Education of the Gifted, 20*(4), 332–362.

Goodnough, K. (2006). Exploring problem-based learning in the context of high school science: Design and implementation issues. *School Science and Mathematics, 106*(7), 280–296.

Goodnough, K. (2010). Investigating pre-service science teachers' developing professional knowledge through the lens of differentiated instruction. *Research in Science Education, 40*(2), 239–265.

Goodnough, K., & Hung, W. (2008). Engaging teachers' pedagogical content knowledge: Adopting a nine-step problem-based learning model. *Interdisciplinary Journal of Problem-based Learning, 2*(2), 61–90.

Goodnough, K., & Hung, W. (2009). Enhancing pedagogical content knowledge in elementary science. *Teaching Education, 20*(3), 229–242.

Hmelo, C. E. (1998). Problem-based learning: Effects on the early acquisition of cognitive skill in medicine. *The Journal of the Learning Science, 7*(2), 173–208.

Hmelo, C. E., & Ferrari, M. (1997). The problem-based learning tutorial: Cultivating higher order thinking skills. *Journal for the Education of the Gifted, 20*(4), 401–422.

Hodson, D. (1998). *Teaching and learning in science: Towards a personalized approach.* Philadelphia, PA: Open University Press.

Hung, W. (2006). The 3C3R model: A conceptual framework for designing problems in PBL. *Interdisciplinary Journal of Problem-based Learning, 1*(1), 55–77.

Hung, W. (2009). The 9-step process for designing PBL problems: Application of the 3C3R model. *Educational Research Review, 4*(2), 118–141.

Hung, W., & Holen, J. B. (2011). Problem-based learning: Preparing pre-service teachers for real-world classroom challenges. *ERS Spectrum, 29*(3), 29–48.

Hung, W., Mehl, K., & Holen, J. (2013). The relationships between problem design and learning process in problem-based learning environments: Two cases. *Asia-Pacific Education Researcher (Springer Science & Business Media B.V.), 22*(4), 635–645. http://dx.doi.org/10.1007/s40299-013-0066-0

Johnson, A. K., & Tinning, R. S. (2001). Meeting the challenge of problem-based learning: Developing the facilitators. *Nurse Education Today, 21*(3), 161–169.

Jonassen, D. H., Tessmer, M., & Hannum, W. H. (1999). *Task analysis methods for instructional design.* Mahwah, NJ: Erlbaum.

Koschmann, T. D., Myers, A. C., Feltovich, P. J., & Barrows, H. S. (1994). Using technology to assist in realizing effective learning and instruction: A principled approach to the use of computers in collaborative learning. *The Journal of the Learning Sciences, 3*(3), 227–264.

Koszalka, T. A., Grabowski, B., & Kim, Y. (2002, April). *Designing web-based science lesson plans that use problem-based learning to inspire middle school kids: KaAMS (Kids as Airborne Mission Scientists).* Paper presented at the 2002 AERA annual meeting, New Orleans, LA.

Lambros, A. (2004). *Problem-based learning in middle and high school classrooms: A teacher's guide to implementation.* Thousand Oaks, CA: Corwin Press.

Magnusson, S., Krajcik, J., & Borko, H. (1999). Nature, sources, and development of pedagogical content knowledge for science teaching. In J. Gess-Newsome & N. G. Lederman (Eds.), *Examining pedagogical content knowledge* (pp. 95–132). London: Kluwer Academic.

Majoor, G. D., Schmidt, H. G., Snellen-Balendong, H. A. M., Moust, J. H. C., & Stalenhoef-Halling, B. (1990). Construction of problems for problem-based learning. In A. M. Nooman, H. G. Schmidt, & E. S. Ezzat (Eds.), *Innovation in medical education: An evaluation of its present status.* New York, NY: Springer.

Marshall, C., & Rossman, G. B. (2006). *Designing qualitative research* (4th ed.). Thousand Oaks, CA: Sage Publications, Inc.

Maxwell, N. L., Mergendoller, J. R., & Bellisimo, Y. (2005). Problem-based learning and high school macroeconomics: A comparative study of instructional methods. *Journal of Economic Education, 36*(4), 315–331.

McGrath, D., & Sands, N. (2004). Taking the plunge: A school district commits to a five-year plan for technology-infused PBL. *Learning and Leading with Technology, 31*(7), 34–36.

Mulholland, J., & Wallace, J. (2001). Teacher induction and elementary science teaching: Enhancing self-efficacy. *Teaching and Teacher Education, 17*(2), 243–261.

National Research Council. (1996). *National science education standards.* Washington, DC: National Academy Press.

Newell, A., & Simon, H. A. (1972). *Human problem solving.* Englewood Cliffs, NJ: Prentice Hall.

Reason, P. (1989). *Human inquiry in action: Developments in a new paradigm research.* Thousand Oaks, CA: Sage Publications, Inc.

Schmidt, H. G. (1983). Problem-based learning: Rationale and description. *Medical Education, 17*(1), 11–16.

Shulman, L. S. (1986). Those who understand: Knowledge growth in teaching. *Educational Researcher, 15*(2), 4–14.

Shulman, L. S. (1987). Knowledge and teaching: Foundations of new reform. *Harvard Educational Review, 57*(1), 1–22.

Spiro, R. J., Coulson, R. L., Feltovich, P., & Anderson, D. K. (1988). Cognitive flexibility theory: Advanced knowledge acquisition in ill-structured domains. In *Tenth Annual Conference of the Cognitive Science Society* (pp. 375–383). Hillsdale, NJ: Erlbaum.

Sugrue, B. (1995). A theory-based framework for assessing domain-specific problem-solving ability. *Educational Measurement: Issues and Practice, 14*(3), 32–35.

Sungur, S., & Tekkaya, C. (2006). Effects of problem-based learning and traditional instruction on self-regulated learning. *Journal of Educational Research, 99*(5), 307–317.

Tabachnick, B. R., & Zeichner, K. M. (1999). Idea and action: Action research and the development of conceptual change teaching of science. *Science Education, 83*(3), 309–322.

Torp, L., & Sage, S. (1998). *Problems as possibilities: Problem-based learning for K–12 education.* Alexandria, VA: Association for Supervision and Curriculum Development.

Trafton, P. R., & Midgett, C. (2001). Learning through problems: A powerful approach to teaching mathematics. *Teaching Children Mathematics, 7*(9), 532–536.

Uyeda, S., Madden, J., Brigham, L. A., Luft, J. A., & Washburne, J. (2002). Solving authentic science problems: Problem-based learning connects science to the world beyond school. *The Science Teacher, 69*(1), 24–29.

Van Gessel, E., Nendaz, M. R., Vermeulen, B., Junod, A., & Vu, N. V. (2003). Basic science development of clinical reasoning from the basic sciences to the clerkships: A longitudinal assessment of medical students' needs and self-perception after a transitional learning unit. *Medical Education, 37*(11), 966–974.

Wilkerson, L., & Gijselaers, W. H. (1996). Concluding comments. *New Directions for Teaching and Learning, 1996*(68), 101–104.

APPENDIX A

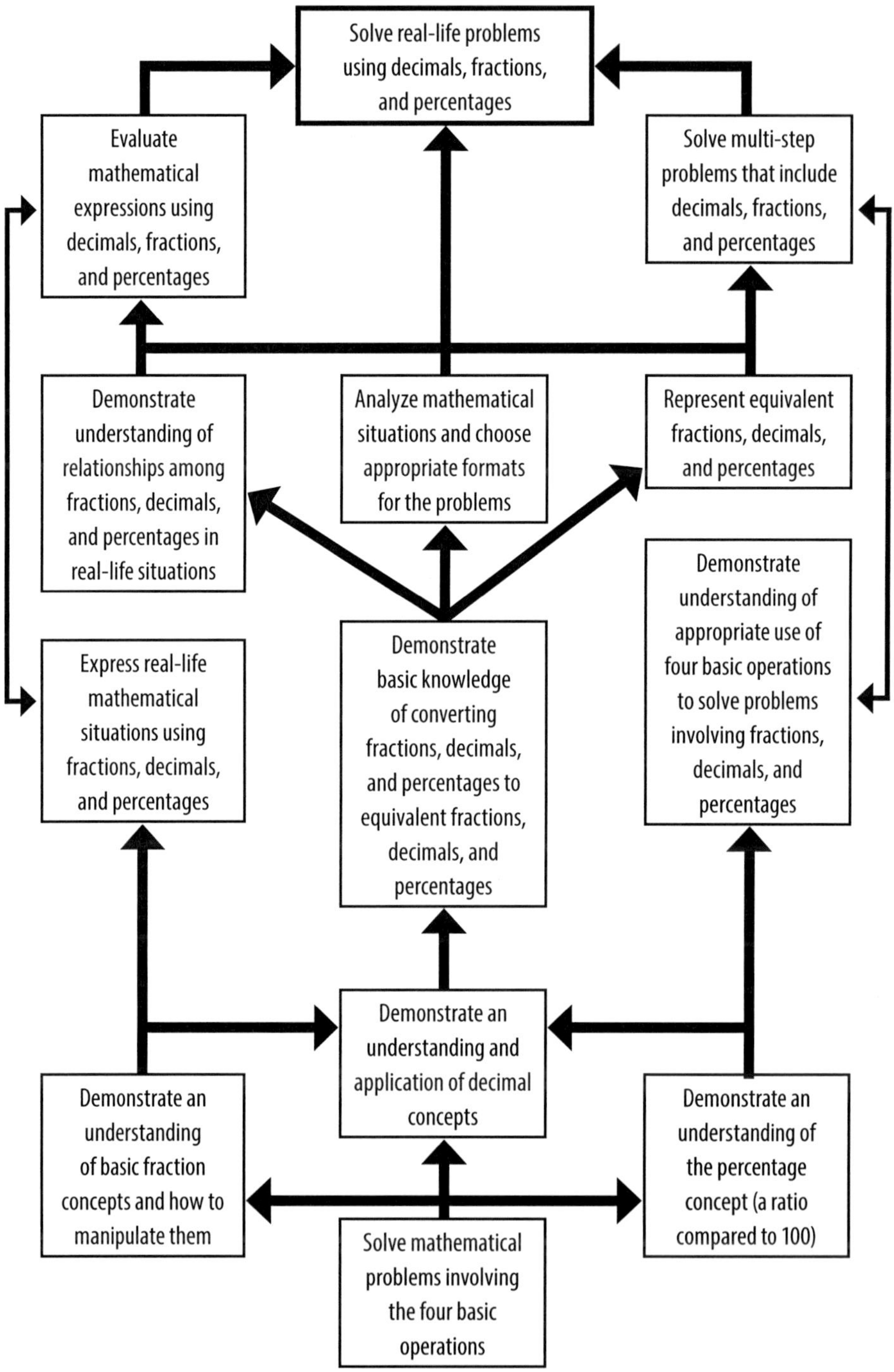

Solve real-life problems using decimals, fractions, and percentages
Evaluate mathematical expressions using decimals, fractions, and percentages
Solve multi-step problems that include decimals, fractions, and percentages
Demonstrate understanding of relationships among fractions, decimals, and percentages in real-life situations
Analyze mathematical situations and choose appropriate formats for the problems
Represent equivalent fractions, decimals, and percentages
Express real-life mathematical situations using fractions, decimals, and percentages
Demonstrate basic knowledge of converting fractions, decimals, and percentages to equivalent fractions, decimals, and percentages
Demonstrate understanding of appropriate use of four basic operations to solve problems involving fractions, decimals, and percentages
Demonstrate an understanding and application of decimal concepts
Demonstrate an understanding of basic fraction concepts and how to manipulate them
Demonstrate an understanding of the percentage concept (a ratio compared to 100)
Solve mathematical problems involving the four basic operations

APPENDIX B

Domain Knowledge (from step 2 →) (from step 5 ↓)			Concepts				Principles				Procedures			
			Decimals (D)	Fractions (F)	Percents (%)	Real-Life Mathematical Situations	Equivalent Relation-ships between D, F, & %	Evaluate Mathematical Expression using Appropriate Rules	Solving Multistep Problems	Conversion Rules for F, D, & %	Convert F to D, D to F, F to %, D to %	Solve using the 4 Mathematical Perations	Prerequisites	Beyond Scope of Objectives
Core	Concepts	Concept of income & expense	☺			☺						☺		☺
		Concept of decimals	☺			☺	☺			☺	☺		☺	
		Concept of percentages (a percentage is a ratio compared to 100)			☺		☺			☺	☺		☺	
		Concept of fractions		☺			☺			☺			☺	
		Budgeting money and time	☺			☺			☺			☺		
		Concept of handling money	☺			☺						☺		
		Relationships between fractions, decimals, and percentages	☺	☺	☺		☺			☺	☺			
		Concept of marketing math (discounts)			☺	☺			☺			☺		
		Greater than, less than, and equal to (for comparing combinations)				☺			☺					
		Concept of how charts/graphs are visual representations of amounts		☺	☺	☺	☺*							☺
	Principles	Rule for finding a percentage of a number			☺					☺	☺		☺	
		Rule for finding a total after a percent markdown or adding in tax or gratuity			☺	☺		☺	☺			☺	☺	
		Rule for converting a decimal to a percentage	☺		☺					☺	☺		☺	

NOTE: ☺ = Addressed in the problem.
*See equivalents.

APPENDIX C
Final Draft of Problem Presentation

Problem: Mother's Day is about four weeks away. You and your "sibling" want to treat your mom to a special day. You decide to take her out to lunch, buy her a gift, and have a fun activity to do together after lunch. Your grandparents are going to chip in $50 to get you started, and they stipulated that the money be divided equally between the food, the gift, and the activity. You each get $25 a month for doing your chores, and this income is available if you choose to buy your lunches. A hot lunch is $.85 per day. On the other hand, you may choose to pack a lunch instead for free. The sales tax where you live is 7%, and the average gratuity for a waiter or waitress in your area is about one-fifth of your total bill.

Transportation will be provided and paid for by your mother. Also, your grandmother is available to take you food shopping, if needed.

Your grandparents would like to see your budget for this day. It should show income and expenses. They'd like to see what fraction of your money will go toward lunch and an activity, and what percentage of your budget will be used on the gift. Included in the budget should be at least one graph or chart showing the distribution of money in fraction and percentage form.

You need to brainstorm and come up with a list of questions to answer. This will help you during your planning. Keep evaluating your options by revisiting your list of questions to make sure you stay focused! Here are two questions to help you get started: How much money do you have? Can this amount be altered by your actions?

You will be grouped in pairs for this activity. Each of you needs to contribute to the project or your solution will suffer (and your grade). When you and your "sibling" meet during each class to put your ideas and research together, you should discuss the ideas that you feel strongly about and back up your ideas with proof. Bring information (menus, flyers, calculations) to show that your ideas will work in the context of the problem. When you are considering different combinations of lunch, activity, and gift, try using "if, then" statements to support your hypothesis generation.

I will meet with each group individually to check your progress and discuss any problems you are having. Be ready to share your "working" budget and itinerary each time we meet, and be able to explain why you are choosing the food, gift, and activity under consideration. You should also have one or two backup plans ready as well.

Well, you have a lot of information and a lot of choices in front of you. Keep your information organized, be flexible with your options, stay within your budget, and you will end up planning a super outing for your mom!

APPENDIX D
Final Revised Problem Statement (Tina)

Every summer, Mrs. Bartlett likes to sit in a chair and enjoy her beautiful garden, where she has lots of plants and flowers with butterflies flying from one to another. However, before Mrs. Bartlett can enjoy her peaceful summers, she always has to fight with hungry caterpillars who love to eat the leaves of her plants in the spring. She noticed that these caterpillars always appear around the same time, eating the plants, and then disappear. Then they appear again the next spring, just like the butterflies who come to visit the flowers in the summer, and then disappear. Mrs. Bartlett thought it would be wonderful if she could get rid of these caterpillars so that she would not have to work so hard to save the plants and so the butterflies would have more flowers to visit in the summer.

You and your teammate are entomologists (bug experts) in training. Your team and other teams of entomologists are called in to help Mrs. Bartlett with her problem. These insects are devouring her plants and flowers. What can your team tell Mrs. Bartlett about caterpillars? What can your team do to help Mrs. Bartlett with her problem without destroying her garden? Mrs. Bartlett will choose the best solution to her problem from all the proposals.

In order to produce an effective and trustworthy solution proposal, your team should use scientific methods, such as continuous, consistent observation, and keep a journal of your research plan, how the plan has been carried out, and whether any revisions to your research plan are needed after a period of doing your research. Mrs. Bartlett will also pay your team a visit and interview you on the progress of your research. So, your team will need to prepare to answer Mrs. Bartlett's questions concerning her problem with caterpillars destroying the plants. And finally, in order for Mrs. Bartlett to select the best solution to her problem, each team will give a presentation of its research and solution to her problem.

Mrs. Bartlett is anxious to find a good solution to keep her plants healthy and attract butterflies to her garden since spring is coming and the caterpillars are about to come out. So, get started and help Mrs. Bartlett!

Karen C. Goodnough has been a faculty member at Memorial University since December 2003. Previously she was a faculty member at the University of New Brunswick and the University of Rochester. She is a former high school science teacher and spent several years working in the area of gifted education. Goodnough's research focuses on collaborative action, problem-based learning, science teaching and learning, and teacher development in STEM education. In 2016 she received the President's Award for Outstanding Research.

Woei Hung is currently a professor in the Instructional Design and Technology Program in the Department of Teaching and Learning at the University of North Dakota. His research areas include problem-based learning, problem solving, problem types and difficulty levels, systems thinking and modeling, and concept mapping and formation. Hung has published numerous journal articles and book chapters in the areas of PBL problem and curriculum design. He is also the current program chair of the Problem-Based Education Special Interest Group (SIG) at the American Educational Research Association.

CONCLUSION

What Is Missing; What Is Needed? Future Research Directions With PBL in K–12 and Teacher Education

Michael M. Grant and Krista D. Glazewski

Introduction

Problem-based learning (PBL) in K–12 and teacher education can be nuanced, challenging to implement, and time-consuming to research rigorously. The chapters in this volume speak to each of these characteristics. In our roles as editors of the *Interdisciplinary Journal of Problem-based Learning (IJPBL),* we enjoy the luxury of considering more PBL research than we are able to publish. To this end, and with the chapters from this volume, we would like to offer comments on what we believe is missing and needed in future research investigations. In this chapter, we use the terms *PBL* and *inquiry* to broadly encompass problem-based learning along with the other complementary pedagogies, such as project-based learning, anchored instruction, and inquiry methods, that share characteristics with PBL. As Brush and Saye note in the introduction, there are specific distinctions between *problem*-based learning and *project*-based learning. Therefore, where necessary in the following sections, we have identified the specific strategy under study or scrutiny.

Even in recent articles, authors continue to call for researchers to investigate the effectiveness of PBL and complementary pedagogies in K–12 (Rico & Ertmer, 2015). Previous PBL research in K–12 has relied on self-report measures as a primary or sole measure; however, this method has moved the field forward very little beyond gauging student attitudes (Belland, French, & Ertmer,

2009; Jerzembek & Murphy, 2013). Still, two trends can be observed in PBL research that offer promise for understanding more of the complexities in PBL and inquiry research and to much extent distinguish these contexts apart from the traditional medical research. One movement in K–12 studies has been away from comparison studies with control groups and toward reporting the complexities of implementations, particularly in the United States (e.g., Acre, Bodner, & Hutchinson, 2014; Gourgey, Asiabanpour, & Fenimore, 2010; Liu, Wivagg, Geurtz, Lee, & Chang, 2012; Pecore et al., 2012). Secondly, there has been an increase in the number of international studies within K–12 contexts (e.g., Beatrice, Amadalo, & Musasia, 2015; Cheriani, Mahmud, Tahmir, Manda, & Dirawan, 2015; Widyatiningtyas, Kusumah, Sumarmo, & Sabandar, 2015).

We are optimistic about the directions of PBL and inquiry research. Nevertheless, we would like to draw close attention to three specific areas of PBL and inquiry research in K–12 and teacher education. We feel these areas need further investigation and exploration in order to strengthen the body PBL and inquiry research and fill voids in both reporting implementations and research findings. First, we identify the need for stronger depictions of PBL and inquiry implementations. Further research should address implementation details, disciplinary goals and PBL, and the variations in implementations. Second, scaffolds and scaffolding as temporary supports are still somewhat ill-defined. More attention to the purposes of scaffolds is needed as well as how they are implemented and faded (if at all). Last, we focus on the limitations of implementing PBL and inquiry in isolation, with dependence on partners and without reports of longitudinal benefits.

Stronger Depictions of PBL

While the range of projects characterized here reflects the complexities and adaptations of PBL across various disciplines, we believe that the body of research will benefit from stronger depictions and descriptions of PBL and inquiry implementations. Because PBL can be so varied (Hung, 2011; Savery, 2015), the descriptions of PBL, problem cases, tutoring, scaffolding, self-direction, and group interactions need much stronger explanations. Readers and researchers need better narratives in order to understand the PBL process (Hung, 2011). It is only with these rich descriptions that readers can determine the utility and relevance of PBL within their own context. Three ways that future studies and reports can enhance the depictions of PBL are:

(1) addressing a lack of implementation details, (2) balancing descriptions of disciplinary learning goals with PBL, and (3) identifying explicitly and describing variations of implementations.

Lack of Details

Published descriptions of PBL implementations typically lack sufficient detail to be valuable to practitioners and researchers. Often due to word limits or page constraints, descriptions of implementations are condensed or abridged; we liken this to a *Reader's Digest* version of the implementation description. In contrast, Lottero-Perdue (see Chapter 4) identifies the components of teaching the *Designing Walls* case, explains the rationales for pedagogy to support these components, and then models the pedagogy and components to preservice teachers. There are ample details within this chapter to elucidate the problem case and the pedagogy to implement the PBL. Furthermore, in our own works and in the works of others, we have noted the implementation that is reported and published typically reflects a final version of the overall process. For example, in these cases, readers do not generally see the multiple versions or iterative nature of a developing problem case. There is not enough space in a published research report to elaborate fully on the iterations and the designer's/teacher's decision making and still include methods, findings, and discussion. The rich details of implementations are needed for readers to wholly contextualize the implementation. A rather uncommon example depicting various iterations is found in Saye and Brush (Chapter 7), in which the authors discuss four iterations of *Decision Point*. Like a case study, readers must determine how and under what conditions the implementation may work in their own contexts (Cresswell, 2012), and their characterization lends insight into iterations across dimensions of problem scope, unit task structure, scaffolding for argumentation and persuasion, perspective taking, and presentation expectations.

In *IJPBL*, we felt there was a need to capture and publish more examples of implementations along with the decision making that led to the implementations. We recently began to publish articles in a section called "Voices from the Field" (e.g., Hutchison, 2016; Persichetti, 2016; Stalker, Cullen, & Kloesel, 2015) in order to capture more of the design processes during the development of a problem case, as well as the decision making and rationales for selecting specific components of a problem. "Voices from the Field" is our attempt to provide a venue for inservice teachers and teacher educators to describe the evolution of their problem cases. Little has been published on how classroom teachers develop their own problem cases, driving questions, and learning tasks (c.f., Goodnough & Hung, 2009; Stalker et al., 2015). The process by which problem cases and inquiry tasks are generated by inservice teachers has not been adequately depicted in the literature.

Balancing Descriptions With Disciplinary Learning Goals

Depictions of PBL and inquiry in journal articles and other published works also compete with descriptions of disciplinary learning goals. It is important to recognize that PBL is an instructional strategy, but it is rarely the goal of learning. Instead, learning goals are most often concentrated on disciplinary content, such as mathematics, science, engineering, or medicine. For example, *Alien Rescue* (Liu et al., 2014; Liu, Williams, & Pederson, 2002) is an inquiry-based hypermedia environment focused on middle school earth science and astronomy. Similarly, Glazewski and colleagues (Glazewski, Shuster, Brush, & Ellis, see Chapter 2), and Ertmer and colleagues (Ertmer, Schlosser, Clase, & Adedokun, see Chapter 6) describe other strategies to improve science-related learning. Space within a journal article or book chapter must address both the disciplinary learning goals and the PBL implementation. So, it is not unexpected that PBL descriptions may be shortened or condensed. Therefore, PBL authors must pay particular attention to how they can provide adequate details about the implementation or teacher professional development. They may also consider splitting the development of the PBL implementation from the research study in order to publish and describe these separately (see "Voices from the Field," mentioned earlier).

In addition, PBL and inquiry methods are often coupled with other initiatives to improve learning or create reform. For example, Strutchens and Martin (see Chapter 1) detail the foundations and rationales for transforming the instructional practices of preservice secondary mathematics teachers that align to standards reforms. From Strutchens and Martin's descriptions, it is difficult to disaggregate the problem-solving strategies and specific PBL learning outcomes from the mathematics education goals. PBL researchers and advocates wish to identify the characteristics of an implementation, and then consider how these characteristics may be generalized or applied in other settings. Admittedly, though, the notion or need to separate the instructional strategy from the discipline may be unwarranted. We acknowledge that a discipline may not make these distinctions. For example, problem identification and problem solving is inherent to mathematics, so the PBL or inquiry strategies may or may not be distinguishable from teaching mathematics. Furthermore, it may be a false assumption that PBL and inquiry strategies can be replicated or transferred to other disciplines.

Saunders-Stewart, Gyles, and Shore's (2012) categories of learning outcomes may help to codify and advance research findings for specific outcomes associated with PBL and inquiry. Saunders-Stewart and colleagues generated 23 categories of learner outcomes broadly organized into four structures, whereby inquiry occurs in a classroom as defined by Manconi, Aulls, and Shore (2008, pp. 249–250): (1) *process* for activities guided by a learner's interest, where generalized skills can be learned; (2) *content* for activities, where learners engage with discipline-specific knowledge and application of this knowledge; (3) *strategy* for activities that support problem solving, organization, metacognition, self-directedness, and self-regulation; and (4) *context* for engagement with activities that require learners to make meaning from experiences within the learning environment, such as data and resources, motivations, collaborations, and reflection.

Identifying Variations in Implementations

Current published research of PBL does not adequately depict or explain the variations in implementations. The implementations differ by many components, including the scale, the scope of the unit, expectations for deliverables or artifacts, and multidisciplinarity. For example, Strutchens and Martin (see Chapter 1) identify opportunities for K–12 students to problem solve in small or discrete ways, while Ertmer and colleagues (see Chapter 6) and Saye and Brush (see Chapter 7) describe larger or more encompassing implementations. Hutchinson (2016) even explains an interdisciplinary implementation in higher education that purposefully crosses a number of disciplines. However, research reports do not provide enough detail to distinguish the different variations among project implementations. In Figure 9.1, we have attempted to identify a number of components as part of PBL implementations. The list presents 12 continua on which variations can occur within a PBL case. This list is not intended to be exhaustive, but, rather, it represents a beginning point for researchers, teacher educators, and professional development designers to consider as elements of an implementation that should be described with more detail in any reports of findings.

We also recognize that specific disciplines may have goals or processes that mediate or influence a PBL implementation. Three recent publications in *IJPBL*

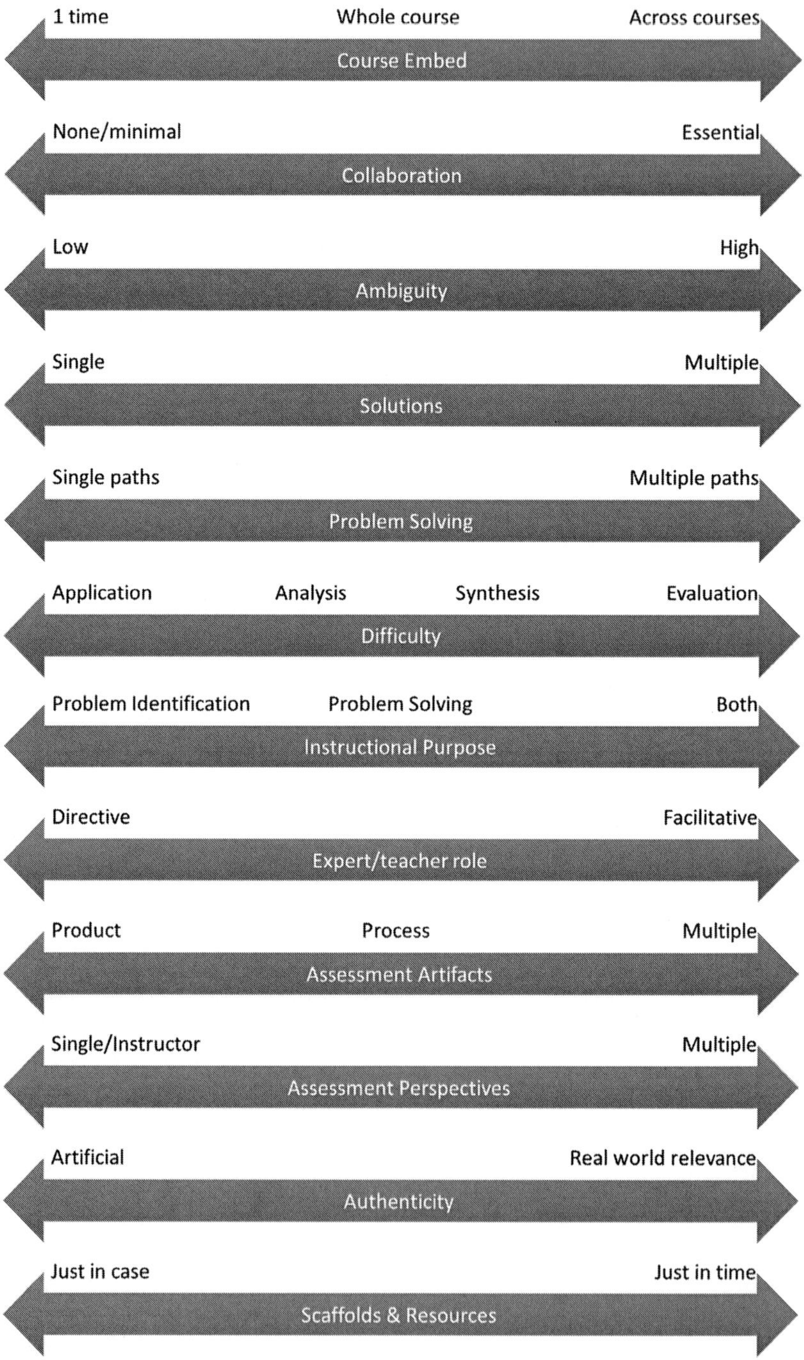

Figure 9.1 Components of variation in PBL implementations

(see, e.g., Galford, Hawkins, & Hertweck, 2015; Makin, 2015; Persichetti, 2016) highlight to us how features of PBL are adopted, adapted, and implemented with very different methods. While outside of K–12 and teacher education, all of these examples emphasize the authenticity PBL can reflect when a professional discipline is employed. This authenticity of a discipline is also evident in Hjalmarson and Diefes-Dux (see Chapter 5) for engineering design. Their chapter also features the evolution of design problems for teacher educators or inservice teachers. The engineering design process as described in their chapter did influence the PBL implementation for the "Million-Book challenge," which manifested in the problem-solving process and differs from the Barrows and Hmelo-Silver cycle (Barrows, 2006; Hmelo-Silver, 2004). Influences were also evident in the *Designing Walls* challenge in Lottero-Perdue's chapter (see Chapter 4).

There is also an unevenness of PBL research across K–12 disciplines. For example, there are more reported implementations of PBL and inquiry in STEM areas (see Chapters 1, 2, 4, 5, and 6) and fewer studies in the humanities (see Chapters 3 and 7) (e.g., Wilder, 2015). Furthermore, English language arts disciplines are unrepresented, both in this volume specifically and in *IJPBL* generally. We remain unsure if this is a direct result from discipline-specific processes, knowledge, or preferences, or if this is from other causes. Broad-scale research that cuts across all disciplines would be useful in order to investigate how and to what degree disciplines use or value PBL and inquiry.

Finally, we acknowledge that teacher pedagogical beliefs (Ertmer, 2005; Ertmer & Ottenbreit-Leftwich, 2010; Ertmer, Ottenbreit-Leftwich, Sadik, Sendurur, & Sendurur, 2012) may also influence implementations, which can lead to variations in the deployment of PBL in classroom settings. Pedagogical beliefs are "teachers' educational beliefs about teaching and learning" (Ertmer, 2005, p. 28). While pedagogical beliefs tend to be stable over time, Anders and Rossbach (2015) reported that discipline-specific beliefs "contribute to a better understanding of the complex association patterns between pedagogical beliefs, pedagogical interactions, and children's development" (p. 308). In the introduction to Goodnough and Hung's chapter (see Chapter 8), they note that the nine-step process for designing PBL can support teachers' enactments of their personal philosophies about teaching and learning. In addition, Tamim and Grant (2013) identified a number of different ways teachers describe their rationales for implementing project-based learning (i.e., to reinforce learning, to extend learning beyond expected goals, to initiate learning, or to purposefully select one of the previous three at different times). Thus, beliefs about teaching and learning can certainly impact PBL implementations, and research that considers how beliefs influence PBL would be beneficial to more fully understanding those implementations.

Scaffolding to Support Disciplined Inquiry

Scaffolding and supports that learners typically require for success are frequently discussed as a critical component of successful implementations of PBL in K–12. However, the projects represented in this volume reported mixed results with regard to helping teachers facilitate scaffolding practices. Two of the projects discussed PBL in science. Ertmer, Schlosser, Clase, and Adedokun (see Chapter 6) discussed their professional development model for PBL with science teachers, which included detailed scaffolding techniques and strategies. However, these practices represented some of the lowest self-reported confidence levels among teachers participating in the professional development activities. These teachers reflected a common tension between planning for scaffolding and independent learning, while simultaneously keeping the scope of the PBL experience manageable. Glazewski and colleagues (see Chapter 2) observed similar tensions among participants as they struggled to maintain a new PBL initiative coupled with development of deeper biology content. In their reflections, individuals were overwhelmingly positive but also expressed struggles with the content expectations, and this was particularly true for those with the least confidence with the science content. However, they were able to both experience their own knowledge building as well as reflect on the importance of doing so in the context of PBL. This, in turn, was enacted in their own practices, as they were able to convert their own struggles into teaching and scaffolding moments for their students.

In both mathematics projects discussed in this volume (Chapters 1 and 5), researchers highlighted the need to elicit thinking, support student reasoning, and sustain productive struggles with consideration for both process and content. Hjalmarson and Diefes-Dux (Chapter 5) examined the resources and tools that teachers designed to bridge practical observation with conceptual understanding. The teachers in their study shifted focus between individual, small group, and whole-class reasoning as they supported and challenged student problem solving. Strutchens and Martin (Chapter 1) described the need to prepare preservice teachers to engage in these shifts of focus as well and presented a "launch-explore-summarize" model for intentionally making decisions about process and content in response to learner needs in their practice.

Preservice teachers also gained experience with peer microteaching in order to develop their capabilities with instructional strategies that lead to both detecting learner needs and supporting them.

Arguably, Saye and Brush (see Chapter 7) presented the most detailed descriptions of scaffolding, as they specified the ways in which they refined their scaffold designs across four iterations of *Decision Point*. After four iterations and implementations, they concluded that scaffolding was most useful when it structured student tasks (e.g., presentations), provided strategies for approaching the problem, engaged learning and empathy, and challenged epistemological assumptions. They became increasing aware of the key role played by the teacher in her soft scaffolding approaches, particularly for deep knowledge construction and critical reasoning. Furthermore, they noted that metacognitive scaffolds intended to prompt reflection or monitor progress went virtually unused. They concluded by noting perhaps one of the most critical observations, which explains the complex interaction between resources, designs, implementations, and the role of the teacher: "Technology may ease certain burdens associated with inquiry, but success hinges on skilled, energetic teachers and motivated learners."

As we reflect on the full range of studies and the examples of scaffolding within the various chapters in this volume, we acknowledge that these practices are driven by disciplinary norms, values, and practices in the context of a commitment to deep student learning. In social studies, where problems are multilogical and interpretive by definition, student knowledge building requires strategies of deliberation, interpretation, and perspective taking. In mathematics, student knowledge building prioritizes content, skill, and process in the context of problems that tend to require different forms of deliberation in order to meet specific and exacting standards. As a result, student inquiry tasks vary considerably along a number of dimensions, including the scope and scale of the problems, activities that lead to knowledge building, and forms of argumentation and evidence. Thus, teacher scaffolding to support learners assumes much different forms across the disciplines.

Brush and Saye (see Chapter 7) use classifications of hard and soft scaffolds to characterize the range of teacher actions to support learner PBL inquiry. Hard scaffolds, as they define them, represent the types of supports and structures that can be planned in advance, such as graphic organizers or modeling for how to confront a specific task. Soft scaffolds reflect just-in-time assistance that learners need when they reach an impasse or seem satisfied with a superficial response. Hard and soft scaffold types can take multiple forms, as seen in the examples in this volume. Hjalmarson and Diefes-Dux (see Chapter 5) describe support in their project when the mathematics teacher asked, “How confident are you in your answer?” The researchers noted that this question allowed students to explain their answers, and thus they were afforded the opportunity to compare solution methods. The teacher’s question initially began as a form of soft scaffolding and was permanently installed as a hard scaffold in her formal documents. This highlights what we can learn from the exploration of iterative implementations of PBL, as well as from the scaffolding practices integrated within those implementations.

Saye and Brush (see Chapter 7) were the only researchers to address the fading of scaffolds in this volume but noted that critical reasoning and complex tasks may need more than one or two exposures before capacity can grow and skills or knowledge can be internalized. In short, they questioned the value of designing scaffolds that are designed to be faded and noted that it is not fully productive to plan for fading given the complexities and advanced skills being targeted. Belland (2011) referenced “transfer of responsibility,” rather than fading, to acknowledge that internal learner processes are gradual and incremental, and may not be realized in our immediate contexts. Thus, while scaffolding remains a critical component of the PBL environment, we are not likely to achieve fading since it is difficult for all learners to reach full independence within the range of targeted knowledge and skills. Thus, we believe that it is acceptable to relegate the goal of fading as one that is aspirational but not critical.

Implementation Isolation, Dependence Versus Sustainability, and Long-Term Impacts

In this final section of our commentary, we address many of the commonly observed patterns across the chapters in this volume. The first addresses the isolative characteristic of the various implementations. The second considers goals of partnership dependence that might conflict with sustainability. Finally, we discuss the need for longitudinal impact of PBL.

Isolation of Implementations

Isolation remains a significant unresolved issue in PBL research. In many reports of PBL research, the implementation takes place with a single teacher in a single classroom apart from other teachers and other disciplines (Holm, 2011; Wilder,

2015). Even when conducted in collaboration with a university researcher or teacher educator, the implementation may be independent from the realities beyond a classroom (Ertmer & Simons, 2006; Grant & Hill, 2006), such as state assessments, pressure to stay on schedule with grade-level colleagues (Bickford, Tharp, McFarling, & Beglau, 2002), and extended time needed to complete PBL units or activities. As a result, reported findings beyond the first implementation of a PBL case is rare. These single or isolated implementations present concerns for furthering PBL research. As mentioned previously, knowledge about how PBL evolves or is implemented successively is not widely reported, which highlights again the unique impact of Saye and Brush's research (see Chapter 7). When teachers are implementing PBL independently, it is unclear how teachers are choosing problem cases (Goodnough & Hung, 2009) and whether these PBL units are continued beyond the initial implementation. One question that remains unanswered is whether teachers who are enacting PBL independently are choosing or developing smaller, shorter, or more discrete problem cases.

When PBL is implemented in partnership with researchers, teacher educators, schools, individual teachers, or preservice or inservice teachers, the partnerships are involved, effortful, reciprocal, and lengthy (e.g., Cognition and Technology Group at Vanderbilt, 1992; Ertmer et al., Chapter 6, this volume; Goodnough & Hung, Chapter 8, this volume; Hjalmarson & Diefes-Dux, Chapter 5, this volume; Krajcik, Blumenfeld, Marx, & Soloway, 1994; Lottero-Perdue, Chapter 4, this volume). Consequently, we question whether the PBL environments are sustainable beyond the partnerships. Directly linked to this sustainability is the difficulty in understanding whether there is a goal to scale the reported implementations beyond a single classroom or school setting. We acknowledge, however, that the expectations to scale may be a biased perspective. Thus, while there does seem to be a generalized expectation that implementations should scale, perhaps this expectation is directly related to federal funding agencies (e.g., National Science Foundation) recommending and/or funding inquiry initiatives and national standards organizations (e.g., Common Core State Standards, Next Generation Science Standards) advocating for inquiry and problem-solving initiatives (e.g., Strutchens & Martin, Chapter 1, this volume; Nariman & Chrispeels, 2016; Newbill, Drape, Schnittka, Baum, & Evans, 2015; Thomasian, 2011).

In contrast, *Alien Rescue* (Liu et al., 2014; Liu, Williams, & Pederson, 2002; Liu, Wivagg, Geurtz, Lee, & Chang, 2012) and *Learning by Design* (Gertzman & Kolodner, 1996; Kolodner et al., 2009; Mehalik, Doppelt, & Schunn, 2008; Puntambekar & Kolodner, 2005) have scaled to multiple schools and contexts, though not without tremendous investment over time. Brush and Saye (see Chapter 3) have scaled the model for problem-based historical inquiry across a full teacher education program that comprises two years, and they have documented changes in the ways preservice teachers think about their instructional practices and instructional priorities, noting shifts toward inquiry-based teaching practices. Thus, we have been able to catch glimpses of sustainability, but it is difficult to determine the critical variables that support that sustainability. We suspect that those variables involve investment, resources, motivation, professional development, buy-in, and time.

A Call for Longitudinal Studies

There is currently little to no research focusing on long-term implementations or longitudinal results with PBL in K–12 classrooms. The evidence for better student learning over time and skills acquisition and application is also not firmly supported (Wilder, 2015). Until recently, whole-school implementation of PBL has been rare. A growing number of public schools have adopted a model of school reform centered on *project*-based learning strategies, integrative curricula, extensive technology integration, and approaches for student engagement (Gourgey, Asiabanpour, & Fenimore, 2010; Mosier, Bradley-Levine, & Perkins, 2016; Ravitz, 2008, 2010). The model programs include New Tech High, High Tech High, EdVisions Schools, and Envisions Schools. The New Tech High School model has grown to include implementations in 21 U.S. states (Mosier et al., 2016). The research, however, has largely focused on case studies and reports of student perceptions of activities, and has not been widely reported in any academic journals (Gourgey et al., 2010).

Specific to project-based learning, Holm (2011) reported student learning gains in schools that have adopted a *project*-based learning model. Similarly, Ravitz (2008, 2010) reported enhanced learning outcomes in whole-school or system-wide implementations of project-based learning. PBL and other inquiry models have not been implemented this widely in K–12 (c.f., Wilder, 2015). However, even with some whole-school implementations, research has not provided strong confirming evidence that PBL has a positive impact on student learning. Furthermore, there is little longitudinal research focusing on how the preparation of preservice teachers to utilize PBL and/or inquiry teaching methods translates into their adoption of those practices once they enter the classroom full time. The ability to conduct these types of long-term research efforts may hinge on both available resources as well as measures that are valid and sensitive to the outcomes of PBL.

Conclusion

As we reviewed the chapters in this volume, we did so with the purpose to both understand more about the similarities among various implementations of PBL in K–12 and teacher education settings as well as to identify gaps in our understanding of PBL implementation in these contexts. That said, we were impressed with the tremendous depth of understanding brought about by these collective works. Not only have we gained deeper insight into the adoption, adaptation, and implementations of PBL, but we appreciate the dual emphases that afford us views in both teacher education settings and in K–12 classrooms. The reciprocal relationship between the two contexts has come into deeper focus for us, thus fostering new understandings across dimensions of PBL depictions, scaffolding, and implementations. We acknowledge that these are not the only dimensions that can assist us with understanding the patterns and gaps in our knowledge, which makes this volume critically important at this time.

References

Anders, Y., & Rossbach, H. G. (2015). Preschool teachers' sensitivity to mathematics in children's play: The influence of math-related school experiences, emotional attitudes, and pedagogical beliefs. *Journal of Research in Childhood Education, 29*(3), 305–322. http://dx.doi.org/10.1080/02568543.2015.1040564

Arce, J., Bodner, G. M., & Hutchinson, K. (2014). A study of the impact of inquiry-based professional development experiences on the beliefs of intermediate science teachers about "best practices" for classroom teaching. *International Journal of Mathematics, Science and Technology, 2*(2), 85–95.

Barrows, H. S. (2006). Problem-based learning in medicine and beyond: A brief overview. *New Directions for Teaching and Learning, 1996*(68), 3–12. http://doi.org/10.1002/tl.37219966804

Beatrice, S., Amadalo, N., & Musasia, M. (2015). Problem based learning technique and its effect on acquisition of linear programming skills by secondary school students in Kenya. *Journal of Education and Practice, 6*(20), 68–75.

Belland, B. (2011). Distributed cognitive as a lens to understand the effects of scaffolds: The role of transfer of responsibility. *Educational Psychology Review, 23*, 577–600. http://doi.org/10.1007/s10648-011-9176-5

Belland, B. R., French, B. F., & Ertmer, P. A. (2009). Validity and problem-based learning research: A review of instruments used to assess intended learning outcomes. *Interdisciplinary Journal of Problem-based Learning, 3*(1), 59–89. http://doi.org/10.7771/1541-5015.1059

Bickford, A., Tharp, S., McFarling, P., & Beglau, M. (2002). Finding the right fuel for new engines of learning. *Multimedia Schools, 9*(5), 18–26.

Cheriani, C., Mahmud, A., Tahmir, S., Manda, D., & Dirawan, G. D. (2015). Problem-based learning—Buginese cultural knowledge model—case study: Teaching mathematics at junior high school. *International Education Studies, 8*(4), 104–110. http://doi.org/10.5539/ies.v8n4p104

Cognition and Technology Group at Vanderbilt. (1992). The Jasper Series as an example of anchored instruction: Theory, program description, and assessment data. *Educational Psychologist, 27*(3), 291–315.

Cresswell, J. W. (2012). *Qualitative inquiry and research design: Choosing among five traditions.* Thousand Oaks, CA: Sage Publications, Inc.

Ertmer, P. A. (2005). Teacher pedagogical beliefs: The final frontier in our quest for technology integration? *Educational Technology Research and Development, 53*(4), 25–39. http://doi.org/10.1007/BF02504683

Ertmer, P. A., & Ottenbreit-Leftwich, A. T. (2010). Teacher technology change: How knowledge, confidence, beliefs, and culture intersect. *Journal of Research on Technology in Education, 42*(3), 255–285. http://doi.org/10.1080/15391523.2010.10782551

Ertmer, P. A., Ottenbreit-Leftwich, A. T., Sadik, O., Sendurur, E., & Sendurur, P. (2012). Teacher beliefs and technology integration practices: A critical relationship. *Computers & Education, 59*(2), 423–435. http://doi.org/10.1016/j.compedu.2012.02.001

Ertmer, P. A., & Simons, K. D. (2006). Jumping the PBL implementation hurdle: Supporting the efforts of K–12 teachers. *Interdisciplinary Journal of Problem-based Learning, 1*(1), 40–54. http://doi.org/10.7771/1541-5015.1005

Galford, G., Hawkins, S., & Hertweck, M. (2015). Problem-based learning as a model for the interior design classroom: Bridging the skills divide between academia and practice. *Interdisciplinary Journal of Problem-based Learning, 9*(2). http://doi.org/10.7771/1541-5015.1527

Gertzman, A., & Kolodner, J. L. (1996). A case study of problem-based learning in a middle school science classroom: Lessons learned. In *Proceedings of the 1996 international conference on learning sciences* (pp. 91–98). Evanston/Chicago, IL. Retrieved from http://www.cc.gatech.edu/projects/lbd/pdfs/pblinmssci.pdf

Goodnough, K. C., & Hung, W. (2009). Enhancing pedagogical content knowledge in elementary science. *Teaching Education, 20*(3), 229–242. http://doi.org/10.1080/10476210802578921

Gourgey, H., Asiabanpour, B., & Fenimore, C. (2010). Case study of manor new tech high school: Promising practices in STEM education for comprehensive high schools. *American Journal of Engineering Education, 1*(1), 47–64. http://dx.doi.org/10.19030/ajee.v1i1.792

Grant, M. M., & Hill, J. R. (2006). Weighing the rewards with the risks? Implementing student-centered pedagogy within high-stakes testing. In R. Lambert & C. McCarthy (Eds.), *Understanding teacher stress in the age of accountability* (pp. 19–42). Greenwich, CT: Information Age Publishing.

Hmelo-Silver, C. E. (2004). Problem-based learning: What and how do students learn? *Educational Psychology Review, 16*(3), 235–266. http://doi.org/10.1023/B:EDPR.0000034022.16470.f3

Holm, M. (2011). Project-based instruction: A review of the literature on effectiveness in prekindergarten through 12th grade classrooms. *InSight: Rivier Academic Journal, 7*(2), 1–13.

Hung, W. (2011). Theory to reality: A few issues in implementing problem-based learning. *Educational Technology Research and Development, 59*(4), 529–552. http://doi.org/10.1007/s11423-011-9198-1

Hutchison, M. (2016). The empathy project: Using a project based learning assignment to increase first-year college students' comfort with interdisciplinarity. *Interdisciplinary Journal of Problem-based Learning, 10*(1), 5–6. http://doi.org/10.7771/1541-5015.1580

Jerzembek, G., & Murphy, S. (2013). A narrative review of problem-based learning with school-aged children: Implementation and outcomes. *Educational Review, 65*(2), 206–218. http://doi.org/10.1080/00131911.2012.659655

Kolodner, J. L., Camp, P. J., Crismond, D., Fasse, B., Gray, J., Holbrook, J., … Ryan, M. (2009). Problem-based learning meets case-based reasoning in the middle school science classroom: Putting learning by design into practice. *Journal of the Learning Sciences, 12*(4), 495–547. http://dx.doi.org/10.1207/S15327809JLS1204_2

Krajcik, J. S., Blumenfeld, P. C., Marx, R. W., & Soloway, E. (1994). A collaborative model for helping middle grade science teachers learn instruction. *The Elementary School Journal, 94*(5), 482–497. http://doi.org/10.1086/461779

Liu, M., Horton, L., Lee, J., Kang, J., Rosenblum, J. A., O'Hair, M., & Lu, C.-W. (2014). Creating a multimedia enhanced problem-based learning environment for middle school science: Voices from the developers. *Interdisciplinary Journal of Problem-based Learning, 8*(1), 1–28. http://doi.org/10.7771/1541-5015.1422

Liu, M., Williams, D., & Pederson, S. (2002). *Alien Rescue*: A problem-based hypermedia learning environment for middle school science. *Educational Technology Systems, 30*(3), 255–270. http://doi.org/10.2190/X531-D6KE-NXVY-N6RE

Liu, M., Wivagg, J., Geurtz, R., Lee, S., & Chang, H. M. (2012). Examining how middle school science teachers implement a multimedia-enriched problem-based learning environment. *Interdisciplinary Journal of Problem-based Learning, 6*(2), 46–84. http://dx.doi.org/10.7771/1541-5015.1348

Makin, D. A. (2015). A descriptive analysis of a problem-based learning police academy. *Interdisciplinary Journal of Problem-based Learning, 10*(1), 16. http://doi.org/10.7771/1541-5015.1544

Mehalik, M. M., Doppelt, Y., & Schunn, C. D. (2008). Middle-school science through design-based learning versus scripted inquiry: Better overall science concept learning and equity gap reduction. *Journal of Engineering Education, 97*(1), 71–85. http://doi.org/10.1002/j.2168-9830.2008.tb00955.x

Mosier, G. G., Bradley-Levine, J., & Perkins, T. (2016). Students' perceptions of project-based learning within the New Tech School model. *International Journal of Educational Reform, 25*(1), 2–15.

Newbill, P. L., Drape, T. A., Schnittka, C., Baum, L., & Evans, M. A. (2015, Fall). Learning across space instead of over time. *Afterschool Matters,* 4–12.

Pecore, J. L. (2012). Beyond beliefs: Teachers adapting problem-based learning to pre-existing systems of practice. *Interdisciplinary Journal of Problem-based Learning, 7*(2), 9–26. http://dx.doi.org/10.7771/1541-5015.1359

Persichetti, A. L. (2016). Producing an online undergraduate literary magazine: A guide to using problem-based learning in the writing and publishing classroom. *Interdisciplinary Journal of Problem-based Learning, 10*(1), 5–6. http://dx.doi.org/10.7771/1541-5015.1546

Puntambekar, S., & Kolodner, J. L. (2005). Toward implementing distributed scaffolding: Helping students learn science from design. *Journal of Research in Science Teaching, 42*(2), 185–217. http://doi.org/10.1002/tea.20048

Ravitz, J. (2008, March 27). *Project based learning as a catalyst in reforming high schools.* Paper presented at the annual meeting of the American Educational Research Association, New York, NY. Retrieved from http://files.eric.ed.gov/fulltext/ED540113.pdf

Ravitz, J. (2010). Beyond changing culture in small high schools: Reform models and changing instruction with project-based learning. *Peabody Journal of Education, 85*(3), 290–312. http://doi.org/10.1080/0161956X.2010.491432

Rico, R., & Ertmer, P. A. (2015). Examining the role of the instructor in problem-centered instruction. *TechTrends: Linking Research & Practice to Improve Learning, 59*(4), 96–103. http://doi.org/10.1007/s11528-015-0876-4

Savery, J. R. (2006). Overview of problem-based learning: Definitions and distinctions. In A. Walker, H. Leary, C. E. Hmelo-Silver, & P. A. Ertmer (Eds.), *Essential readings in problem-based learning: Exploring and extending the legacy of Howard S. Barrows* (pp. 5–16). West Lafayette, IN: Purdue University Press.

Stalker, S. L., Cullen, T., & Kloesel, K. (2015). Using PBL to prepare educators and emergency managers to plan for severe weather. *Interdisciplinary Journal of Problem-based Learning, 9*(2). http://dx.doi.org/10.7771/1541-5015.1441

Tamim, S. R., & Grant, M. M. (2013). Definitions and uses: Case study of teachers implementing project-based learning. *Interdisciplinary Journal of Problem-based Learning, 7*(2), 71–101. http://doi.org/10.7771/1541-5015.1323

Thomasian, J. (2011). *Building a science, technology, engineering, and math education agenda.* Washington, DC: National Governors Association. Retrieved from http://files.eric.ed.gov/fulltext/ED496324.pdf

Widyatiningtyas, R., Kusumah, Y. S., Sumarmo, U., & Sabandar, J. (2015). The impact of problem-based learning approach to senior high school students' mathematics critical thinking ability. *Journal of Mathematics Education, 6*(2), 30–38. Retrieved from http://jims-b.org/wp-content/uploads/2015/09/03-Full-IndoMS-JME-62-Reviandari-Widyatiningtyas.pdf

Wilder, S. (2015). Impact of problem-based learning on academic achievement in high school: A systematic review. *Educational Review, 67*(4), 414–435. http://doi.org/10.1080/00131911.2014.974511

Michael M. Grant recently joined the faculty at the University of South Carolina as program coordinator for the Educational Technology program. Previously, he spent 12 years in the Instructional Design and Technology program at the University of Memphis. His research considers three complementary areas: the design and development of technology-enhanced learning environments, graphic and instructional designs to support learning, and key learner characteristics. His most recent scholarship has focused on how to design, develop, and implement inquiry learning environments and mobile teaching and learning in K–12 and higher education. Grant earned his PhD in instructional technology from the University of Georgia and a BS and master's of industrial education from Clemson University. He is currently the editor of the *Interdisciplinary Journal of Problem-based Learning* and the executive secretary for the Association for Educational Communications and Technology. He can be contacted via his website at Viral-Notebook.com and through Twitter (@michaemgrant).

Krista D. Glazewski is an associate professor of instructional systems technology at Indiana University, Bloomington. Her work and interests are centered primarily on problem-based and inquiry-based learning within K–12 contexts with teachers and students. She has more than 15 years' experience in public education, first as a middle school teacher and later as a teacher educator.

INDEX

Page numbers in *italics* refer to figures and tables.

L

M